Jade Culture of the Dongyi東夷
tribe through the Black skin jade

Jade Culture of the Dongyi東夷 tribe through the Black skin jade

publication date 12. 21. 2018.

publisher Ahn Gyeong-jeon **Place of issue** Sangsaengbooks pub. **author** Jung Gun-jae, Ph.D.
translated by *mireene*
address 29beon-gil 36, Seonhwa-dong, Jung-gu, Daejeon, Republic of Korea
phone 070-8644-3156 **fax** 0303-0799-1735 **Registered publication** March 11, 2005 (175)
ISBN 979-11-86122-80-8

Jade Culture of the Dongyi東夷
tribe through the Black skin jade

Sangsaengbooks

RECOMMENDATION

Park Seok Jae

Co-chairman of the Right History Council for future
Ex-President Korea Astronomy and Space Science Institute

The fact that the Sānshèngzǔ三聖祖 era was history prove in jade!

According to Huántángǔjì桓檀古記, the history of Shànggǔshǐ 上古史(Ancient history) in Korea, Huánguó桓國 was controlled by Huányīn桓因, Bèidá倍達 was controlled by Huánxióng桓雄 and Cháoxiǎn朝鮮 by Tánjūn檀君. The time when Huányīn桓因, Huánxióng桓雄, and Tánjūn檀君 were called Sānshèng三聖, and they ruled the era of Sānshèngzǔ三聖祖 era. Those who learned that Tánjūn檀君 Cháoxiǎn朝鮮 was a myth, not a history, would be unfamiliar with the Sānshèngzǔ三聖祖 era.

Based on 'Wǔxīngjùlóu五星聚婁' record in 'Huántángǔjì桓檀古記,' Korean astronomers have shown that the Tánjūn檀君 Cháoxiǎn朝鮮 is not a mythical country. If you look at the astronomical software, you can see that there was actually Wǔxīngjiéjí 五星結集 during the Tánjūn檀君 Cháoxiǎn朝鮮dynasty. In other words, 'Huántángǔjì桓檀古記' is not a memorial, but also proved that Tánjūn檀君 is a history, not a myth.

Based on the records of 'Tiānwénlèimiǎo天文類秒's Wǔxīngjùlóu五星聚婁' Korean astronomers also proved that Huánxióng桓雄 Bèidá倍達 and Tánjūn檀君 Cháoxiǎn朝鮮 are closely related to Hóngshān紅山 civilization. The remains of this civilization were discovered in the last century, thousands of years ahead of the Huánghé黃河 civilization.

The discovery of Hóngshān紅山 civilization was a historic event that brought attention to the world. A vast variety of jade ornaments and relics have been unearthed from the site, which is a good match for the term 'Yùqì玉器 era'. Therefore, accurately describing and evaluating jade culture has become one of the most important tasks to correct our history.

One of the best jade cultural experts in the world is Jung Gun-jae, a professor who wrote the book, 'the jade-culture of the Dongyi東夷 tribe' In the book, Jung is proving with jade that the Sānshèngzǔ三聖祖 era was a real history. In a word, we have done almost more by ourselves than our astronomers put together.

Professor Jung is not satisfied with this and wants to let the world know the excellence of our history by publishing books in English. The fact that there are people like Professor Jung in our country proves that our nation is a descendant of Heaven. I am happy to recommend Professor Jung's 'the jade-culture of the Dongyi東夷 tribe' with confidence.

RECOMMENDATION

Yoon Sung Joon

Coodinator - between government companies and, international relationship Now korea japan international economy association special advisor Before studied in Us , Japan, and china Advisor to the Prime Minister of Japan on foreign government policy for East Asia

It's been 35 years since I'd met Dr. Jung Gun Jae. My original hometown is Jeju island and I also studied in Japan just like Dr. Jung.

During Japanese occupation of Korea, 70 to 80 thousand went to Kobe, Japan, and my father was born there. He came back to Jeju when he was very young – there are lots of stories regarding Jeju Island – After I came back from Japan, I worked for FKI(the Federation of Korean Industries) media company. Including 7 years of study in Japan, I also studied in China and the US over 2 years.

I have little knowledge of 'the Black Skin Jade Hongsan Pre-Historic Culture', and I don't think I am qualified to write any book recommendation. However, Dr. Jung wanted me to write a recommendation with the perspective of experiences in China, Japan, and the US.

Recently, I happened to find out few historical reasons why my father was born in Japan. [It was interesting experience for me to understand historical reasons behind my father's birth.] [Just like how I find it interesting to understand my father's birth history], I believe 'the Black Jade' would have tremendous stories behind that we had never imagined. 'the Black Skin Jade' is the jewel of humanity which existed as pre-historic civilization from areas based on northeast China.

Dr.Jung had studied Chinese history specialized in China Militia in 'Hitochubashi'–spun-off business and economy school of University of Tokyo, offering history and anthropology major programs–Dr. Jung had studied in the University of Huadong Education after 'Hitochubashi'. I believe there are few scholars who has firm understanding of the East Asian history including Korea, Japan, and China. With the basis of complete understanding of the East Asian history, I believe Dr. Jung was able to understand the true meanings of 'the Black Skin Jade'.

It is an exciting thrill to find out the history of Korean race is hidden behind the history of China which had led over 5,000 years based from Huang He civilization. Dr. Jung had discovered many historical artifacts that can shake the foundation of the 'Imnailbonbu' theory of Japan or the 'East North Project' theory of China. The explanation of his discoveries is clearly described and well explained in this book.

I'd visited the Alamo Cenotaph in San Antonio, Texas in the US long time ago. The United States of America is a fairly new country with the history written over the Native American history. However, it was very impressive to learn how small number of Americans had fought to conserve its historical site over the battle with Mexicans out-numbering 30 to 40 times. Korea, Japan, and China are making enormous efforts to register their cultural heritage with UNESCO World Heritage Center nowadays.–It is truly great event to find out the 'Black Skin Jade' culture, which is closely related to the Korean race, flourished since pre-historic ancient era.

There is wind of change in Korean peninsula with 'Peace' and 'Co-existence'. It is not important now at all to imply on 'who did it', 'who outstood', nor 'who ruled'. I hope this book becomes the role model for uplifting the 'Spirit' of sharing and becoming one with outstanding common heritage we all inherited. Congratulation on the publication of this book!

Thank you very much!

RECOMMENDATION

Lee Geum Hwa

2013~2016 china 10-point national people treasure,
2013~2016 china the products of civilization protection certificate of award, black
skin jade culture korean president, china antiquity collection association member

I express my infinite respect for Dr. Jung Geon Jae' book.

It is already 15years since we discovered these ancient treasures. Plus, plenty of episodes that we has looked for the excavation scenes, have passed like wind, while crisscrossing the entire desert zone in Mongolia.

Dr, Jung had lived in the same village and had been close to their brother with the late Kim Hui Yong. He wrote the very book that is the current result of great discovery with 20 year's exerting himself to the utmost about the ancient mill scale jade from the inner Mongolia desert zone.

Indeed, it has been success of the adventures for me as a female to look for the ancient treasures at the extreme region of Wulanchabu烏蘭察布, Hohhot呼和浩特 of the capital of Inner-Mongolia. In that excavation site, when as a female, I finally discovered them, to be honest, it is the best ecstasy, the best memory and the best impression simultaneously.

The jade of the material for the stature is precious itself. In particular, the ancient jade is so priceless that we cannot purchase even with astronomical amount.

This Black skin jade is the best work among esthetical arts, which is never available to be found out in Modern days.

Dr. Jung Geon Jae', in this book, it includes the secret pertaining the ancient Black skin jade, that is to say, the secret of lying at the root of the history from the ancient to the contemporary.

There are still lots of people insisting the relavance with the old stone age and new stone age and the extraterrestrial...

However, the ancient treasures is repeating the very secret that the only people have touched and researched more than the hundreds in person...

Introduction

Beginning to receive the attention of the international community around both countries of Korea and China in the 21st century, Black skin jade黑皮玉 Culture is considered to be the same as Hóngshān紅山 Culture or the part of Pan Hóngshān汎紅山 Culture in some cases because it not only has apparently exactly the same form as Jadeware such as yùlóng玉龍 (C-shaped dragon), jade earrings (玉玦), sun god (太陽神), jade bird (玉鳥), gōuyún-type jade jewelry (勾雲形玉佩) etc. which are the representative artifacts of Hóngshān Culture but has in common in terms of jade materials called Xiuyanyù岫岩玉. And it is true that not only a series of jade carving forms such as yùlóng玉龍, jade earrings (玉玦) etc. which are representative jadeware had a certain social order with the common formative production format but the society at that time represents the emergence of the early ancient country characterized by status discrimination with jade as the peak and occurrence of political power.

Recently, as for the Neolithic Age jade culture territory around the Northeastern region of China, the jade culture of the Neolithic Age developed around the Liáo-hé遼河 region is the independent culture that existed as a historical entity in a certain area for at least 5000 years enough for a Chinese professor Sūbǐngqí蘇秉琦 said in his book «Zhōngguówénmíngqǐyuánxīntàn中國文明起源新探», "The discovery of Yànshān燕山 Northsouthern District, "Língyuán凌源-Jiànpíng建平-Kāzuǒ喀左" small triangular area over a period of about 5000 years from Cháhǎi查海, Xīnglóngwā興隆窪-Zhàobǎogōu趙宝溝 type of 8000 years ago to Yànxiàdū燕下都 of about 2000 years ago made us watch it carefully and it had an impact on two major challenges in this Chinese history about uninterrupted continuous mystery and trajectory of five thousand years of Chinese civilization, how was a Chinese unified multi-ethnic country formed."

In particular, the fact is that the argument about 'ZhōngguótŏngyīduōmínzúGuójiā中國統一多民族國家' among this arguments indirectly reveals they were other ethnic groups not the Chinese nation in the past although of course, currently some minorities in the unified Chinese society.

In addition, it is no wonder Neolithic jade culture for the northeastern area of current China is historically important because it corresponds to a great turning point when an ancient country appears for the first time in Northeast Asia enough for most historians or archaeologists in China, Korea and Japan to recognize that the civilized and social stage of Hóngshān Culture is 'the original form of an ancient country or Chúxíng雛形 (miniature) of an ancient country.

With respect to the appearance of the Jadeware society including Hóngshān Culture, a Korean professor Lee, Hyeong-gu said, "The emergence making of Jadeware has a huge meaning. It means the opening of a so called theocratical society where a monopolist communicating with the heavens rules an ancient country and specialization is made and social position class occurs in the process of monopolizing and producing Jadeware. It is Dōngyí東夷 Tribe who created it. Furthermore, Jadeware artifacts were discovered in large quantities along with other artifacts of the Dōngyí Tribe line such as Stone Mound Tomb, Comb-pattern Pottery, Mandolin-shaped bronze dagger, (Mirror of the early Iron Age) etc. in the Hóngshān Culture Area of Inner Mongolia and Liáo-hé Region and a variety of Jadeware was excavated including jade earrings (玉玦), Yùzhūlóng玉猪龍 (Pig shape jade dragon),

Yùbì玉璧 (jade disk with a hole in the center), Yùhuán玉環 (jade ring), Yùpèi玉佩(jade jewelry), Yuguī玉龜 (jade turtle), Mandolin-shaped jade dagger etc. which are representative Jadeware of Hóngshān Culture along with altar, Nǚshénmiào女神廟 (Goddess grave), Stone Mound Tomb group etc. especially in the Niúhéliáng 牛河梁 historic site excavated in the 1980s." («Jīngxiāngxīnwén京 鄉新聞» 2007,12,14, Korea).

The humankind in the Neolithic Age believed that a bird is a device moving the spirit to the gods of heaven after a man dies as an envoy who can pass between the heaven above the head and ground below. Therefore, they selected snakes, birds, wild boars, cattle, bears, tigers, sheep, etc. among ground animals directly related to the existence and prosperity of their kin groups or social groups to use them as Dìshén地神 (God of the earth), their guardian and animals selected as Dìshén or Dìmǔ地母 should have a dignified and courageous shape as the animals for common worship of the whole ethnic group and became more sanctified as gradually deified and united with ancestral gods. The birth of such gods between heaven and earth not only eliminated the worry and fear over a long period of time in the spirit and material areas of people but enabled the appearance of the primitive religious system reflecting the elementary recognition and interpretation for their surrounding natural environment of mankind.

Under such circumstances, Wūrén巫人 (shaman), who appeared as the actual ruler in the ground in the society at that time, conducted the process of carrying out sacrificial rites and Shénqì 神器 symbolizing the marvelous ability of gods of heaven and earth was made of jade not general minerals. Finally, Hóngshān Culture, Black Jade Culture and shamans already added a meaning to jade as Shénqì, that is, Shénwù神物 not as a mineral state and let the whole world know that they themselves are divine beings by exclusively dominating the communication with the gods of heaven. In particular, shamans seem to have been able to maintain the social order as zhìzhě智者(wise men) knowing the state of the heavens and the earth by telling people that gods are also supernatural capabilities created by them through the mutual relation between jade and shamans and carrying out religious work with jade and conveying God's will at the same time.

Although jade carving of Black skin jade Culture that appeared in the late 20th century slightly later than Jade culture-centered Hóngshān Culture is attracting attention mainly by both countries of China and Korea, it is revealed that the official announcement such as archaeological excavation reporting for Black skin jade Culture in China has not been made until now. In spite of this overall situation, however, Black Skin Jade statues seem to have attracted intensive attention mainly by some academics and experts because of their Black skin and mysterious molding beyond the imagination so difficult that even modern men in the 21st century difficult to understand. As for such black skin of jade carving of Black skin jade Culture, national institutions or representative institutes of China·Korea·U.S scientifically found already that Black Skin Jade artifacts were not made in modern times through a variety of latest experimental results such as black skin jade material inspection, black skin jade surface component inspection (Korea Seoul National University National Center for Inter-University Research Facilities, China National Geological measuring-centered, Shanghai Museum etc.), black skin jade surface public peeling experiment etc. In order to secure the scientific basis for

Black skin jade Culture, the author also took samples from the same black skin jade Bànrénbànshòu半人半獸 (half man and half beast) sculpture two times in 2007 and 2009 and was informed of the first and second age-dating experimental results of 14300±60 years ago by Seoul National University National Center for Inter-University Research Facilities and 3150±40 years ago by U.S. GEOCHRON LABORATORIES, respectively. These age dating results over two times are the scientific experimental results by radioactive isotope age dating for black skin jade sculpture officially conducted by research institutions representing Korea and the United States for the first time in the world, securing a chronological space that jade carving of Black skin jade Culture is ancient artifacts of at least 5,000 years ago. In particular, the age dating results for Black Jade Culture sex figure statues carried out by the U.S. CIRAM (CIRAM ANALYSIS CERTIFICATE 0415-OA-21N-2) in June 2015 are even more surprising. According to these experimental results, "Conclusions /

The raw material consist of tremolite-actinote (nerphite) and chlorite. It could correspond to a metamorphic stone, such as chlorite-actinote schist. We talk about "jade" nephrite.

From the investigations of the surface replica, we have observed natural alteration features, such as dissolution, micro-fracturing and amorphisation of the nephrite and chlorite. Furthermore, we did not dedect chroline, sulphur or fluorine, which indicate a chemical etching.

The weathering degree of the stone is relatively low, but the decay originates from natural and long-term processes.

The results indicate that the weathering of the stone originates from natural and long-term processes, after the carving phase."

These series of scientific experimental results are not only the clue for black skin of jade carving of Black Jade Culture but important materials that can support records of «Shānhǎijīng山海經 (Classic of Mountains and Seas)» 中山經, "嬰用吉玉, 彩之, 饗之 (When offering good jade, color it beautifully and bless so that the gods of heaven can enjoy it.)", 西山經 "其祠之禮, 用一吉玉瘞, 糈用稷米 (The etiquette of performing ancestral rites is to bury one good jade in the ground and use nonglutinous millet as rice to be cooked for a sacrifice) and "郭曰又加以繪綵之飾也 (Guō says that it was decorated by coloring it again)", the note of Guōpú郭璞 (Eastern Jin, 276-324) cited by Wúrènchén吳任臣(Qing,1628-1689) «Shānhǎijīngguǎngzhù山海經廣注». Eventually, these materials could prove the fact that jade was used extensively as various uses in the society before «Shānhǎijīng» appeared and jade was colored and colored jade was buried in the ground. Especially by finding the literature basis that jade was colored in «Shānhǎijīng», the Wūshu巫書 of Dōngyí東夷 Tribe, the important literature basis that can examine the historical nature of Black skin jade Culture was ensured. Henceforth, we would like to expect the research participation and results of jade culture related experts.

Jade Totem Society:

Together with Hóngshān Culture, Black skin jade Culture is mainly excavated in Liáo-hé遼河 Area and jade carvings showing the ultimate of a three-dimensional space art as well as jade manufacturing technology prove that the world's highest level of the Neolithic Age jade culture already existed in the Northeastern area of the current Chinese continent as the historical entity about

5000 years ago.

It means that the old saying 'Serving gods with jade' is the evidence and the main character is a shaman. After all, shaman, sky (god) and Yù (jade) can be regarded as the Trinity. Therefore, it was considered that jadeware was a creation in the form of ideas and their life was given by the heaven and spiritual animals, landscape and land etc. are exchanged each other like mystical creatures. Clan or tribal societies at that time created shénqì used in ancestral rites and various objects such as animal totem, nature worship, ancestor worship etc. they worshiped into jade carving, extraordinary three-dimensional space art of the diverse and rich form. Hóngshān Culture was the 'Jade Totem' society where its subjects took charge of the material culture with funeral customs burying jade belonging to the spiritual culture category in the tomb and had private ownership with an emphasis on the spiritual culture. As the 'Jade Totem society' that expressed worship rituals for all natural phenomena including ancestral spirits, animals in the form of nature etc. through jade, it can be regarded as a civilized society in the phase of the initial ancient country with a certain level of social order with jade as its peak. For the emergence of jade Shénwù神物, that is, Shénqì神器, Yángbǎidá 楊伯達, president of Chinese Cultural Relics Society Jadeware Committee argues, "Ancient Jadeware, of course, is part of stoneware. At first, it was used as a tool. Since there was no way to tell its beauty and mystical properties, it was considered Shénwù through which people could communicate with the heaven, Jiēshén 祭神, Shénshì神事, Tōngshén通神. It was at least 8000 years ago that jade was regarded as Shénwù."

In particular, Niúshǒurénshēn牛首人身 (Cow head and human body) Sun God Jade carving shape, the representative artifact among half god half beast shapes of Black skin jade Culture and Hóngshān Culture is well known enough to appear in Gāojùlì高句麗(Goguryeo) tomb murals. For such sun god black jade carving, a Chinese professor Xiàdéwǔ夏德武 argues in «Zhōngguóshénmìdehēipíyùdiāo中国神秘的黑皮玉雕»," Of the formative arts of Pan Hóngshān汎紅山 Culture black skin jade carving, the most striking expression is commonly known as "Sun God" black skin jade carving. This kind of black skin jade carving expression is a combination of "Cow head (Niúshǒu) and human body (Rénshēn)" of a kind of supernatural phenomenon. Objectively, this kind of black skin jade carving accounts for about 30% of Hóngshān Black skin jade carving. In fact, the formation of Rénshòu人獸(human and beast) combination shows the shape of the totem ancestors of an ancient ethnic society. Examples: Xióngshì熊氏 sculpture combining a bear and human, Xuānyuánshì軒轅氏 sculpture combining fish and human, Fúxīshì伏羲氏 sculpture combining human head and dragon body, Shǐwéishì豕韦氏 sculpture of pig head and human body, Huāntóushì讙头氏 sculpture of bird head and human body, Such complex molding appears everywhere in black skin jade carving and Cow head and human body (Niúshǒurénshēn) Statue is Shénnóngshì神農氏 Statue."

Therefore, the totem shape of early myths was changed into Bànrénbànshòu 半人半獸 and even transformed into the shape of Rénjiànshén人間神 (human god). This is a symbol of vitality of the myth and expression of human thinking development at the same time.

As a way to explain the Black skin jade culture and Hóngshān Culture society the most effectively, it was largely divided by area from the perspective of the 'Jade Totem' society as follows:

1. Nature worship

Sun-shaped jade disk with a hole in the center, gōuyún-type jade jewelry and rainbow-shaped jade emperor etc. based on nature worship are included.

2. Animal Totem

Yùlóng玉龍 (C-shaped dragon) of snake totem, Yùxiónglóng玉熊龍 (bear-shaped dragon made of jade) and bear crown jade Shénrén神人 of bear totem, Niúshǒurénshēn牛首人身 of cattle totem, Yùniǎo玉鳥 of bird totem, Yùniǎoxíngjué玉鳥形玦, Rénmiànniǎo人面鳥 (human face, bird body) and Rénmiànyúshēn人面魚身 (human face, fish body) of fish totem etc. are included. Original animal shaped and Bànrénbànshòu半人半獸 shaped jadeware based on the worship of animals is supposed to be a collective symbol of a certain specific tribal society. In particular, this type of jadeware is not only standard jadeware representing two cultures in Black skin jade culture and Hóngshān Culture jadeware but accounts for the most majority.

3. Ancestor worship

The figure formation made of jade is closely related to each other of reproduction worship, genital organ worship, sex worship, ancestor worship given by God to human beings so the prosperity of reproduction, that is, survival issue of a tribe was the most important key task determining the continuous existence of a clan. Therefore, the appearance of such a jade figure shape is a progressive conclusion reflecting the transition process of sex worship rituals the most directly in order to express the reproductive ability and other divine power given by God to human beings to the gods of heaven and it seems to have been made of jade with the best symbolic value in the Black skin jade culture and Hóngshān Culture society.

The dual sculpture or complex sculpture shape appearing in Black skin jade culture (including Hóngshān Culture) is not only the social relics for meeting and parting according to natural disasters, alliance, war, marriage, peace among different animal totem tribal groups but contemporary self-portrait representing the society at that time created by various consciousness worlds such as heavenly gods worship, nature worship, ancestor worship, reproduction worship of 'Jade Totem' Society.

Together with Hóngshān Culture, especially Black skin jade Culture is mainly found in Liáo-hé遼河 Area and jade carvings showing the ultimate of a three-dimensional space art prove that the world's highest level of the Neolithic Age jade culture already existed in the Northeastern area of the current Chinese continent as the historical entity about 5000 years ago.

Recently in «Hēipíyùfēngyúnlù黑皮玉器風雲錄», a Chinese professor Chényìmín陳逸民 is not only explaining black skin jade carving a bird with Yùshòuxíngjué玉獸形玦 on its head and image 'The heaven ordered Xuánniǎo to set up a statue (天命玄鳥, 降而生商)' appearing in «Shījīng詩經» Shāngsòng商頌 by associating the birth myth of a nation with black skin jade carving but it has a lot of similarity with Gāojùlì高句麗(Goguryeo) national myth that occurred between the Liáo-hé遼河 and Héběi河北.

In «Angtti-Oedipus's Mythology», a Korean professor Jeong, Jae-seo鄭在書 explains, "The most primitive form is expressed as the shape of Rénmiànniǎo人面鳥 (human face, bird body) which is a God bird as well as Guàiniǎo怪鳥(mysterious bird) in

«Shānhǎijīng». The examples include unidentified Rénmiànniǎo in the Qiānqiū千秋, Wànsuì萬歲, Sānshìzhǒng三室塚, Wǔyǒngzhǒng舞踊塚 mural drawn in the Déxīnglǐ德興里 burial mound. Their shapes are all derived from «Shānhǎijīng»."

However, what surprising us more is the fact that the historical and cultural mutual affinity of Gāojùlì高句麗(Goguryeo) tomb murals · «Shānhǎijīng» · Black skin jade culture (Hóngshān Culture) cannot be completely denied through the mutual comparison verification for cattle totem such as half man and half beast statue (Chinese Sun God) of Black skin jade culture Niúshǒurénshēn 牛首人身 and Yándì炎帝 Statue of Niúshǒurénshēn牛首人身 of Gāojùlì(Goguryeo) murals, bird totem such as Réntóuniǎoshēn 人頭鳥身 (human head and bird body) and black skin jade bird and Rénmiànniǎo人面鳥 such as Qqiānqiū千秋, Wànsuì萬歲, jílì 吉利, Fùguì富貴, snake totem such as black skin jade dragon and Moon God, Sun God appearing in the Gāojùlì(Goguryeo) tomb murals as well as bear totem appearing in the founding process of Gǔcháoxiǎn古朝鮮(Gojoseon) and Jadeware relics of Hóngshān Culture and Black skin jade culture. In other words, the historical and cultural subject of a series of jade culture from the Neolithic Age to the historic era is highly likely to be the ancestors of Gāojùlì(Goguryeo), that is, Dōngyí Tribe, the ancestors of East Asian and Korean people.

Recently, the direction of research on jade culture in China is moving from individual Jadeware of jade culture to the whole jade culture. Professor Léi guǎngzhēn雷廣臻 argues, "The secret of Hóngshān Culture and other prehistoric cultures could be solved by confirming the exact geographical position of '海 (sea)' of «Shānhǎijīng». Through many years of research, he recognized that a place where '海 (sea)' of «Shānhǎijīng» is pointing is Bóhǎi 渤海 and a place written in «Shānhǎijīng» Hǎiwàixījīng海外西經 (overseas west longitude) is Hóngshān Culture Area of Dàlínghé 大凌河、Lǎohāhé老哈河 and the contents occurred in the ancient Hóngshàn indigenous people period. According to his interpretation, Bóhǎi渤海 designated by '海 (sea)' is generalized among old documents; only Bóhǎi渤海 in Chinese Dominion can configure this direction situation such as a place surrounded by the sea and forming all directions of South, West, North, East (that is, Hǎiwàinánjīng海外南經, Hǎiwàixījīng海外西經, Hǎiwàiběijīng海外北經, Hǎiwàidōngjīng海外東經)."

The purpose of this study is to newly identify the historical affinitive relationship mainly around Dōngyí東夷 Tribe and the culture subject of Black skin jade culture and Hóngshān Culture that built its own cultural area and existed as the historical subject in a certain area called Liáohé River Basin of the current Chinese Continent for at least over 5000 years.

In order to accomplish the above research purpose, therefore, this is a full-scale study attempted for the first time under the assumption that the society at that time was the 'Jade Totem' society mainly by analyzing jade culture of a series of international nature developed in Northeast Asia of China, Korea and Japan such as jade earrings, rounded jade, Guī圭, Yùyī玉衣 (clothes made of jade,Yùxiá玉匣) of the Korean peninsula and the Japanese archipelago and Gāojùlì(Goguryeo) tomb murals, «Shānhǎijīng», a series of jade culture artifacts including half man and half beast statue (Black skin jade culture) mainly found around the Northeastern region of current China.

Contents

Chapter 1 East-asia Jade Culture / 25

1. Hongshan Culture / 26

2. Black Skin Jade Culture / 68

3. Jade Culture in Yellow River, Yángzǐ River Area / 100

Chapter 3 Jade Culture of the Korean People / 283

Chapter 1

East-asia Jade Culture

1 HONGSHAN CULTURE

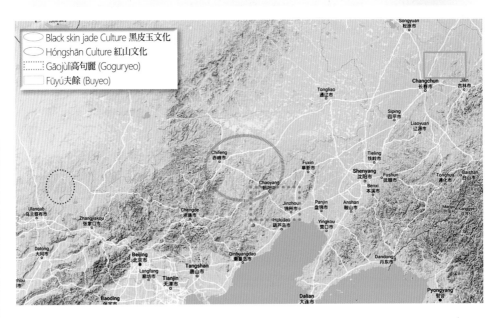

Legend:
- Black skin jade Culture 黑皮玉文化
- Hóngshān Culture 紅山文化
- Gāojùlí高句麗 (Goguryeo)
- Fūyú夫餘 (Buyeo)

[1] Xīnglóngwā Culture-Cháhǎi Culture-Zhàobǎogōu Culture :

(1) Xīnglóngwā Culture 興隆窪文化

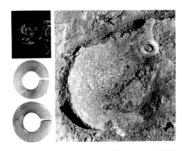

○ Jade earrings: Xīnglóngwā (8000 years ago) Jade earring inserted into the right eye. Nnǚwū女巫 (Girl shamen).

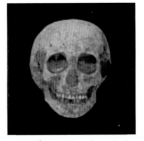

○ Bìyù碧玉: Hóngshān Culture Niúhéliáng牛河梁 (5000 years ago) Bìyù inserted into both eyes. Molded goddess statue.

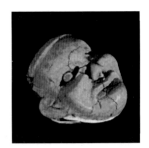

○ <Rényǔshèhuìxúnyù 人與社會尋玉>《China CCTV-10》 The 239th. 2010,10,20.

* These are the oldest juézhuàngěrshì玦狀耳飾 in Asia and items excavated from Liáoníngshěng Fùxīnshì Cháhǎi 遼寧省 阜新市 查海 Historic site belonging to Xīnglóngwā Culture of Northeastern China and are the old type with thick cross section using kidney stone. Jué玦(earring) of Wényánlǐ文岩里 (Munam-ri) juézhuàngěrshì is estimated to be imported from China Northeastern Province, the Maritime Province and elsewhere and the period is also thought to be similar to this. On the other hand, these were excavated in a state of being worn in a human bone in Běiyīnyángyíng北陰陽營 ruins of Jīngliángǎng青蓮崗 Culture corresponding to the late Neolithic period of China. Given coastal sand zone, no human bones are left in Wényánlǐ (Munam-ri) ruins but the worn condition can be guessed in the excavated situation. Therefore, Wényánlǐ (Munam-ri) juézhuàngěrshì is more greatly related to China in terms of burial custom and materials, forms and is highly likely to be imported from Northeastern China and the Maritime province.

■ «GāochéngWényánlǐyíjì高城文岩里遺蹟» National Research Institute of Cultural Heritage, 2004,12,29. Korea.

* Based on the writing in «Zhōuyì周易» xìcí系辞, Chinese Yánxiángfù颜祥富 said in his book «Hóngshānwénhuàyùqìyánjiū红山文化玉器研究», "Yīn and Yáng陰陽 culture is the basis of the Eight Trigrams八卦 for divination. "Fúxī made the Eight Trigrams for divination" is inseparable from Yīn and Yáng culture and explains the fact that Yīn and Yáng culture already existed before Fúxī (4000 BC or much earlier). When is the specific origin of Yīn and Yáng culture. There is no clear answer yet. Many jade earrings excavated from Xīnglóngwā Culture (6200 years BC)Historic site were analyzed and as a result, the big and small, Yīn and Yáng phenomenon evenly existed in each jade earring. This explains that these Xīnglóngwā Culture former inhabitants already used Yīn and Yáng.

❀ **Yellow River area:** HénánWǔyángGǔhú河南舞阳贾湖 Historic site (8600-7600 years ago).

Lǜsōngshíqiú綠松石球 found in head left and right eyes of a middle-aged woman. 3 pieces from the right eye, 2 pieces from the left eye. 1 piece outside the left lower jawbone (Guessed it fell from the left eye).

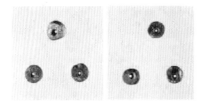

■ <HénánWǔyángGǔhúYízhǐ2001niánfājuéjiǎnbào河南舞阳贾湖遗址2001年发掘简报> «Huáxiàkǎogǔ华夏考古» 2007 (2)

❀ **Liúguóxiáng劉國祥 Chinese Academy of Social Sciences Archeological Institute:** Dry-field farming origin area 8500 years ago-4000 years ago)

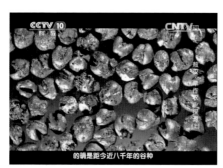

○ Grain excavated from Xīnglóngwā

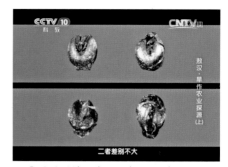

○ Grain in Hóngshān culture and XiàjiādiànLower Culture period

The seeds of grains planted by people during the Xiàjiādiàn Lower Culture 夏家店下层文化 period were inherited from Hóngshān Culture and the seeds of grains are not the only ones they inherited and typical jadeware of Hóngshān Culture period has been found around Xiàjiādiàn Lower Culture tombs and among the highest rating tombs and the fact explains that jadeware used by people during the Hóngshān ulture period continued to be used also in the Xiàjiādiàn Lower Culture period.

(2) Cháhǎi Culture 查海文化

🏵 Dragon (lóng The product of Liáohé遼河 Civilization born while praying for a good harvest 8000 years ago.)

These ruins of 8000 years ago amounting to about 10,000 píng坪 are also Northeast's first agricultural district ruins.

A dragon born by Hóngshān People who started the agricultural life 8,000 years ago from the ritual worshipping a dragon governing water while praying for a good harvest. Shíilong石龍 (Stone dragon) identified in China Liáoníng Province Cháhǎi ruins located in the lower foothills of river upstream. Found between the residential area and residential area, it proved that Hóngshān Culture is the origin of dragon faith.

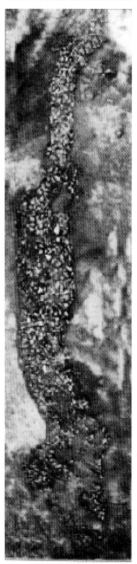

Dragon Culture Origin 1,000 years earlier than Zhōngyuán中原

When and where did a dragon deified by Asians appear. Based on the facts revealed so far, dragon ruins of 8000 years ago in China Liáoníngshěng Cháhǎi are regarded as the origin because they are the oldest. Cháhǎi Historic Site 20km away to the northeast from China Liáoníngshěng Fùxīn was the stage of action of Dōngyí Tribe and is connected to Bóhǎi渤海 Gulf by being led to Dàlínghé in the west, Liáohé in the east and bordered with Inner Mongolia grasslands in the north. Unlike now, it must have been a liveable natural environment because water was abundant at that time. Already 8,000 years ago, the ethnic community where Neolithic people lived was formed here and this place is named as Zhōnghuádìyīcūn中華第一村 with Xīnglóngwā (Neolithic culture of 8,000 years ago belonging to Liáohé Civilization) in China because it is the oldest town and is regarded as the base of Liáohé Civilization. This group residence place was found and was given its name of Cháhǎi Culture. It was found that about 100 households have formed groups in this Historic Site and a dragon-shaped sculpture found in the town center created a sensation in Chinese academics. It is so called Shílóng and is similar to the present dragon shape. The dragon shape was created by stacking stones a little larger than a fist and the length is 19.7m, the wide part is 2m and narrow part is 1m. Chinese scholars name it as 'Zhōnghuádìyīcūn, Zhōnghuádìyīlóng中華第一龍'. According to them, this place Cháhǎi is the origin of Chinese dragon. Until Cháhǎi dragon ruins were found, Shílóng of 7000 years ago of Húběishěng湖北省 Chéncūn陳村 was considered to be the oldest and regarded as the birthplace of Chinese dragon while referring to it as 'Best dragon in Yángzǐ River Basin'. And considering the dragon shape created by stacking shells found next to the body of Hénánshěng河南省 Xīshuǐpō西水坡 No.45 Tomb, a Neolithic tomb of 6000 years ago, it was recognized the homeland of dragon culture that has been led in Zhōngyuán for thousands of years.

Target of the religion dominating the spirit world

But Chinese scholars were greatly embarrassed because Cháhǎi dragon ruins were found and the history of dragon was moved forward 1,000 years and the origin of dragon was found to be the Northeastern Region not Zhōngyuán. Cháhǎi, the Liáoxī遼西 Region is the stage of action of Dōngyí Tribe and the source of the Northeast culture. Soothing their excited mind, Chinese people regard the home of the dragon culture as Northeastern China, Hóngshān Culture in a broad sense. Another reason why China regards this place as the origin of the dragon culture is because the dragon pattern decorated with relief in the pottery as well as Shílóng was found in the Cháhǎi ruins. This dragon pattern pottery sherd is the fragment of Comb-pattern Pottery.

■ «Yùshānrìbào蔚山日報» January 11, 2012, Korea.

❀ Home of Dōngyí東夷, Cháhǎi

Called as 'First Chinese Village (Cháhǎi)', 'First Huáxià Village (Xīnglóngwā)', this is a place respected by the village of China's founder by Chinese People. However, these two are the places that opened the dawn of Bóhǎi Civilization that became the lifeline of East Asian Civilization embracing even China and Japan as well as our nation.

'First Chinese Village' is 'First Dōngyí Village'

Comb-pattern Pottery with engraved a dragon or snake swallowing a toad and pottery sherd with engraved dragon.

All of them were found in Cháhǎi. Specifically speaking, it could be called as 'First Dōngyí Village' not 'First Chinese Village' or 'First Huáxià Village.'

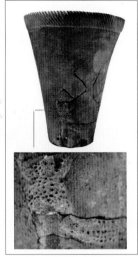

○ Both Comb-pattern Pottery with engraved a dragon or snake swallowing a toad and pottery sherd with engraved dragon were found in Cháhǎi.

❀ Yellow River 黃河 Area: Dragon

Neolithic tomb Hénán河南 Xīshuǐpō西水坡 No.45 Tomb 6000 years ago

Excavated in Púyáng濮陽 Xīshuǐpō西水坡 in 1987, 6400 years ago,

■ «Guāngmíngrìbào光明日報» 2009,11,20.

○ Home of Dōngyí, Cháhǎi

■ «Jīngxiāngxīnwén京鄕新聞» 2007,10,26, Korea.

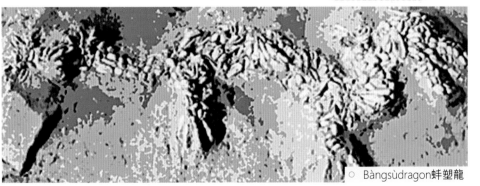

○ Bàngsùdragon蚌塑龍

(3) Zhàobǎogōu趙寶溝 Culture (7400 years ago-6500 years ago)

❀ Yùgū玉箍

❀ Shíxióng石熊 (Stone bear): Typical memorial ritual vessels during Zhàobǎogōu Culture (7000 years ago)

■ «Nèiměngguchénbào内蒙古晨报» 2013,10,23. 14.5cm

❀ Excavated from Áohànqí敖漢旗 Xiǎoshān小山 Historic Site(6800 years ago), Cǎiwén彩紋 Pottery.

Chinese archaeological community: China's first perspective drawing" Original form of "lóngfènglù龍鳳鹿".

 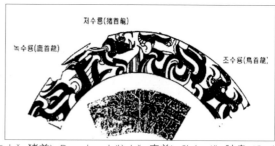

○ Perspective drawings of pig head (zhūshǒu猪首), Deer head (lùshǒu鹿首), Shénniǎo神鳥 (God bird) Língwù靈物.
○ Artifact of the times marking a new era in ritual format and art paintings.
○ Gāojiāwōpùxiāng高家窩鋪鄉 Zhàobǎogōu趙寶溝: Earlier by more than one thousand years than lónghǔduīsù龍虎堆塑 found in Hénán Xīshuǐpō河南 西水坡 6000 years ago.

🎡 **Dragon (lóng)** The product of Liáohé Civilization born while praying for a good harvest 8000 years ago.

The dragon-shaped pattern is also shown in the ceremonial goblet shaped pattern of 7,000 years ago excavated from Áohànqí敖漢旗 Xiǎoshān in 1986. The heads of deer, pig, bird etc. were engraved on the body of a dragon and this are called Lùshǒulóng鹿首龍, Zhūshǒulóng猪首龍, Niǎoshǒulóng鳥首龍. These engraved patterns are regarded as the main totem animals of people of the era and considered to be Shénlíngtúxiàng神靈圖像 (Spiritual iconography) created by faith worship. Therefore, the name of this pottery is also 'Shénshǒutú'àn神首圖案' Given the dragon expressed as the body here, a dragon seems to have been more emphasized than any other animals.

■ «Yùshānrìbào蔚山日報» January 11, 2012, Korea.

🎡 **Táofèngbēi陶鳳杯: "Zhōnghuádìyīfèng中華第一鳳" 6800 years ago**

■ «Rénmínwǎng人民網» 2004,6,22.

○ 17.6cm

○ Yūjiànshè於建設: "lóngfèng appeared in Chìfēng赤峰 in prehistoric times, Following the surprising emergence of Xīnglongwa "Huáxiàdìyīwénhuàjùluò華夏第一文化聚落" of 8000 years ago and Zhàobǎogōu "Zhōnghuádìyīlóng" Bìyùlóng碧玉龍 32 years ago in Chifeng, and 40 years ago surprisingly "Táofèngbēishì陶鳳杯式 fèngzàoxíng鳳造型" of about 6400 years ago appeared today.

[2] Hóngshān Culture:

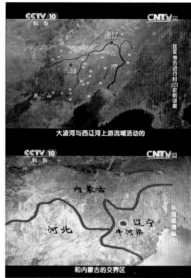

○ Korea The Common Root of Korea-China-Mongolia
■ «Seoul Shinmun» 2007.04.17. Korea.

■ China «CCTV-10» 2014,8,16.11,07.

🌀 **Sūbǐngqí**蘇秉琦: The owner of the goddess grave is a Hóngshān person of 5000 years ago. It is a god statue modeled after a real person and not a god created by the descendants through imagination. She is a woman ancestor of Hóngshān People and also the common ancestor of the Chinese nation.

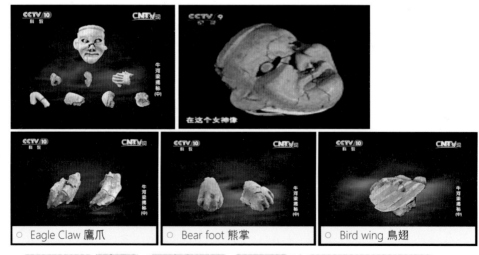

○ Eagle Claw 鷹爪 ○ Bear foot 熊掌 ○ Bird wing 鳥翅

■ «Tànsuǒfāxiàn探索發現» 五千年文明見證-牛河梁揭秘(中) «CCTV-10» 2014,08,16.

❀ Professor Xuēzhìqiáng薛志强: There is "Jade" first and then, "Ritual", indicating that Xīnglóngwā Culture jadeware is one important origin of Chinese ritual civilization.

■ <lùnxīnglóngwénhuàzàiZhōngguówénmíngqǐyuánzhōngdedìwèiyǔzuòyòng论兴隆文化在中国文明起源中的地位与作用>《大连大学学报》第29卷 第5期 2008,10 (大连大学韩国学研究院)

❀ Guōdàshùn郭大顺 (Liáoníngshěng Cultural Relics Archeological Institute)< Hóngshānwénhuàde"wéiyùwéizàng"yuLiáohéwénmíngqǐyuántèzhēngzàirènshi红山文化的"唯玉爲葬"與遼河文明起源特征再認識>

■ 《Wénwù文物》1997年第8期.

Hóngshān Culture Niúhéliáng Historic Site: Wéiyùwèizàng唯玉爲葬 (holding a funeral only with jade). Wéiyùwéilǐ唯玉爲禮.

Niúhéliáng first point already robbed tomb only one Wūrén巫人 (shaman) (5500-7500 years ago)

❀ Guōdàshùn郭大顺: Individual centered grading society.

■ 《Tànsuǒfāxiàn探索發現》五千年文明見證-牛河梁揭秘(下)《CCTV-10》 2014,08,17.

Large tombs, middle tombs and small tombs of Niúhéliáng are clearly different in size, grave goods but the most important thing is that there is a central tomb there and the large tomb of each point is located in the middle and this grading system was further developed and this is one grading system with a focus on one person rather than only some distinction.

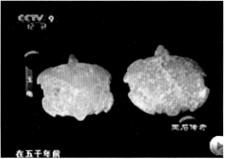

❀ Hóngshān Culture Wéiyùwèizàng唯玉爲葬: Divided into 4 grades (Types and quantities of grave goods, structural type, size of Hóngshān Culture Stone Mound Tomb)

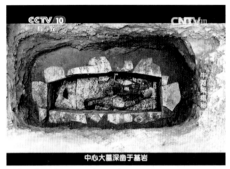

○ center tomb second grade

○ third grade fourth grade

■ 《Tànsuǒfāxiàn探索發現》五千年文明見證-牛河梁揭秘(下) 《CCTV-10》 2014,08,17.

❀ Niúhéliáng 1st point No.1 Stone Mound Tomb No.21 Tomb (5500-7500 years ago) Stone Mound Tomb: Animal Face jade jewelry.

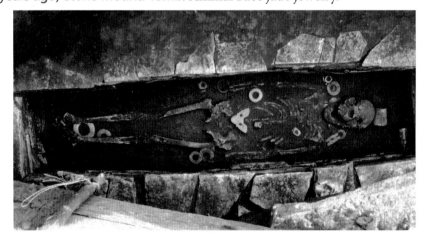

Citing professor Guōdàshùn's claim in <Niúhéliángyízhǐyùqìjìshùchūtàn牛河梁遗址玉器技术初探>, Dèngcōng邓聪(香港中文大学), Liúguóxiáng刘国祥(中国社会科学院考古研究所) analyze that the owner of No.1 tomb M21 tomb in Niúhéliáng Historic Site 2nd point is a shaman from Lake Baikal Jíhēi吉林黑龍 District and excavated jadeware is divided into A Xiùyánxì岫岩係 jadeware and B Baikal-Jíhēixì jadeware in the following picture.

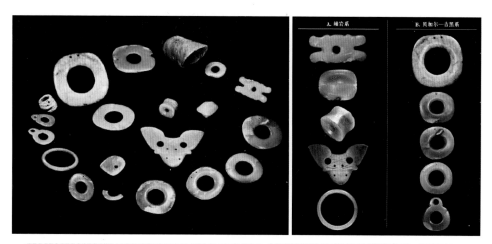

■ «NiúhéliángHóngshānwenhuayízhǐfājuébàogào牛河梁紅山文化遺址發掘報告» (1983-2003), 2013, 北京文物出版社.

As a great finding related to the origin of a series of jade culture with a focus on Neolithic Hóngshān Culture and Black Skin Jade Culture that existed as a historical entity for at least 5000 years in the Northeast Region of the current Chinese Continent, this proves the historical fact that the jade culture area at that time covered a wide area of Russia Siberia as well as current Mongolia and I want to look forward to future study findings.

⊛ Niúhéliáng 2nd point No.1 tombs No.4 grave Stone Mound Tomb (5500-7500 years ago).

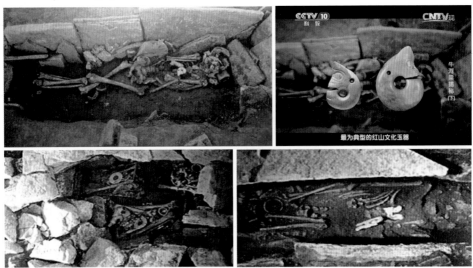

○ 2nd point No.1 tombs No.7 grave 2nd point No.1 tombs No.14 grave

○ 5th point No.1 Tombs Already robbed tomb

⊛ Niúhéliáng 16th point No.4 tomb: Língyuánshì凌源市, Stone Mound Tomb.

⚛ Great performance of Niúhéliáng Historic Site 16th point excavation:

Occupation layer: Upper layer (Xiàjiādiàn Lower Culture 夏家店下層文化, Chéngzǐshān城子山). Middle layer (Hóngshān Culture Stone Mound Tomb). Lower layer(Hóngshān Culture life ruins)

Niúhéliáng Historic Site 16th point is located in the southwest among Niúhéliáng Hóngshān Culture Historic Site groups and is away from Niúhéliáng 1st point Goddess grave in Northeast by the straight-line distance of about 4000m and belongs to Liáoníngshěng Língyuánshì Língběizhèn凌北鎮 Sānguāndiànzǐcūn三官甸子村.

Historic Site is the mountaintop hilly land away about 2 lis里 in village northwest and topography is tilted to the northwestern side and the elevation is 555.5m. The Historic Site is called "Chéngzǐshān城子山" in the area because it was used as a fortress in Xiàjiādiàn Lower Culture after Hóngshān Culture and traces of pikestaves still remained at top of the mountain. In order to understand the whole story of the Historic Site more deeply, the structure and placement of Hóngshān Culture Stone Mound Tomb should be revealed more intensively. Through the approval of the national cultural relics bureau, Liáoníngshěng Cultural Relics Archeological Institute and we excavated 15 pieces of jadeware and 2 pieces of Turquoise ornaments in 4 ash pits, 6 Hóngshān Culture tombs, 16 points archaeological excavations of excavation area 1575m² over two years of last year and this year and found about 470 object props made of various materials such as stone, bones in 8 Xiàjiādiàn Lower Culture chambers, 3 holes, 94 ash pits, 4 ash ditch. Historic Site is divided into 3 occupation layers. The upper layer is Xiàjiādiàn Lower Culture layer and middle layer is Hóngshān Culture Stone Mound Tomb and lower layer has life ruins and stone mount ruins such as Hóngshān Culture ash pit.

■ «Zhōngguówénwùbào中国文物报» September 5, 2013

⚛ Yèshūxiàn叶舒宪: <Wolf Totem or Bear Totem? Analysis and Reflection of Chinese Ancestral Totems 狼图腾,还是熊图腾?关于中华祖先图腾的辨析与反思>

In prehistoric culture on Mongolian grassland, a variety of Hóngshān culture represented by Chìfēng赤峰 most prominent. 8000-4000 years ago, it leads from Xīnglóngwā Culture to Xiàjiādiàn Lower Culture and jadeware culture has lasted for 4000 years. What if examining human totem under today's northern grassland ecology. That is, every jadeware of Hóngshān Culture belongs to it.

■ Chinese Academy of Social Sciences Gazette中国社会科学院院报2006,8,2.

🐚 Independent jade culture: Yellow River Basin, Jade lǐqì禮器 production traditional development impossible.

Shānxī山西 Táosì陶寺 Culture: Zhōngyuán中原 District First, Jade lǐqì禮器 system appeared.

Yèshūxiàn叶舒宪 <Huánghéshuǐdào yǔ Yùqìshídàide Qíjiāgǔguó黄河水道与玉器时代的齐家古国>

1. For archeological excavation, there is only Dúshān獨山 jade mine in Hénán Nányáng南陽 District of Southern Zhōngyuán District because Jade mineral resources are scarce in Zhōngyuán District and jade lǐqì禮器 use of Zhōngyuán Civilization in ancient times is rather very small. Looking at a large quantities of jadeware samples excavated from Erlǐtóu二里頭 and Yīnxū殷墟 Fùhǎomù妇好墓, it can be found that only one or two pieces of jadeware were made by using jade materials. Due to the limitation of these physical conditions, the tradition of large scale jade lǐqì (ritual vessels) production could not be developed like cultures other than Zhōngyuán in the same time or slightly later than Yǎngshào仰韶 Culture which is the most influential in Zhōngyuán District 7000-5000 years ago from now, that is, Hóngshān Culture, Língjiātān凌家滩 Culture and Liángzhǔ良渚 cultures.

2. Most Yǎngshào Culture jadeware that can be seen so far was jade tools or small ornaments. 4000 years ago from now, large combination Jade lǐqì system represented by yùbì玉璧 (jade disk with a hole in the center), yùcóng 玉琮 appeared in Zhōngyuán District for the first time in Táosì Culture of Shānxī Xiāngfén襄汾, Línfén临汾 xiàjìncūn下靳村 and Ruìchéng芮城 Pōtóucūn坡头村 Miàodǐgōu庙底沟 2nd culture. And then, as more mature and diverse Jade lǐqì system and Hénán Yǎnshī偃師 èrlǐtóu二里頭 Culture jadeware appeared in the middle of

Zhōngyuán 3700 years ago from now and dàyùzhāng大玉璋 about 50cm long and dàyùdāo大玉刀 about 60cm long appeared in Zhōngyuán country location for the first time, consistent Jade lǐqì tradition of three generations of XiàShāngZhōu夏商周 could be achieved through the middle role of Erlǐtóu Culture.

■ «Gǔyùshōucángyǔyántǎo古玉收藏与研讨» a total of 13 terms, 2012,12.

[3] Xiǎohéyán小河沿 Culture

(1) Bok, Gi-dae <About Xiǎohéyán小河沿 Culture> :

Before and after 24th century BC (Chìfēng赤峰 Area)

	Chìfēng赤峰 Area	except Chìfēng赤峰 Area
about 24th century BC	Xiàjiādiàn Lower Culture	Xiàjiādiàn Lower Culture
	Xiǎohéyán Culture	
30th century BC	Hóngshān Culture	Hóngshān Culture

Xiǎohéyán Culture : Trace of crushed strata in Hóngshān Culture
Xiàjiādiàn Lower Culture : Trace of crushed ruins layer in Xiǎohéyán Culture.

Regionally, a case of Hóngshān Culture → Xiǎohéyán Culture → Xiàjiādiàn Lower Culture is a phenomenon that appears a lot around Chìfēng Area and a case leading to Hóngshān Culture Xiàjiādiàn Lower Culture is a phenomenon that appears a lot areas outside aforementioned Chìfēng Area.

In order to estimate the upper limit age of Xiǎohéyán Culture based on the results investigated so far, the layers of ruins should be identified first. These layer relations of culture can be traced in Inner Mongolia línxīxiàn Báiyīnchánghàn (內蒙古 林西縣 白音長汗) ruins. In these ruins, traces of Hóngshān Culture Layer crushed by Xiǎohéyán Culture Layer were found. Also, not a few parts among Hóngshān Culture elements were shown as a modified form in Xiǎohéyán Culture elements. Therefore, it can be seen that age of Xiǎohéyán Culture is later than that of Hóngshān Culture. And it can be seen to be very similar to objects of mid and late Dàwènkǒu大汶口 Culture of

Shāndōng山東 Peninsula. Looking at octagonal starts or signs etc., for example, two cultures can be regarded as almost the same period. Mid and late age of Dàwènkǒu Culture that has been studied so far is estimated to be 30th century BC. Then, the upper limit age of Xiǎohéyán Culture should be regarded as the similar period. Next, looking at the lower limit age, traces of Xiǎohéyán Culture ruins layer crushed by Xiàjiādiàn Lower Culture ruins layer appeared in Nántāidì南台地. Given such overlapping phenomenon of ruins, it can be seen that Xiǎohéyán Culture is earlier than Xiàjiādiàn Lower Culture. Then, the lower limit of Xiǎohéyán Culture will be regarded as before and after 24th century B.C. «Dangun Studies» No.21,2007. Korea.

@ Suǒxiùfēn索秀芬, Lǐshǎobīng李少兵
■ <Xiǎohéyánwenhuaniándàiheyuánliú小河沿文化年代和源流 «Biānjiāngkǎogǔyánjiū邊疆考古研究» 1st term in 2008.

Destroying Xiǎohéyán Culture strata, Xiàjiādiàn Lower Culture residence in Nántáidì南台地 Historic Site proves that Xiǎohéyán Culture is earlier than Xiàjiādiàn Lower Culture.

@ Petroglyphs: Reproduction worship.

Six types of reproduction worship Petroglyphs were found in Inner Mongolia Chìfēng赤峰 Wēngniútèqí翁牛特旗 Dàhēishān大黑山. Things attracting the most attention among things found those days and Petroglyphs are genital organs and signs around them represent the first state of life or the age of maturity of life. The local elderly say that the stars above the head is correlated with life and death of each individual. According to the measur-

○ Reproduction worship petroglyphs found in Inner Mongolia
■ «Zhōngguóxīnwénwǎng中國新聞網» 2013,10,3.

ing results, they belong to the late Hóngshān Culture to the Xiǎohéyán Culture period.

(2) Possibility of primitive character appearance.

❀ Wújiǎcái吳甲才: (Researcher of Inner Mongolia Chìfēngshì Wēngniútèqí Humanities and History Institute)

Petroglyphs of about 10,000 pieces were found in Chìfēng Hóngshān Culture District. Followed by Yīnshān陰山 Petroglyphs of 50,000 pieces, this is one of two largest districts with the greatest Petroglyphs amount in China or the world. West Yīnshān陰山 Petroglyphs, East Hóngshān Petroglyphs. Inner Mongolia Dàhēishān Petroglyphs characters likely to be the China's first characters.

Wújiǎcái said that Petroglyphs exhibited this time are the history of 4200 years ago from 5500 years ago from now, leading to Xiǎohéyán Culture period belonging to later Hóngshān Culture. Because of this, the advent of Petroglyphs character signs makes people recognize that ancient Chinese characters certainly prove the history of 5000 years ago.

❀ Chìfēng赤峰 Wēngniútèqí翁牛特旗 Dàhēishān大黑山 character petroglyphs: Round head, cross character.

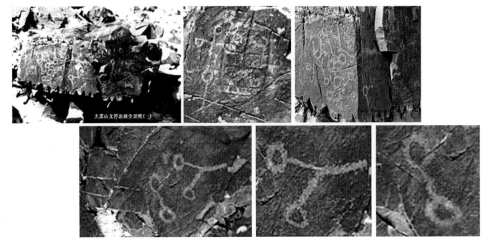

❀ **Xiǎohéyán Culture**: Shípéngshān石棚山 sign character pottery found (4900 years ago).

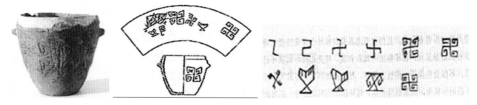

❀ **Xiǎohéyán Culture**: Sign characters (5000-4200 years ago)

In a single drawing sign, there is one shape quite resembling a upside down bird among these 7 drawings. This drawing sign resembled "至" and "帝" among Jiǎgǔwén甲骨文. Yīnshāng殷商 uses "a black bird 玄鳥" as totem and therefore, supreme "帝" is a swallow shape and the head part was made with and inverted triangle and drawing sign, a bird flying backwards above Táoguǎn 陶管 of Xiǎohéyán Culture also has the upside down head and this may be related to bird worship totem of indigenous people during the Xiǎohéyán Culture period. Some scholars think that Yīnshāng殷商 culture originated from Northern China and is closely related to Hóngshān Culture, Xiǎohéyán Culture and Xiàjiādiàn Lower Culture and this is one perspective of the academic world and not discussed here. But, primitive character signs on Xiǎohéyán Culture pottery has certain relationship with Jiǎgǔwén. Overall, character drawing signs of Xiǎohéyán Culture are important clues and materials in Chinese character origin research.

■ <FùhéwénhuàyuHòuHóngshānwénhuà富河文化与后红山文化> «Inner Mongolia Education Publisher» 2008,1,15.

❀ Liúbīng劉冰: (Director of Chìfēngshì Museum)

Shūhuàtóngyuán書畫同源 (same origin of calligraphy and painting)
It went through Xiàjiādiàn Lower Culture in the first of Shípéngshān石棚山
Primitive Táowén陶文 and then, went southward with Shāng商 ancestors and
finally formed Jiǎgǔwén characters and Jīnwén金文 of Shāng Dynasty System
after undergoing the evolution of about a thousand years.
Primitive funeral oration Shípéngshān 30km in the north of Chìfēngshì
"織, 豆, 田; 窯, 窯, 窯, 豆".
Early hieroglyphics = Shūhuàtóngyuán書畫同源

❀ Chénhuì陳惠: <NèiměnggǔWēngniútèShípéngshāntáowénshìshì內蒙古翁
牛特石棚山陶文試釋> Inner Mongolia Chìfēng Wēngniútèqí Shípéngshān
porcelain sign character (Appeared with deer picture) of 4900 years ago.

Signs of 7 letters came out only in a piece of earthenware among them and
signs include an antiquated style such as 飛, 燕, 己, 乙 etc. in addition to 田, 卍.
wànxíng卍形 letters: symbol of Báizhái白翟 tribe

❀ Chinese professor Yánwénmíng嚴文明 (Peking University): <What was early
China like?>

Since the shape of zhūlóng猪龍 or xiónglóng熊龍 is very special and unified among Hóngshān Culture jadeware, most disputants accept it as the totem
of Hóngshān people. This shows that Hóngshān Culture people had unified
religious faith. When combined with a certain power system, such faith can
produce a huge capacity. This point is impossible in traditional clan villages.
Because of this, it can be said to be reasonable that a certain country regime occurred already in the Hóngshān Culture period. It declined rapidly during the
Xiǎohéyán Culture period after Hóngshān Culture because if using too many
people and materials, it is generally difficult to maintain in a long-term.
■ «Guāngmíngrìbào光明日報» 2010,1,14.

❀ Chinese Wángqiáng王强: <Shìlùnshǐqiányùshíqìxiāngqiàngōngyì试论史前玉石器镶嵌工艺 «Southern Cultural Relics» 3rd term in 2008.

In the Xiǎohéyán Culture perdio, jadeware started to decline and excellent genuine goods were also reduced and the application of inlay technology was not shown either. Not a few jadeware was excavated from other Northeastern Districts such as Xīnlè新樂 Culture, Xiǎozhūshān小珠山 Culture, Xiǎonánshān 小南山 Historic Site but inlay craft is not seen either.

❀ Xiǎohéyán Culture: Excavated jadeware

○ Yùyú玉魚. Chìfēng Xiǎohéyán, 22.7cm.

○ Niǎoxíngyùdāo鳥形玉刀. Chìfēng Xiǎohéyán, 29.3cm.

❀ Shinohara篠原昭·Shima島亨: <神々の発光-Chinese Neolithic Age Hóngshān Culture Jadeware Sculpture> Tokyo 山羊舎.

○ Yùbì玉璧. Xiǎohéyán Culture. Diameter 12.1cm.

○ Yùzhuó玉镯 (Jade bracelet) Xiǎohéyán Culture. Diameter 7.6cm.

■ Owned by Chìfēngshì Museum

❀ Bok, Gi-dae: Octagonal star (Inner Mongolia línxīxiàn Báiyīnchánghàn内蒙古 林西縣 白音長汗) ruins, very similar to mid, late objects of Dàwènkǒu Culture, Almost the same period. <About Xiǎohéyán Culture小河沿文化>

■ «Dangun Studies» No.21, 2007. Korea.

@ Chénguóqìng陳國慶: <An Analysis of Correlation between Xiǎohéyán Culture and Other Archaeological Cultures 淺析小河沿文化與其他考古學文化的互動關係> (Jílín University Biānjiāng Archaeological Research Center)

The octagonal star pattern of Xiǎohéyán Culture was found in the largest quantities from Dàwènkǒu Culture and the areas are also extensive and in addition, the relationship is quite close to Xiǎohéyán Culture and Dàwènkǒu Culture listed in the above.

小河沿文化
大汶口文化
凌家灘文化
松澤文化

■ Xiǎohéyán Culture-Dàwènkǒu Culture-Sōngzé松澤 Culture- Língjiātān凌家灘 Culture «Biānjiāngkǎogǔyánjiū邊疆考古研究» 1st term in 2009.

@ Biyùduōtóuqì碧玉多頭器 (Jade ritual vessel): Aohànqí敖漢旗 Sàlìbāxiāng萨力巴鄉. A symbol of power.

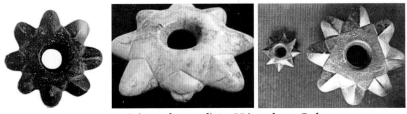

The most important Lǐqì (ritual vessel) in Hóngshān Culture
Jilin Province, Large octagonal type jadeware (vision of the universe)

■ «Aohàn cultural relics purification» Bìyùduōtóuqì (Lǐqì), diameter:11cm. Aohànqí Museum.

[4] Xiàjiādiàn Lower Culture夏家店下層文化

(1) Hóngshān Culture and Xiàjiādiàn Lower Culture

❀ **Zhūhóng朱泓 (China Jílín University):** Xiàjiādiàn夏家店 Lower Culture remains (134 pieces: 5000 years ago)

We tried the constitutional anthropological analysis of 134 human bones from Xiàjiādiàn Lower Culture. According to the research findings, they were largely divided into two tribes and the old Northeast type around Liáohé civilization was found to account for more than 2/3.

❀ **Korean professor Bok, Gi-dae:** "More than 60% of ancients in the Liáoxī遼西 area are the old Northeast type affinitive with Koreans"

■ «Dangun Studies» No.21. 2007. Korea.

Scientific experiment results: Human succession relations. Constitutional anthropological analysis. Race classification.

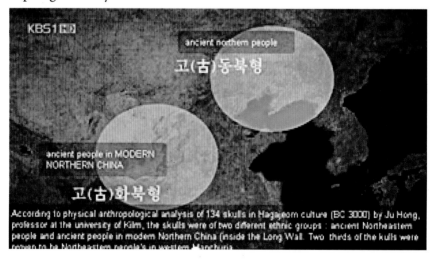

@ **Korean professor Bok, Gi-dae:** <An Essay on the Relevance between Hóngshān Culture and Xiàjiādiàn Lower Culture>

Xiàjiādiàn Lower Culture: Association with Hóngshān Culture (Sānzuòdiàn 三座店shíchéng石城, Gōuyún-type jade jewelry (Cloud-type jade jewelry), Tāotièwén饕餮紋, Inherited Xiàjiādiàn Lower Culture jadeware and Hóngshān Culture jadeware as they are. Hóngshān Culture is the culture with very developed jadeware.

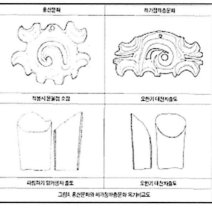

○ Paper citation, life-size jade

○ <An Essay on the Relevance between Hóngshān Culture and Xiàjiādiàn Lower Culture>

■ «Cultural Historiography» No.27.

@ Liúguóxiáng劉國祥 (Chinese Academy of Social Sciences Archeological Institute): Grains inherited from Hóngshān Culture, jadeware.

The seeds of grains planted by people during the Xiàjiādiàn Lower Culture period were inherited from Hóngshān Culture and the seeds of grains are not the only ones they inherited and typical jadeware of Hóngshān Culture period has been found around Xiàjiādiàn Lower Culture tombs and among the highest rating tombs and the fact explains that jadeware used by people during the Hóngshān Culture period continued to be used also in the Xiàjiādiàn Lower Culture period. Looking at the use function of these jadewares, they are all about the communication between man and God and such medium between heaven and earth is to pray for rain and hope abundant agricultural production and Hóngshān Culture and Xiàjiādiàn Lower Culture has a kind of cultural transmission relationship.

■ «Tànsuǒfāxiàn探索發現» 敖漢-旱作農業探源(上) «CCTV-10» 2014,06,07.

@ Xiàjiādiàn Lower Culture: Excavated from Chìfēngshì Áohànqí Dàdiànzǐ大甸子 Xīnglóngwā興隆窪.

○ Yùgū玉箍 Qūmiànyùpáishì曲面玉佩飾   ○ Excavated from Dàdiànzǐ No.833 Tomb

Excavated from Dàdiànzǐ Cemetery No.659 Tomb, 7.1cm, Owned by Chinese Academy of Social Sciences Archeological Institute

(2) Existence of mature character signs.

Sānzuòdiàn三座店 shíchéng shard characters (4000-3400 years ago)

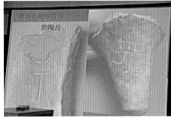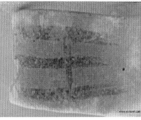

○ Cǎitáo彩陶 character sign Xiàjiādiàn Lower Culture Cǎitáo

🌀 **Guōzhìzhōng郭治中 (Inner Mongolia Cultural Relics Archeological Institute) character signs (Hieroglyphic signs)**

left image; lower part "丌Gi" Hieroglyphic signs, upper part "柴chái" Hieroglyphic signs.

There were mature character signs during the Xiàjiādiàn Lower Culture period.

○ Xiàjiādiàn Lower Culture Sānzuòdiàn Mountain fortress Historic Site, Chi (mǎtíxíngshíchéngqiáng 馬蹄形石城墙)

🌀 **Tiányànguó田彦國 (Áohàn pre history museum 敖漢史前文化博物館):**

Chéngzishān城子山 Mountain Fortress, the center of Xiàjiādiàn Lower Culture.

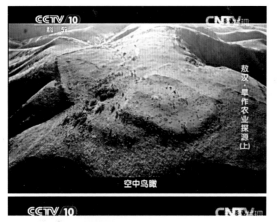

○ Xiàjiādiàn Lower Culture center Chéngzishān, The largest ritual mountain fortress Historic Site of 4000 years ago.

○ Aohànqí敖漢旗 Sìjiāzǐzhèn四家子鎮 Cǎomàoshān草帽山. Ancestors honored by ancestral rites were buried in the altar.

○ Shírén石人: Excavated from Cǎomàoshān. He is a kind of ancestral god and is a god statue jointly served during ancestral rites by Hóngshān People.

■ «Tànsuǒfāxiàn探索發現» 敖漢-旱作農業探源(上) «CCTV-10» 2014,06,07.

※ Anzhìmǐn安志敏 (Chinese Academy of Social Sciences): <Lùn"wénmíngdesh ǔguāng"héNiúhéliángyízhǐdekǎogǔshízhèng論"文明的曙光"和牛河梁遺址的考古實證>

■ «Běifāngwénwù北方文物» Total 69 terms,1st term in 2002.

Age of Xiàjiādiàn Lower Culture Niúhéliáng copper decoration, Yětóng冶銅 crucible wall was measured and as a result, it turned to be a thousand years later than Hóngshān Culture. A piece of copper decoration was excavated from a surface stone coffin of one Stone Mound Tomb witnessed at that time and seemed almost not to belong to the Hóngshān Culture Relics. But copper decoration was not generally mentioned in the materials released in the past and new information started to be provided in recently published "yěliàn冶鍊 Ruins and Copper Products of Hóngshān Culture". (SūBǐngQí蘇秉琦主編 «Zhōngguótōngshǐ中國通史» 第2券, 上海人民出版社,1994)

In particular, Yětóng crucible wall revealed during the excavation in 1987 was already confirmed to belong to Xiàjiādiàn Lower Culture and is later by a thousand years than Hóngshān Culture at the same time through chemical experiment and carbon-14 dating. (LǐYánXiáng李延祥等 <Niúhéliángyětónglúb ìcánpiànyánjiū牛河梁冶銅爐壁殘片研究> «Wénwù文物» 12th term in 1999) And it is already undoutful fact that Niúhéliáng Historic Site has the cultural ruins of different ages. In addition, there are other circumstantial evidence and for example, jadeware found in large quantities here has been regarded as a representative artifact among Hóngshān Culture Stone Mound Tomb groups but does not match almost completely among papers published already because of the lack of certification by the official report.

[5] Liáodōng遼東 (Jílín吉林, Hēilóngjiāng黑龍江) Area

(1) Liáodōng Peninsula遼東半島

Snake type jade earrings: Snake Totem proven in «Shānhǎijīng山海經» records. Jadeware excavated from Tiánjiāgōu田家溝 No.9 Tomb.

■ «Dàliánrìbào大連日報» 2013,2,21.

Since 2009, Liáoníng Cultural Relics Archeological Institute has conducted archaeological excavations targeting Língyuánshì凌源市 Tiánjiāgōu Hóngshān Culture cemetary continuously over the years and as a result, snake shaped jade earrings were first excavated in the right ear of the tomb owner. These snake shaped jade earrings are the size of combining the index finger and middle finger of an adult and the color is white and snake head mouth, eyes are clearly visible and they are every lustrous. But the lower part is sloppy. The age is before and after 5300-5000 years. The legend on snake earrings during the ancient period in «Shānhǎijīng» proves that the record of «Shānhǎijīng» on the excavation of snake shaped jade earrings is not wrong. Hongshan Culture Yùjué玉玦 of 5000 years ago from now, which has consistently lasted from Xīnglóngwā Culture of 8000 years ago that first appeared that experts already pointed out, is a kind of earring ornament representing the status of upper figures in the ancient society and these high figures are Wūxí巫覡 (shaman) at that time. The original form of Yùjué is a snake and is a result of snake worship custom which was fashionable in the society at that time and snake shaped jade earrings excavated from Tiánjiāgōu are Shénqì神器 at that time.

❀ 'Xiǎozhūshān小珠山-Měisōnglǐ美松里 (Misongri)' Culture type (5000 B.C.): Gǔcháoxiǎn古朝鲜 (Gojoseon) period. Southern Liáoníngshěng.

○ Xiǎozhūshān, yùxuánjī玉璇璣 excavated from Xiǎozhūshān Historic Site, yùshífǔ玉石斧

❀ Qūyù曲玉 (Korea;Gokok.Japan;Magatama):

Neolithic Bìyù碧玉 system Qūyù used Měisōnglǐ (Misongri) ruins.

In Měisōnglǐ (Misongri) ruins, Qūyù type Shǒushì首飾, the jade and stone material of Bìyùxìtǒng碧玉系統 was excavated and its color is white and the front was well ground and there is a hole on one side. It is a small thing 16㎜ long, 7㎜ wide and 4㎜ thick. Qūyù (Gokok) made in a distinct form in Bronze Age was said to come from Japan, but it can be said that this was used early in Korea by yùshí玉石 unshaped Qūyù (Gokok) of Bìyù system excavated from Měisōnglǐ (Misongri) ruins ruins of Neolithic Age, the very early period. «Korea National Culture Encyclopedia» Central Academy of Korean Studies

❀ Gǔcháoxiǎn古朝鮮 (Gojoseon) Period:

Liáoníngshěng, Měisōnglǐ (Misongri) type pottery. 'Xiǎozhūshān'-Měisōnglǐ (Misongri) culture type. Liáoníngshěng (Centering on Dāndōng丹東.Dàlián大連 district): North Korea set the same cultural area.

Considering that winding pattern excavated from Hòuwā後窪, Shàngmǎshí上馬石, Xiǎozhūshān小珠山, Xīnlè新樂 ruins etc. of Liáoníngshěng centering on Dāndōng.Dàlián district and that of Měisōnglǐ (Misongri) are the same, North Korea set the same cultural area. This cultural type is called Xiǎozhūshān-Měisōnglǐ (Misongri) type'. Referring to the radiocarbon dating of Xīnlè ruins, Neolithic Age of Měisōnglǐ (Misongri) ruins was recorded to correspond to B.C. 6000. This is 1000 years earlier than the conventional claim considering that the upper limit of Neolithic Age was regarded as B.C.5000 and belong to the earliest time among period classifications of North Korea. And Měisōnglǐ (Misongri) ruins which were considered to correspond to the late Neolithic Age (second half of B.C.3000) until the mid-1980s appeared as the earliest Neolithic ruins in Korea. And then, Měisōnglǐ (Misongri) type pottery was found to be widely distributed in Liáodōng area including the northern Korean Peninsula and became the relics representing the Gǔcháoxiǎn (Gojoseon) period. The age of ruins is B.C.8-7th century and corresponds to the Gǔcháoxiǎn (Gojoseon) period.

■ Yìzhōu義州 Měisōnglǐ (Misongri) ruins «Archeology Dictionary», 2001.12, National Research Institute of Cultural Heritage, Korea.

⚘ Shànxíngtóngfǔ扇形銅斧 (fan-shaped Bronze ax) = excavated with Mandolin -shaped bronze dagger: Distributed around Liáoníngshěng.

Bronze axes are divided into fax axes with the fanwise head part and rectangular bronze axes showing overall rectangle but fax axes are typical and are excavated with Mandolin-shaped bronze dagger. These special types of axes are distributed around Liáoníngshěng and most of them are found in the ruins of Mandolin-shaped bronze dagger Culture. Korean fan axes seem to have been produced under the influence of Liáoníngshěng Bronze Age Culture.

(2) Jílín吉林 area: Dōngyí東夷 Shǎohào少昊 belongs to Hóngshān Culture.

⚘ **Professor Jeong, Jae-seo:** Shǎohàoguó belongs to Hóngshān Culture of Northeast.

«Shānhǎijīng» Dàhuāngdōngjīng大荒东经 :

"Outside of East Sea, large valley, Shǎohào少昊's country, Shǎohào Little Emperor Zhuānxū颛顼 came here."

Outside of the East Sea is the living site of Shǎohào Niǎoyí鸟夷 village. The distinction of inside and outside of the East Sea belongs different cultural areas. "Dōnghǎizhīwài东海之外" here not only means "7 continents and 5 oceans all over the world" but mainly territory other than "East Sea", for example, two letters of Hǎiwài海外 were written in front of all northeast states such as overseas Sùshèn肃慎 overseas Fūyú夫餘 (Buyeo) etc. Hóngshān Culture of Liáohé Basin belongs to the outside of the East Sea and Lóngshān龍山 Culture and Dàwènkǒu Culture of Yellow River Basin to the inside of the East Sea. Therefore, Shǎohàoguó is not in Shāndōng山東 Dàwènkǒu or Lóngshān Culture but belongs to Hóngshān Culture of northeast. Dōngyí includes Tàihào太昊 . Shǎohào少昊 . Ddìjùn帝俊 . Yì羿.

■ «Angtti-Oedipus's Mythology» p.260 Changbi, 2010,9. Korea.

❀ **Researcher Liúguóxiáng刘国祥 (Chinese Academy of Social Sciences Public Archeology Research Center Executive deputy director):**

The originality of Shíilóng石龍 found in Zuǒjiāshān左家山 Culture Historic Site in the grounds of Jílínshěng is very excellent. It is clearly pointed out in his thesis. Jílínshěng is an important area in Northeast district prehistoric jadeware research because it is located in China Central Northeast District and the east and southeast face the territory of the Soviet Union, Cháoxiǎn朝鲜, respectively and north, west and south are bordered with Hēilóngjiāng黑龍江, Inner Mongolia, Liáoníng, respectively.

■ 《Chángchūnrìbào長春日報》 2012,2,16.

❀ **Professor Léiguǎngzhēn雷廣臻 (Cháoyáng Teachers' High School) <Relationship between Hongshan Culture and Emperor Culture>**

《Shānhǎijīng》 Dàhuāngběijīng大荒北經 Zhuānxū顓頊 burial plot. Fūyú夫餘(Buyeo) cultural area.

We say that <Hǎiwàiběijīng海外北經> and <Dàhuāngběijīng大荒北經> are the same direction. A described object in one direction and Fūyú (Buyeo) Culture of Jílín, Liáoníng District fit each other. In 《Shānhǎijīng》, there is a lot of description about Fūyú (Buyeo) and according to the record of <Hǎiwàiběijīng>, "Shān山 of Wùyú务隅, Dì帝 Zhuānxū was buried in Yáng and Jiǔpín九嬪 in Yīn." According to the record of <Dàhuāngběijīng>, "Shān of Fùyú附禺, Dì帝 Zhuānxū and Jiǔpín were buried." Two recorded "Wùyú" and "Fùyú" all refer to "Fúyú (Buyeo)". Dì Zhuānxū was buried here.

■ 《Cháoyáng朝陽日報》 2010,4,22.

❀ **Park, Sun-hee (Sangmyung University, Korea): <The Origin of Seal and Gǔcháoxiǎn (Gojoseon) Culture shown in Hóngshān Culture Artifacts>**
《Comparative Folklore Studies》 Vol. 49. Korea.

1. Unlike other regions, the nature of cultural ruins is closely associated with large-scale political structures or religious rituals in Hóngshān Culture Region

so various animal-shaped jadeware and jade seal must have been excavated. In this region, a magical ceremony targeting nature and animals is likely to have been made. In contrast, only ornaments and impractical production tools may have been made into jadeware and buried because tombs in Jílínshěng region and Hēilóngjiāngshěng region are tombs only burying bodies.

2. Large amount of jadeware was also excavated with embossed earthenware in Neolithic tomb ruins of Hēilóngjiāngshěng. Excavators excavated 97 jadeware in 25 places from the Neolithic ruins in Hēilóngjiāngshěng and analyzed that the material of jadeware is Xiuyanyù岫岩玉 of the Yālùjiāngbiān鴨綠江邊 because it is very fine. Excavators thought that a tribe who created jade culture in Hēilóngjiāngshěng may be indigenous culture earlier than Gǔ Fūyú古夫餘 or Dōngyí Tribe.

3. Qūyù曲玉 (Gogok) and bones, leaf-shaped button decoration made of stone and beads made from shells, bracelets etc. were excavated a lot in Zuǒjiāshān ruins of Late Neolithic Age and Xīpǔgǎng西浦港 ruins 4th layer (3,780 BC-3,530 BC), showing that clothing decoration is more colorful than before and glamorous and a variety of formative beauty was pursued.

✿ Jílín Region: Closely related to Xīnglóngwā Culture, Xīnlè Culture, Hóngshān Culture <Owned by National Museum Historic Site where "China's Best Shíilóng" was excavated. Nóngān農安 Zuǒjiāshān Culture stoneware found>

Excavated relics: Pottery, stoneware, boneware in large quantities.
Carbon (C14) age dating: 6,755 years, 4870 years respectively (Two samples)
Shídiāolóng石雕龍 excavated: Taken by National Museum after excavation. Paying attention to two pieces of Shídiāolóng among excavated relics. 6000 years ago Zuǒjiāshān 2nd term cultural artifacts (Characterized by Hóngshān Culture Yùzhulong玉猪龍).

■ «Chángchūnrìbào長春日報» 2012,2,16.
■ Excavated by Jilin University archaeological research community in 1985

⊛ **China's best Shíílóng excavated: Jílín Nóngān Zuǒjiāshān Culture (5000-4000 years ago)**

Zuǒjiāshān Culture : One place among important archaeological cultures in second Sōnghuājiāng松花江 Basin and entire Northeast District.

○ Neolithic Excavated from Nóngān Zuǒjiāshān in 1985 .4.4cm, 3.8cm.
○ Black stone Cánrén蚕人 (Cocoon-shaped figure). Wild goose type pèishì佩飾.

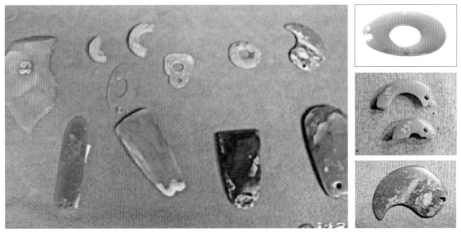

○ Yùyú玉魚 ornaments, Yùfǔ玉斧(jade ax). Excavated from Báichéng白城 Region, Prehistoric jade-ware.
■ «Chángchūnrìbào長春日報» 2010,5,20. 2009,11,10

⊛ **Professor Dèngcōng邓聪, Professor Wánglìxīn王立新:**

Yùjué玉玦 (7000 years ago. Báichéng Museum). Jílínshěng first.
Route: Hēilóngjiāng-Northeastern Plain-Yellow River downstream Shāndōng Area-Mid and downstream of Yángzǐ River–Northern Guǎngdōng

Bei River water system

Traces "cut with a strap buried in sand" were commonly found on one piece of Yùjué excavated from Historic Site of 6000 years ago from now and this is the first trace "cut with a strap buried in sand" identified in Jílín for the first time. This type of processing technique is commonly seen in the Neolithic culture of 8000 years ago from Northeast Asia, northern Japanese islands to Russia beach District, China Hēilóngjiāng District etc. Traces "cut with a strap buried in sand" were found for the first time among prehistoric jadeware excavated from Jílínshěng. The age of this Yùjué is evaluated to be at least 7000 years ago and it may be one of the earliest jadeware found in Jílín.

Sand buried strap cutting technology: Northeastern Province Chìfēng Áohànqí Xīnglóngwā (8000 years ago). In 2004, he and Lǚhóngliàng吕 红亮, Chénwěi陈玮 conducted the jadeware cut experiment, Co-paper <yǐróuzhìgāngshāshéngjiéyùkǎo以柔制刚砂绳截玉考> describes the jadeware cut experiment as follows: Given current ancient materials, the cutting technology was originated from the Northeast and spread to the west again and went down to Yellow River along Northeastern Plain from the south of Hēilóngjiāng and reached the vast range of whole area of Shāndōng, mid and downstream of Yángzǐ River basin and Northern Guǎngdōng Běijiāng北江 and Neolithic jadeware line cut traces could be found.

■ «Chángchūnrìbào長春日報» 2009,11,10

⊛ Xītuánshān西團山 ruins: Connecting Xīnglóngwā-Hóngshān Culture-Gǔcháoxiǎn (Gojoseon) culture

The jadeware line cutting technology found in China Chìfēng Áohànqí Xīnglóngwā Historic Site of 8000 years ago from now representatively the earliest in the same kind of craft age in the world so far and earlier by 5000 years than Central America. Jade ornaments were also unearthed in large quantities from Jílínshěng Xītuánshān tomb ruins belonging to 5th century B.C. to 4th century B.C estimated to be relics of Sùshèn肅慎 Tribe. Ornaments of Xītuánshān Culture made of stone and jade account for largest proportion and bronze and ornaments made of bronze were the least. Among jade ornaments, Báishíguǎn白石管 accounts for an absolutely large quantity, 1559. Such large amount of jade products also shown in Late Gǔcháoxiǎn (Gojoseon) reveals that jade ornaments of early Neolithic Xīnglóngwā ruins bloomed in Hóngshān Culture and led to Gǔcháoxiǎn(Gojoseon) Culture again.

○ yùfǔ玉斧 21.5cm. 18.3cm. 14.3cm. 20.5cm.
○ Excavated from Jílínshěng Zhènlàixiàn镇赉县 Jùbǎoshān聚宝山. Báichéng City Museum. Owned by Zhènlàixiàn Cultural Relics Management Office. Owned by Zhènlàixiàn Cultural Relics Management Office. Excavated from Jílínshěng Dàānshì大安市, Owned by Báichéng City Museum.

☸ Liúguóxiáng劉國祥 (Chinese Academy of Social Sciences Archeological Institute) : Hóngshān Culture Largest Yùsì玉耜(40cm). Yùsì owned by director Sūnshùlín孙树林, president of Jílínshěng Hóngshān Culture Research is the largest Shísì石耜 (Digging tool) in the Hóngshān Culture period and belongs to an important treasure of the country.

■ «Chángchūnrìbào長春日報» 2011,1,25.

☸ Bok, Gi-dae: large octagonal star shape jadeware <About Xiǎohéyán小河沿 Culture>

Object of mid and late Xiǎohéyán Culture and Shāndōngshěng Dàwènkǒu Culture, Very similar (octagonal star. sign etc.). The layer relationship of this culture can be tracked in Inner Mongolia línxīxiàn Báiyīnchánghàn 林西縣

白音長汗 ruins. In these ruins, traces of Hóngshān Culture Layer crushed by Xiǎohéyán Culture Layer were found. Also, not a few parts among Hóngshān Culture elements were shown as a modified form in Xiǎohéyán Culture elements. Therefore, it can be seen that age of Xiǎohéyán Culture is later than that of Hóngshān Culture. And it can be seen to be very similar to objects of mid and late Dàwènkǒu Culture of Shāndōng Peninsula. Looking at octagonal starts or signs etc., for example, two cultures can be regarded as almost the same period. Mid and late age of Dàwènkǒu Culture that has been studied so far is estimated to be 30th century BC.

■ «Dangun Studies» No.21, 2007. Korea.

❀ Liúguóxiáng: Large octagonal type jadeware (Reflecting Hóngshān Culture vision of the universe) «Chángchūnrìbào長春日報» 2012,5,22.

○ Belonging to Late Hóngshān Culture and 5500 years ago to 5000 years ago from now.

(3) Hēilóngjiāng Region: jadeware Historic Site 266 places, jadeware 173 pieces of jadeware excavated.

❀ Yújiànhuá于建华: More than 100 kinds of perfect jadeware excavated. <Neolithic jadeware excavated from Hēilóngjiāng Province and Related Issue>

■ «Northern Cultural Relics» 4th term in 1992.

Excavation of Hēilóngjiāngshěng Neolithic jadeware is relatively early. In the early 1950s, Senior scholars such as Lǐwénxìn李文信, a Chinese eminent archaeologist found a bunch of sophisticated jadeware in Yīlánlóukěnhǎdá依兰楼肯哈达 cave ruins and showed it to people. And then, due to the development of China's archeology industry especially for recent 10 years, soundness of Cultural Relics Agency and efforts of relevant personnel, relatively complete jadeware close to almost one hundred kinds have been excavate on the vast land of Hēilóngjiāngshěng.

🐚 Liúguóxiáng <Study on Hēilóngjiāng Prehistoric Jadeware>
■ «Chinese History Museum» 1st term in 2000

In China prehistoric Northeast District jadeware development process, Hēilóngjiāngshěng prehistoric jadeware occupies an important position. According to the current data statistics, prehistoric jadeware points excavated from the grounds of Hēilóngjiāngshěng are a total of 266 places, total number of jadeware excavated is 173 pieces, main kinds are Fǔ斧, Chǎn铲, Bēn锛, Záo 凿,Bǐxíngqì匕形器, guǎn管, zhū珠, Huáng璜, round jade with Shuāngniǔ双钮 tooth, oval vessel, Yùbì玉璧 (jade disk with a hole in the center) etc.

🐚 Park, Sun-hee (Sangmyung University, Korea): Hēilóngjiāngshěng 97 Neolithic ruins, 97 jadeware excavated <The Origin of Seal and Gǔcháoxiǎn (Gojoseon) Culture shown in Hóngshān Culture Artifacts>
■ «Comparative Folklore Studies» Vol. 49,Korea.

Large amount of jadeware was also excavated with embossed earthenware in Neolithic tomb ruins of Hēilóngjiāngshěng. Excavators excavated 97 jadeware in 25 places from the Neolithic ruins in Hēilóngjiāngshěng and analyzed that the material of jadeware is Xiuyanyù岫岩玉 of the Yālùjiāngbiān鴨綠江邊 because it is very fine. Excavators thought that a tribe who created jade culture in Hēilóngjiāngshěng may be indigenous culture earlier than GǔFūyú古夫餘 (GoBuyeo) or Dōngyí Tribe. And then, moving to Hēilóngjiāngshěng in the division process of Fūyú (Buyeo) located in Liáoxī遼西 Area, they further developed jade culture by following the tradition of this indigenous culture. As a good example, according to «Sānguózhì三國志» <WūwánXiānbēidōngyíchuán

烏丸鮮卑東夷傳> Fūyú (Buyeo) part, red jade and beautifuil beads as big as Jujube are produced in East Fūyú (Buyeo) and people have regarded Yùbì玉璧 and Yùguī玉圭, Yùzàn玉瓚 inherited from previous generations as treasure.

@ **Professor Sin, Yong-ha**: Originated from Yezú濊族 Nènjiāng嫩江, Hēilóngjiāng Area <The Formation of Gǔcháoxiǎn (Gojoseon) Country>

"Ye濊" was a tribe originated from Nènjiāng Basin. "Ye River' is the old name of present 嫩江 (Nèn River, tributary of Sōnghuājiāng松花江). The land where Ye Tribe was originated was the land where Fūyú (Buyeo) Country was founded. The name can be seen in the records of «Hòuhànshū後漢書», "Fūyú (Buyeo) was originally the land of Ye" and "there is an old castle in Fūyú (Buyeo) and its name is Yechéng濊城. Usually it is the land of Yemò濊貊" in «Jìnshū晋書» " "Ye" Tribe started the economic life of fishing and hunting first and therefore, moved around rivers along water plants and deer, wild boar etc. Cháshān Dīngruòyōng 茶山 丁若鏞 recorded "Ye is a place name or water name. Therefore, the military leader called himself YeWáng濊王."

■ «Society and History» Vol. 80 (2008) Korean Sociological Association

@ **Hēilóngjiāngshěng Xiǎonánshān小南山 (Neolithic Age 75000-5000 years ago) Historic Site.**

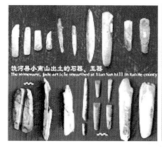  

In zhǔfēng主峰 in 1991, 117 pieces of various grave goods were found in a couple's tomb and among them, 62 pieces of jadeware, 72 pieces of jadeware

currently collected and taken in Xiǎonánshān Historic Site amount to 45.3% of jadeware found in the entire Province and 12 kinds and it is the best Historic Site showing the most abundant, diverse kinds among jadeware excavated from Historic Site of the entire provice.

❧ Hēilóngjiāng Area Yùbì: Tàiláixiàn泰来县 Tàiláizhèn泰来镇 Dōngmínggǎcūn东明嘎村.

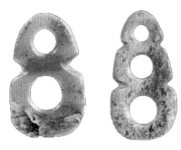

○ Tàiláixiàn Dōngwēnggēnshān东翁根山, Shàngzhìshì尚志市. jade disk 5.91cm. Owned by Tàiláixiàn Museum.

○ Jadeware excavated from Dōngmínggǎ tomb jade disk 9.37cm. Owned by Hēilóngjiāng Province Cultural Relics Archeological Institute

○ Yùbì 4.32cm. 4.57cm. 7.15 – 8.93cm.
○ Excavated from Tàiláixiàn Dōngwēnggēnshān ruins. Owned by Tàiláixiàn Museum

❧ Fūyú夫餘 (Buyeo) Kingdom: <See Fūyú Kingdom in Yìlóuwángchéng挹娄王城 —Fènglín凤林 Ancient Castle cǎifǎngjì采访记>

■ «Jiāngchéngrìbào江城日报» 2010, 7, 21.

Fènglín Ancient Castle Site floor plan Produced by Hēilóngjiāngshěng Cultural Relics Archeological Institute

According to the introduction of Wángxuéliáng王学良, this is the largest semi-basement palace currently found in China. It fully proves the fact that Yìlóu挹娄 People, Mǎnzhōu滿洲 ancestors already entered the civilization era and constructed "Yìlóuwángchéng".

He says that Fènglín Ancient Castle Site and relative Pàotáishān炮台山 Sacred Place the largest and magnificent "Big Dipper" memorial service altar currently found in China as confirmed by several archaeological experts through the actual investigation. A Chinese eminent astronomer, astronomical archaeological expert Yīshìtóng伊世同 recognized that Fènglín acred place is the administrative point and Pàotáishān sacred place is a memorial place and Yìlóuwángchéng is consistent with "worship of Heaven, courtesy, wisdom" the dead were saying. In July 2001, a prominent astronomical archaeological expert Yīshìtóng presented a clear answer at that time when investigating in Pàotáishān: Correction was carried out by using astronomy annual equation and as a result, 8 mountaintop holes represent "Tàiyī太一" or "Tiānyī天一" star typically referred in future generations, that is, North Star at that time. Yīshìtóng said there is no doubt because Big Dipper bearing is clearly marked in Historic Site. Although Pàotáishān Sacred Place was built during the Hàn 漢, and Wèi魏 Dynasty, the constellation marking of the North Star reflects the constellation grid of about 4500 years ago from now and shows the transmission relationship of astronomical knowledge of the ancestors who lived in the Northeast during the Hàn Dynasty. Pàotáishān Big Dipper altar is the largest and earliest altar among the altars of the same kind first found in China. What is the relationship between Ffènglín Ancient Castle and it?

[6] Korean Peninsula

❀ Gyeonggi Provincial Museum Curator Lee, Hun-jae: Yùzhūlóng玉猪龍 excavated from Jīngjīdào Pōzhōu Zhōuyuèlǐ 京畿道 坡州 舟月里. Ornaments of the Neolithic people, Jadeware.

Yùzhūlóng is Jadeware symbolizing an animal head. Originally, Yùzhūlóng was named after 'Yùzhūlóng (Dragon and Pig) known in China Liáoníng Neolithic Age Hóngshān Culture and means 'Pig and dragon made of jade.' Jadeware in Pōzhōu Zhōuyuèlǐ 坡州 舟月里 may be also included in the classification of Yùzhūlóng of Hóngshān Culture. There is a groove for a string in two places of the middle hole and the groove shape has something in common with the technique of jade products excavated from Xiǎozhūshān 2nd group Ojiācūn 吳家村 in China. The shape of jadeware in Pōzhōu Zhōuyuèlǐ 坡州 舟月里 is similar to that of Jadeware of Neolithic Hóngshān Culture in Liáohé Basin in Northeastern China. Hóngshān Culture belongs to the late Neolithic Age of China and is mainly distributed in Chìfēngshì in Liáoxī遼西.

Whether Zhōuyuèlǐ舟月里 jadeware ornaments that came out to the world by localized heavy rain in 1996 are trading goods of Neolithic Age or those brought by migrants or those directly processed by Neolithic People of the Korean Peninsula is a task to be further studied. One obvious fact is that people who lived in Zhōuyuèlǐ (Juwolri) in Neolithic Age used jadeware like today's modern people. They may have kept perfect and beautiful eternal life in mind.

2 BLACK SKIN JADE CULTURE

Together with Hóngshān Culture, Black skin jade Culture is mainly excavated in Liáohé遼河 Area and jade carvings showing the ultimate of a three-dimensional space art as well as jade manufacturing technology prove that the world's highest level of the Neolithic Age jade culture already existed in the Northeastern area of the current Chinese continent as the historical entity about 5000 years ago.

Niúshǒurénshēn牛首人身 (Cow head and human body) Sun God, the representative artifact among half god half beast shapes of Black skin jade Culture and Hóngshān Culture jade carving is well known enough to appear in Gāojùlì 高句麗 (Goguryeo) tomb murals. For such sun god black jade carving, a Chinese professor Xiàdéwǔ夏德武 argues in «Zhōngguóshénmìdehēipí yùdiāo中国神秘的黑皮玉雕», " Of the formative arts of Pan Hóngshān Culture Black skin jade carving, the most striking expression is commonly known as "Sun God" black skin jade carving. This kind of black skin jade carving expression is a combination of "Cow head Niúshǒu牛首 and Rénshēn人身" of a kind of supernatural phenomenon. Objectively, this kind of black skin jade carving accounts for about 30% of Hóngshān Black skin jade carving. In fact, the formation of Rénshòu人獸 (human and beast) combination shows the shape of the totem ancestors of an ancient ethnic society. Examples: Xióngshì熊氏 sculpture combining a bear and human, Xuānyuánshì軒轅氏 sculpture combining fish and human, Fúxīshì伏羲氏 sculpture combining human head and dragon body, Shǐwéishì豕韦氏 sculpture of pig head and human body, Huāntóushì讙头氏 sculpture of bird head and human body, Such complex molding appears everywhere in black skin jade carving and Niúshǒurénshēn牛首人身 (Cow head and human body) Statue is Shénnóngshì神農氏 Statue.

Most of all, however, the thing attracting the most attention is black skin of

Black Skin Jade Culture jade carving. As for black skin of Black skin jade Culture, National Institutions or University Institutes of the two countries of Korea and China already found through a variety of scientific experimental results such as black skin jade material inspection, black skin jade surface component inspection (Seoul National University National Center for Inter-University Research Facilities, China National Geological measuring Center, Shanghai Museum etc.), black skin jade surface public peeling experiment etc., "Black skin created a film and jade was not discolored into black. Black skin has been buried in the soil over a long period of thousands of years and changed physically and chemically." In addition, according to recent age dating results for the sex figure statue by U.S. CIRAM, "The material is jade (nerphite) and surface is caused by natural and long-term weathering and artificial corrosion is not observed."

Based on the above test results, «Shānhǎijīng山海經» 中山經, "嬰用吉玉, 彩之,饗之 (When offering good jade, color it beautifully and bless so that the gods of heaven can enjoy it.", 西山經 "其祠之禮, 用一吉玉瘞, 糈用稷米 (The etiquette of performing ancestral rites is to bury one good jade in the ground and use nonglutinous millet as rice to be cooked for a sacrifice). "郭曰又加以繒綵之飾也 (Gwak says that it was decorated by coloring it again)", the note of Guōpú郭璞 (Eastern Jin東晋, 276-324) cited by Wúrènchén吳任臣 (Qing 清,1628-1689) «Shānhǎijīngguǎngzhù山海經廣注». If compared with Guōpú's record of "jíyù吉玉 is colored jade" each other, it could be proved that jade was used extensively as various uses in the society before «Shānhǎijīng» appeared and jade was colored and colored jade was buried in the ground. Especially by finding the literature basis that jade was colored in «Shānhǎijīng», the Wūshu 巫書 of Dōngyí東夷 Tribe, the important literature basis that can examine the cultural relevance of Black skin jade Culture was ensured.

[1] Yùlóng玉龍 : Snake, dragon totem.

 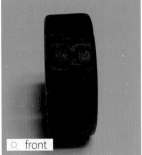

○ Side ○ front

○ Black Skin Jade Culture

(1) Yùjué玉玦: Áohànqí敖漢旗 Xīnglóngwā-Wényánlǐ文岩里 Gāochéng高城, Jiāngyuán江原-Niúhéliáng牛河梁-Wēngniútèqí 翁牛特旗

 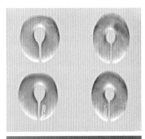

○ 8000 years ago.; Xnglóngwā. Wényánlǐ, Korea.

○ 6000 years ago;
○ Andǎoli 安島里 Lìshuǐ麗水 Quánnán 全南 Korea.
○ Japan 日本 Sāngyě桑野Kuwano ruins

○ 5000 years ago;
○ Yùshān Chǔróng 蔚山 處容里i, Yùshān蔚山. Ulsan Museum
○ Chinese Liángzhǔ良渚 Culture (5300-4300 years ago)

(2) Yùlóng玉龍:

7500-5500 years ago. Hóngshān Culture Niúhéliáng

   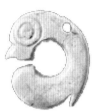 

○ 4000 years ago-3500 years ago Collected from Xiàjiādiàn Lower Culture Wēngniútèqí翁牛特旗 Sānxīngtālā三星他拉 (1971,8)

○ Collected from Wēngniútèqí Sānxīngtālā Claimed to be excavated from Dōngguǎibànggōu東拐棒溝
○ National Museum of China. Wēngniútèqí Museum
○ Black Skin Jade Culture Yùlóng (C-shaped dragon):

◎ Official name: Yùlóng玉龍

Korean Yùlóng : "World's best Yùlóng", "Bóhǎi渤海 Yùlóng like Flying" Professor Lee, Hyeong-gu

■ <The Root of Korean Culture> 《Jīngxiāngxīnwén京鄉新聞》 1989,2,3. Korea.

○ Chinese Yùlóng : China Palace Museum, Tribal totem. Hóngshān Culture Early clan art major work.

○ Gāojùlì (Goguryeo) tomb murals: Moon god and Sun god. China, Claimed to be Fúxī伏羲, Nǚwā 女娲.

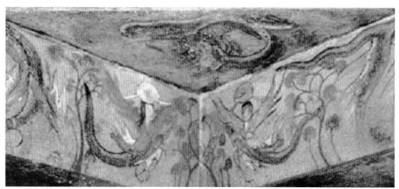

○ Jí'ān集安 Gāojùlì (Goguryeo) tomb murals No.5 Tombs No.4 Moon god and Sun god.

○ Jí'ān集安 Gāojùlì (Goguryeo) tomb murals No.5 Tombs No.5.

☺ Zhūnǎichéng朱乃誠: (Chinese Academy of Social Sciences Archeological Institute) <Hóngshānwénhuà shòumiànjuéxingyùshìyánjiū紅山文化獸面玦形玉飾研究>

As the research of Hóngshān Culture Shòumiànjuéxingyùshì獸面玦形玉飾 progresses, it was found that there is no direct relationship between Sānxīngtālā Yùlóng and Hóngshān Culture Shòumiànjuéxingyùshì. Sānxīngtālā Yùlóng is not Hóngshān Culture jadeware and the period may be the Xiàjiādiàn Lower Culture period.

1. Sānxīngtālā三星他拉 Yùlóng and Hóngshān Culture Shòumiànjuéx-ingyùshì have no direct change relationship.
2. Sānxīngtālā三星他拉 Yùlóng is not Hóngshān Culture jadeware.

(3) Yùshòuxíngjué玉獸形玦 : Step of undefined official name.

China: Yùshòuxíngjué. China Palace Museum. Expressing deified animals.
Animal worship.

○ Court collections during the Qing Dynasty: Neolithic Hóngshān Culture. Explaining the fact of non unearthed relics.
○ China Yùzhūlóng玉猪龍: Niúhéliáng牛河梁 2nd point No.1 tombs No.4 grave (5500-7500 years ago)

○ Yùzhūlóng 7.2cm, 10.3cm. Yùgū 8.6cm

○ British Museum: Yùlóng玉龍.

❀ Yùshòuxíngjué玉獸形玦: Reflecting a variety of animal totem.

Bear (Yùxiónglóng), Pig (Yùzhūlóng), Bird (Yùniǎoxíngjué) etc..

❀ Yùshòuxíngjué + Figure statue: Tribal chief of a variety of animal totem.

○ 40cm Front Side

❀ Yùshòuxíngjué + Animals: Tribal group society with different animal totems.

[2] Yùniǎo玉鳥 (jade bird) Shénniǎo神鳥 (God bird): Heavenly gods.

Shòu獸=God of the earth. 天父地母 (Combination of heaven and earth).

Bird totem tribe Dōngyí東夷 Tribe: Supreme 天帝. Father of the Sun. Leader of various gods

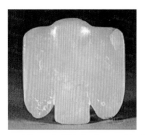

○ Yùyīng玉鷹 (jade eagle): Shanghai Museum.
○ Beijing Palace Museum (2.5cm, Hóngshān Culture, Eagle Related)

○ Excavated from Liáoníng Cemetery Niúhéliáng牛河梁, 5500-6000 years ago.

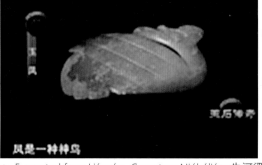

○ "The most complete first discovered Yùfèng玉鳳 (Jade Phoenix). The original of Yùfèng is a noble and rare animal. The target animal of jade carving of Hóngshān Culture is a highly realistic art and Phoenix appeared finally when reaching a certain artistic level." «People's Daily Overseas Edition人民日報 海外版» May 21, 2011.

  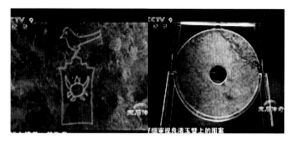

- ○ Yùniǎo玉鳥 on the altar:
- ○ Liángzhǔ良渚 Culture Fēiniǎo飛鳥 (Chief priest, Dominating divine right).

- ○ North America West Coast, China Hèlánshan贺兰山, Yǎngshào仰韶 Culture táopíng陶瓶

- ○ Black Skin Jade Culture Yùniǎo

❀ Yùniǎo (Shénniǎo) + animals: Combined with tribal groups worshipping other animal totems

❀ Yùniǎo + Sun God : Sun God tribal chief.

❀ Yùniǎo + Figure statue : Tribal chief, Group leader.

[3] Bànrénbànshòu半人半獸
(獸人;half man and half beast):

(1) Niúshǒurénshēn牛首人身 (Cow head and human body)(Yándì炎帝; Gāojùlì 高句麗Goguryeo tomb murals) : Cattle totem.

■ 《Shānhǎijīng山海經》

Běishānjīng北山經 ; 有獸焉,其狀如牛,而赤身,人面,馬足,名曰窫窳,其音如嬰兒,是食人.

Xīshānjīng西山經 Xīcìèrjīng西次二經 ; 其七神皆 人面牛身

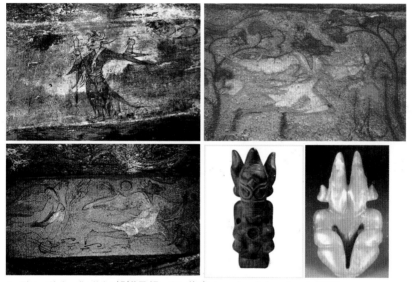

○ The 《Cháoxiǎnrìbào朝鮮日報》 Jí'ān集安 Area local shooting in 1993.
○ Gāojùlì No.5 Tombs No.5 tomb mural
○ Black Skin Jade Culture 35cm. Hóngshān Culture7.7cm

֍ Niúshǒurénshēn: 《Shānhǎijīng》 Dōngyí myth. Original possibility of Korean myths.

"In the mythical age, many ethnic groups co-existed in the Chinese Continent. The contents covered by Chinese mythology can be seen to be East Asian Culture. There was no border in the mythical age. Thinking that Chinese mythology has nothing to do with us too exclusively can be seen to be the idea after the modern ethnic concept has formed. I think we can bind together with the common roots only when escaping from one country-centered mythical theory." The author's core argument is that Chinese mythology is the common assets at the East Asian level because the Ancient Chinese continent was a stage where numerous tribes co-existed. In the extension, comparing with the gods of Gāojùlì (Goguryeo) tomb murals, he reveals that the gods of Yándì炎帝·Chīyóu 蚩尤 system in Dōngyí myth of «Shānhǎijīng» are highly correlated with Korean mythology. He says that they may be 'the (some) original of Korean mythology.'

■ Professor Jeong, Jae-seo «Angtti-Oedipus's Mythology» Changbi, Korea.
■ Hankyoreh, 2010.9.10.Korea.

🌀 **Black Skin Jade Culture Sun God** : CCTV official report.

■ <Shìbókànguóbǎo世博看国宝: HóngshānGǔyù红山古玉> 国宝档案 «CCTV-4» 2010.8.17.

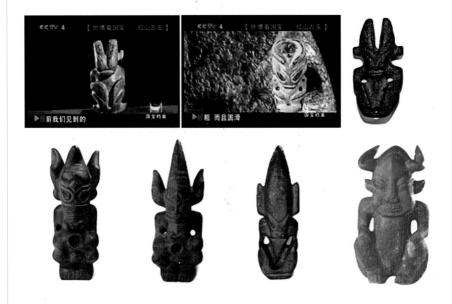

🌀 **Niúshǒurénshēn Sun God + Calf** : Sun God + God man

(2) Xióngshǒurénshēn熊首人身: Bear totem. Black Skin Jade Culture

(3) Zhūshǒurénshēn猪首人身: Pig Totem
(Shǐwéishì 豕韦氏. Fēngxīshì封豨氏)

«Shānhǎijīng» Zhōngshānjīng中山經;Zhōngcìqījīng中次七經 皆豕身而人面.

(4) Yángshǒurénshēn羊首人身(Sheep head and humanbody): Gǔqiāngzú古羌族.

■ «Shānhǎijīng»

Xīcìsanjīng西次三經 其神狀皆 羊身人面,
Dōngshānjīng東山經 Dōngcìsānjīng東次三經 其神狀皆人身而羊角.

(5) Guī龜 totem: Emperor Xuānyuánshì軒轅氏 related.

Deer totem: Lùshǒurénshēn鹿首人身

Dog totem : Dog head goddess statue wearing a scepter on the head.

Horse totem: Mǎshǒu馬首 (horse head) Statue with Mǎshǒurénshēn馬首人身(Horse head and human body) Statue on the head.

○ Chényìmín «Hóngshānyùqìshōucángyǔgǎnshǎng紅山玉器收藏與感賞» Shanghai University Press, 2004,4.

○ «Shānhǎijīng» Hǎinèidōngjīng 海內東經: Léizé雷澤's Great Spirit lightning

○ Léishén雷神. Guīshēnréntóu龜身人頭 (Turtle body and human head).

(6) Bànrénbànyú半人半魚 (half human and half fish): Dīrénguó氐人国.

○ Jeong, Jae-seo «Angtti-Oedipus's Mythology» Changbi. 2011. Korea.
○ Rénshǒuyúshēnyǒng人首魚身龍 (唐,陶俑)48cm, Excavated from Jiāngsū江蘇 Nánjīng南京 in 1950

(7) Frog totem: Nǚwā女娲 with a frog on the head

The goddess statue with a frog on the head is Hóngshān Culture sex worship and idol of reproduction worship. The head part of this carving is very big and one frog is put on the head and the statue body stands bent and has protruding breasts and this kind of carving with unusually large female genitals has a very clear and sincere purpose, substantially reflecting sex and reproduction worship of primitive village people and the frog right on the head is the best explanation of the reproduction worship. Particularly vigorous reproductive performance of a green frog already received the attention of prehistoric men.

■ Chényìmín «Hóngshānyùqìshōucángyǔgǎnshǎng» p.129,130.Shanghai University Press, 2004.

🐚 **China's first snake civilization 8000 years ago:** Cháhǎi查海 indigenous people totem

Snake totem clan + Toad totem clan = Village configuration.

The tubular táoguǎn陶管 in the pattern of snake biting a toad 8000 years ago was found in Fùxīn阜新 Cháhǎi Historic Site in the 1980s of the 20th century. This is the earliest snake shape among things found so far. This artifact is already a primitive art work and also totem worship work. This táoguǎn seems to express that the Cháhǎi communit is a village composed of two clans of toads and snakes and Cháhǎi indigenous people already expected very powerful reproductive potential of toads and expected an animal with strong power like snakes to protect their clan.

■ «Dàliánrìbào大连日报» 2013,2,21.

[4] Yùshénrén玉神人

Yùshénrén: Neolithic jade culture human statue Life-size comparison (10:1, Unit cm)

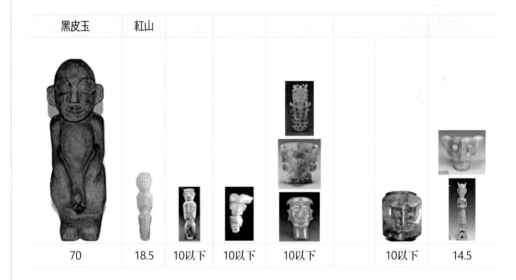

黑皮玉	紅山					
70	18.5	10以下	10以下	10以下	10以下	14.5

(1) Yùshénrén: Wūrén巫人.

Chinese Zhōuxiǎojīng周曉晶: Yùshénrén, Shaman(Wūrén).

"Yùrén玉人 is to carve a Wūrén statue. The tomb owner is to lead live shamans, wear jade carvings of the shamans of dead ancestors and wish the protection and cooperation to the soul of the shamans to perform shénshì神事."

⚜ Liúguóxiáng劉國祥 "Yùrén puts two hands on the chest and strikes a praying pose and is Wūrén governing shénshì神事."

"Chinese Jade Studies Jade Culture 4th Academic Conference" thesis, Liáoníngshěng Museum<Hóngshānwénhuàdòngwùxíngherényùqìyánjiū紅山文化動物形和人形玉器研究> Dàlián大連 University. 2004,5,18-20.

■ Water jar woman and her daughter 26cm. poor book «Black Skin Jade» p.154.

🌀 Yùshénrén : Nánnǚliǎngtóuyìtǐ男女兩頭一體

○ Nánnǚliǎngtóuyìtǐ Yùshénrén(Jade god man) 20cm

○ poor book «Black skin jade» p.35. «Shānhǎijīng山海經»

🌀 Yùshénrén: Main character of myths and legends.

Lǐsuǒqing李鎖清: Huángdì黃帝 (yìtóusìmiàn一頭四面)

"Huángdì is the god of lightning among mythical legends and became the emperor of the center later. He is said to be able to see every direction of North, South, East and West at the same time because he has four faces."

■ «Zhōngguólìshǐwèijiězhimí中國歷史未解之謎» p.12,Guāngmíngrìbào光明日報Publisher, 2004,1. China

@ **Yùshénrén : Chinese official report.**

■ <Shìbókànguóbǎo世博看国宝-HóngshānGǔyù红山古玉> 国宝档案 «CCTV-4» 2010.8.17.

○ (right) Excavated from Chìfēngshì Bālínzuǒqí巴林左旗. Stone Statue 19.4cm. Collected in 1980. Excavated from Bālínyòuqí巴林右旗.

@ **Yùshénrén: Excavated from Hóngshān Culture Niúhéliáng.**

Black Skin Jade Culture Figure statue.

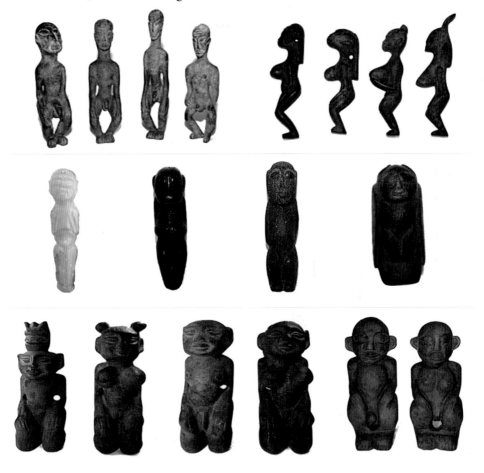

✿ Goddess 女神

■ «Cháoxiǎnrìbào朝鮮日報» 2009.1.31., Korea

✿ Pregnant goddess 姙婦女神

✿ Boy, girl god.

○ Thinking girl (Front, back) 41cm

✿ Male god 男神

🌀 **Yùshénrén**: Goddess wearing a crown.

🌀 **Yùshénrén**: Figure god wearing a crown

○ Rénmiànniǎo人面鳥 (human face, bird body)«Black skin jade» p.166

○ Qing (Estimated to be Mid-17th century-19th century) 5.7cm. Owned by Smithsonian Museum Freer Gallery

FREER SACKLER THE SMITHSONIAN'S MUSEUMS OF ASIAN ART

🌀 **Yùshénrén**: Shaman

○ Táng唐 (600-1000) 4.8cm. 5.0cm. Smithsonian Museum Freer Gallery
○ Commentary Materials of Smithsonian Museum Freer Gallery:

This ornament probably represents a shaman and he can play a role of a middleman and force of good and evil living in the world. This may have been a headdress a shaman enjoyed wearing or the part of Taoistic preist's ceremonial costume.

(2) Sexual intercourse figure statue: Sex worship 性崇拜

■ «Black skin jade» p.160

(3) Genital organ worship; 生殖器 崇拜

○ Eagle female genital organ Black Skin Jade Culture

[6] Yùlǐqì玉禮器 (jade ritual vessels)

(1) Gōuyún-type jade jewelry 勾雲形玉佩 (Cloud-type): Hóngshān Culture Center Niúhéliáng 5th point

Wéiyùwèizàng唯玉爲葬 (holding a funeral only with jade): Funeral system. Status order society. Type of tomb: Stone Mound Tomb

○ Niúhéliáng 5th point No.1 Tombs Already robbed tomb.
○ Smithsonian Museum Freer Gallery H:5.7cm

❧ Guōdàshùn <Hóngshān Culture Gōuyún-type jade jewelry Research 红山文化 勾云形玉佩研究>

Gōuyún-type jade jewelry:

Symbolizing the combination of priesthood + sovereignty.

Excavated location: Above the right shoulder. Excavated in the same location as Fǔyuè斧鉞.

Function: Related to quánzhàng權杖, Gōuyun-type jade jewelry, Fǔyuè, Gōuyún jade jewelry, Shénqì神器 such as Yuguī玉龜, excavated only in the central tombs(中心 大墓).

❧ Professor Léiguǎngzhēn雷广臻 <Relationship between Hóngshān Culture and Emperor Culture>

■ «Chángyángrìbào朝陽日報» 2010,4,22.

«Zuǒzhuàn左傳» zhāogōng昭公17th year: "In the old days, Huángdìshì黄帝氏 examined clouds so by recording clouds such as Yúnshī雲師, Yúnmíng雲名, he operated clouds by dividing them into areas and displayed a series of objects by classifying or using clouds. Things called Yún(cloud) were all referred to as Yún雲"

According to «Zhōuyì周易», "Clouds came from a dragon and wind from a tiger." It means that a dragon changed from clouds. If this explanation is established, the Gōuyún-type jadeware is related to clouds and if related to clouds, it means that it is associated with a dragon and being associating with a dragon means that it is also associated with the Yùxiónglóng玉熊龍 we are talking about. Among Jiǎgǔwén甲骨文, jīnwén金文, the character "Yún" looks a lot like a bent animal without feet such as dragon, snake type. According to Huángdìshì, there is a relationship between cloud totem, Gōuyún-type jadeware found a lot in Hóngshān Culture and these two kinds of culture.

(2) Sānkǒngyùbì 三孔玉璧

○ Fùxīn Hútóugōu胡頭溝. Black Skin Jade Culture

☸ **Yùxuánjī玉璇璣**: Astronomical equipment.

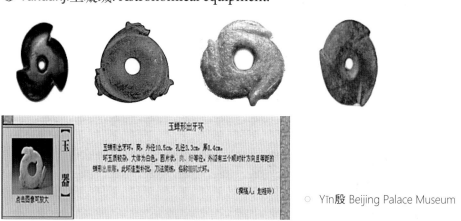

○ Yīn殷 Beijing Palace Museum

☸ «Shǐjì史記» Vol. 1 五帝本紀 1st

於是帝堯老, 命舜攝行天子之政, 以觀天命。舜乃在璿璣玉衡, 以齊七政。

King Yáo堯 was old and ordered them to take the politics of the emperor and examined the allotted span of life. Thanks to his Xuánjīyùhéng, King Shùn 舜 controlled seven emotions.

Xuánjī璿璣: Astronomical observation equipment, Celestial globe.

Yùhéng玉衡: Fifth star of the Big Dipper

Xuánjīyùhéng: Celestial globe

Yángjiāluò楊家駱 zhǔbiān主編 «XīnxiàoběnShǐjìsānjiāzhùbīngfùbiānèrzhǒngyī新校本史記三家注幷附編二種一» 台灣鼎文書局印行.

❀ «Mèngzǐ孟子» : Shùn舜 Dōngyí東夷 Tribe. Age of civil wars (475 B.C-221 B.C) Lílóuxià離婁下: 舜生於諸馮, 遷於負夏, 卒於鳴條, 東夷之人也.

King Shùn was born in Zhūféng, was defeated by Xia Dynasty and moved and died in Míngtiáo and who is a Dōngyí person.

(3) Yùhuáng玉璜: Half of Yùbì玉璧

(4) Yùyuè玉鉞: Symbol of power.

○ Pig and dragon small hatchet

[7] Scientific experiment:

(1) Age dating experiment:

Seoul National University National Center for Inter-University Research Facilities. U.S. GEOCHRON LABORATORIES.
Same yùdiāo玉雕 carving phase: Requested Sampling age dating (Korea, U.S.)

<1> 1st carbon dating:

World's first. 14300 ± 60 years (SNU07-R131.2007,12,18).

Korea Chunnam Techno University Northeast Cultural Institute Professor Jeong, Gun-jae

Experiment: Korea Seoul National University National Center for Inter-University Research Facilities. Sampling in the presence of KBC-TV.

<2> 2nd carbon dating:

Korea Chunnam Techno University Northeast Cultural Institute Professor Jeong, Gun-jae

Experiment: U.S. GEOCHRON LABORATORIES. 3150 ± 40 years (GX-33119-AMS.2009.7.23.)

<3> 3rd carbon dating: China, Neolithic period

Experiment: U.S CIRAM ANALYSIS CERTIFICATE 0415-OA-21N-2 (New York, June 3, 2015)

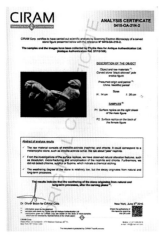

(2) Surface component analysis:

The results indicate that the weathering of the stone originates from natural and long-term processes, after the carving phase.

Experiment 1 : China National Geological measuring Center Analysis report (June 26, 2000). Request agency: Geological agency

Sample Name, Old jade skin (古玉殻). Date of receipt June 6, 2000.

Reporting Date June 26, 2000.

Experiment 2 : Request agency: Bǎiyuè柏岳 Experiment report: Analysis of Hóngshān Black skin jade elements

Shànghǎi Museum : Black skin jadeware materials experiment (Without separating the skin and body). U.S.TN Corporation QuanX type Sèsànyíngguāng 色散螢光 Fluorescence analysis.

Experiment 3 : Bǎiyuè: Skin and body separate analysis experiment report. To distinguish the authenticity of Black skin jade carving.

Black skin: Including 35 kinds of elements such as phosphorus, chromium, nickel, manganese, titanium, silicon, copper etc.

"Black skin was not made artificially but has been buried in the soil over a long period of thousands of years and changed physically and chemically."

Experiment 4: Seoul National University National Center for Inter-University Research Facilities. Given that black skin components of 9 Black skin jade artifacts are not constant, they are materials which are not completely identical in different time and places. This result eliminates the claim to some degree that this Black skin jade may be a forgery made in modern times.

Experiment 5 : U.S CIRAM ANALYSIS CERTIFICATE 0415-OA-21N-2 (New York, June 3, 2015)

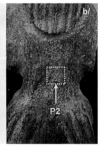

Conclusions

The study and the analysis of two samples taken on a carved stone figure have showed that :

The raw material consist of tremolite-actinote (nerphite) and chlorite. It could correspond to a metamorphic stone, such as chlorite-actinote schist. We talk about "jade" nephrite.

From the investigations of the surface replica, we have observed natural alteration features, such as dissolution, micro-fracturing and amorphisation of the nephrite and chlorite. Furthermore, we did not dedect chroline, sulphur or fluorine, which indicate a chemical etching.

The weathering degree of the stone is relatively low, but the decay originates from natural and long-term processes.

The results indicate that the weathering of the stone originates from natural and long-term processes, after the carving phase. The material of the above Black skin jade sex statue is jade (nerphite) and surface is caused by natural and long-term weathering and artificial corrosion is not observed.

(3) Public peeling experiment :

○ China Art Collector Association, Jadeware Collection Committee

■ «Zhōngguóshénmìdehēipíyùdiāo中國神秘的黑皮玉雕» p.152, 萬國學術出版有限公司. 2009, Beijing.

■ Black skin jade is the best authentic jade 黑皮玉也是古玉珍品 «Běijīngrìbào北京日報» 2010,1,31.

❧ **Professor Xiàdéwǔ夏德武**: Argued Black Skin Jade Culture, Pan Hóngshān Culture 汎紅山文化.

Given in two aspects, including Black skin jade carving in the category of Pan Hóngshān Culture means as follows:

1. The formative characteristics of Black Skin Jade Culture jade carving Hóngshān Culture jadeware excavated from Inner Mongolia Chìfēng District Niúhéliáng simliar in many aspects and belong to the same early cultural phenomena of Liáohé Basin.

2. There are archaeological excavation reports about Black Skin Jade Culture jade carving yet and because of this, it is difficult to conclude the period of this cultural phenomenon and independent cultural properties. (Black Skin Jade Culture was first published by Bǎiyuè, January 2001, «Zhōngguóshōu cáng中国收藏» 37th term magazine).

■ Jadeware Collection Committee zhǔbiān «Zhōngguóshénmìdehēipíyùdiāo中國神秘的黑皮玉雕» Introduction p.6, 萬國學術出版有限公司. 2009.

❧ **Chinese Chényìmín**: Hóngshān Culture = Black Skin Jade Culture

In particular, Black Skin Jade Culture receiving the attention of the international community has apparently exactly the same form as jadeware such as yùlóng玉龍 (C-shaped dragon), jade earrings, sun god, Yùniǎo玉鳥(jade bird), Gōuyún-type jade jewelry etc. which are the representative artifacts of Hóngshān Culture and the only difference is the seemingly skin color. For the similarities of two cultures, Chényìmín argues, "Given the similarities between Black Skin Jade Culture and Hóngshān Culture such as jade quality, patterns, unique carving techniques, drilling etc., two cultures are consistent completely."

■ «Hóngshānyùqìshōucángyǔgǎnshǎng紅山玉器收藏與鑑賞» pp.80-82, 上海大學出版社. 2044,4.

(4) Site excavation:

Inner Mongolia Archaeological Excavation Group.

China CCTV local shooting.

Test site excavation 1st, 2nd. (2009,9. 2010,6) (Chényìmín «Hēipíyùfēngyúnlù 黑皮玉風雲錄» p.189)

1st Closed excavation (2009,9, 23-24). Wūlánchábù烏蘭察布 Museum.

2nd Test excavation (2010,6) Wūlánchábùméng烏蘭察布盟 Archaeological Group.

3rd Test excavation (2014,3): CCTV Special Scene shooting

3 JADE CULTURE IN YELLOW RIVER, YÁNGZǏ RIVER AREA

[1] Jade culture

(1) Zhōngyuán中原 Culture jadeware: Mostly jade tools, small ornaments.

Yǎngshào仰韶culture (7000-5000 years ago): Mostly jade tools, small ornaments.

Táosì陶寺 Culture, Miàodǐgōu廟底溝 2nd culture (4000 years ago): Jade lǐqì禮器 system, appeared first in Zhōngyuán District.

Erlǐtóu二里頭 Culture (3700 years ago): Zhongyuan country location for the first time, Dàyùzhāng大玉璋 (50cm), Dàyùdāo大玉刀 (60cm) appeared

❀ **Jadeware in Yángzǐ River District:** Tradition of large scale jade lǐqì(ritual vessels) production.

Língjiātān凌家灘 Culture (5500-5000 years ago) :

Liángzhǔ良渚 Culture (5000-4500 years ago) :

❀ **Zhōngyuán District:** Yellow River Basin, first dynasty<yuǎngǔdeshēngyīn遠古的聲音>

■ «CCTV-10» 探索.發現 2009,7,3.

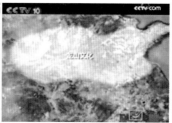

○ Yǎngshào仰韶 Culture (6000 years ago)
○ Lóngshān龍山 Culture (4000 years ago)
○ Erlǐtóu二里頭 Culture (3800-3500 years ago)
○ Hénán Yǎnshī偃師 assumed to be the first Xià夏 capital city.

* Given that the same symbol was excavated in Yǎngshào culture ruins(Shǎnxīshěng陝西省 Bǎogyeshi宝鶏市 Běiwěigēn北尾根, chánganwǔlóu 長安五樓, Hélìshēnyě郃儞莘野,Tóngchuānshì銅川市 Lǐjiāgōu李家溝, Líntóngqū臨潼区 Jiāngzhài姜寨, Língkǒu零口, yuántóu垣頭), it is assumed that characters existed in Zhōngyuán during the Xià era.

✿ Lǐbóqiān李伯謙 (Peking University): grave goods副葬品 (jadeware) is basically different.<Zhōngguógǔdàiwénmíngyǎnjìndeliǎngzhǒngmóshì中國古代文明演進的兩種模式-紅山, 良渚, 仰韶大墓場隨葬玉器觀察隨想>

Grave goods副葬品 (jadeware) of Yǎngshào Culture Miàodǐgōu type tomb is basically different from Hóngshān Culture and also basically different from Liángzhǔ Culture and is the same as the situation where Língbǎo靈寶 xīpō西坡 royal mausoleum is revealed so it is not essentially even the target to discuss the combination because types are very simple and just one kind of yùyuè玉鉞. Grave goods副葬品 (jadeware) quantity of Yǎngshào Culture Miàodǐgōu type tombs cannot be said when compared to Liángzhǔ Culture royal mausoleum and is relatively left behind when compared with Hóngshān Culture royal mausoleum. In tombs generally equivalent to Língbǎo xīpō size and Hóngshān Culture, Liángzhǔ Culture, there is only one Yùyuè and the most M11 is just 3 pieces. And there is no jadeware at all except pottery in M27, M29, the royal mausoleum showing larger burial chamber than that of Hóngshān Culture and Liángzhǔ Culture.

🕮 Zhūnǎichéng朱乃誠: <HóngshānwénhuàShòumiànjuéxíngyùshìyánjiū紅山文化獸面玦形玉飾研究>

■ 《kǎogǔxuébào考古學報》 1st period in 2008. China.

Yellow River Basin Erlǐtóu Culture: Claimed to have affected Liáoxī遼西 District Xiàjiādiàn Lower Culture Sānxīngtālā三星他拉 Yùlóng玉龍.

The period of Xiàjiādiàn Lower Culture is close to that of Erlǐtóu Culture in Liáoxī District. The period of Xiàjiādiàn Lower Culture and Erlǐtóu Culture is similar and effect relationship with cultural exchanges exists. For example, Táojué陶爵 excavated from Inner Mongolia Áohànqí敖漢旗 Dàdiànzǐ大甸子 Xiàjiādiàn Lower Culture tomb in 1977 and Erlǐtóu Culture Táojué are all the same in the shape, dignity and Erlǐtóu Culture explains exchanges and influence relationships for Liáoxī District Xiàjiādiàn Lower Culture. Sānxīngtālā Yùlóng has the same characteristics only as Erlǐtóu Culture dragon sign and it means that Liáoxī District Xiàjiādiàn Lower Culture where Sānxīngtālā Yùlóng is distributed was also influenced by Erlǐtóu Culture and it can be guessed that Sānxīngtālā Yùlóng was born under the influence of Erlǐtóu Culture. It is no wonder that the period of Sānxīngtālā Yùlóng is close to that of Erlǐtóu Culture and also corresponds with Xiàjiādiàn Lower Culture.

🕮 Yèshūxiàn叶舒宪: <HuánghéshuǐdàoyuyùqìshíQíjiāgǔguó黄河水道与玉器时齐家古国>

■ 《Gǔyùshōucángyǔyántǎo古玉收藏与研讨》 total 13, 2012,12.

Yellow River Basin: Jade Lǐqì production traditional development impossible.

Shānxī Táosì Culture: Zhōngyuán District First, Jade lǐqì system appeared.

For archeological excavation, there is only Dúshān獨山 jade mine in Hénán Nányáng南陽 District of Southern Zhōngyuán District because Jade mineral resources are scarce in Zhōngyuán District and jade Lǐqì use of Zhōngyuán Civilization in yuǎngǔ遠古 period is rather very small. Looking at a large quantities of jadeware samples excavated from Erlǐtóu and Yīnxū殷

墟 Fùhǎomù妇好墓, it can be found that only one or two pieces of jadeware were made by using jade materials. Due to the limitation of these physical conditions, the tradition of large scale jade Lǐqì production could not be developed like cultures other than Zhōngyuán in the same time or slightly later than Yǎngshào Culture which is the most influential in Zhōngyuán District 7000-5000 years ago from now, that is, Hóngshān Culture, Língjiātān Culture and Liángzhǔ cultures. Most Yǎngshào Culture jadeware that can be seen so far was jade tools or small ornaments. 4000 years ago from now, large combination Jade Lǐqì system represented by Yùbì玉璧 (jade disk with a hole in the center), Yùcóng玉琮 appeared in Zhōngyuán District for the first time in Táosì Culture of Shānxī Xiāngfén襄汾, Línfén临汾 Xiàjìncūn下靳村 and Ruìchéng芮城 Pōtóucūn坡头村 Miàodǐgōu 2nd culture. And then, as more mature and diverse Jade Lǐqì system and Hénán Yǎnshī Erlǐtóu Culture jadeware appeared in the middle of Zhōngyuán 3700 years ago from now and Dàyùzhāng大玉璋 about 50cm long and Dàyùdāo大玉刀 about 60cm long appeared in Zhōngyuán country location for the first time, consistent Jade Lǐqì tradition of three generations of XiàShāngZhōu夏商周 could be achieved through the middle role of Erlǐtóu Culture.

(2) Shāndōng山東 Peninsula Dàwènkǒu大汶口 Culture (6300-4500 years ago): Yùcóng玉琮, yùxuánjī玉璇璣.

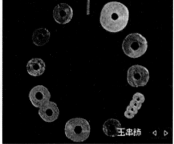

○ Yùcóng 49.7cm. National Museum of China

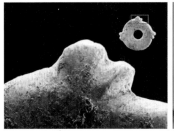

○ Zhōuhé周河 Historic Site Yùyábì玉牙璧

🌀 Shāndōng Peninsula Lóngshān Culture:

○ Owned by Beijing Palace Museum and Tiānjīnshì Museum
○ Xúchūnlíng徐春苓, Vice Researcher of Tiānjīnshì天津市 Museum:
○ Yīngjuérénmiànpèi鷹攫人面佩 (Jade jewelry of an eagle holding the human head).
○ It may be Zúhuī族徽 (A pattern symbolizing a tribe) of Shǎohào少昊 Clan or ancestrial god statue about 4000 years ago. Zúhuī or ancestrial god statue was also created by primitive mankind as their protective god of their village by borrowing their imagination. Naming an animal as a clan or ancestrial god statue is one important contents of a primitive society.

■ <Lóngshānwénhuà龍山文化Yngjuérénmiànpèi鷹攫人面佩>国宝档案《CCTV-4》 2012,5,7.

🌀 Shāndōng Lóngshān type Yázhāng牙璋 distribution.

Dèngcōng邓聪 (香港中文大学), Luánfēngshí栾丰实, Wángqiáng王强 (山东大学)

<DōngYàzuìzǎodeYázhāng东亚最早的牙璋—山东龙山式牙璋初论>

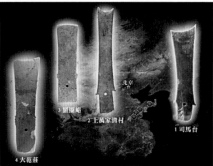

○ Shāndōng Lóngshān type Yázhāng distribution (5000-4300 years ago)
○ Yázhāng excavated Historical Site

(3) Zhōngyuán Area:

<1> Shǎnxī Shímǎo石峁 jade culture (5000 years ago-4000 years ago): Yázhāng

■ Jadeware excavated from Shǎnxī Shénmù神木 Shímǎo Historic Site «Zhōngguówénhuàbào 中国文化报» 2014,6,9.

Late Qing Wúdàchè吴大澂 «Gǔyùtúkǎo古玉圖考» : «zhōulǐ周禮» Grounds, named Yázhāng.

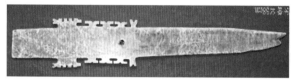 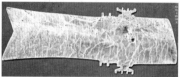

○ 56cm

Sūnzhōuyǒng孙周勇, Deputy Director of Shǎnxī Province Archeological Institute:

6 pieces such as Yùchǎn玉鏟, Yùhuáng玉璜 etc. excavated from Shímǎo Historic Site Yùchǎn. 4000 years ago, Shénmù Shímǎo Historic Site is a very important jade culture center in China Northern District.

Shénmù Shímǎo, Liángzhǔ Culture, Qíjiā Culture (4000-5000 years ago) Large village groups (or Chief Country).

<2>Táosì陶寺 Culture (4600-4000 years ago) Yùbì: Midstream of Yellow River.

■ Zhūshūpiànhú朱書片壺 character found (Royal authority generation). <Yùshíchuánqí 玉石传奇> Vol.2, 巫神之玉 «CCTV-9» 2011,1,8

Chinese Cultural Relics Society Jadeware Research Committee Gǔfāng古方: Claimd to form Yùshízhilù玉石之路 4000 years ago.

Royal authority generation: Táosì Culture. Shānxī山西 Province representing Zhōngyuán Area

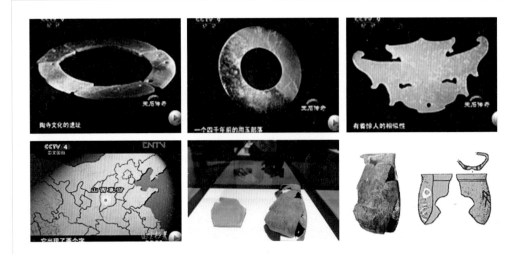

🌀 Táosì Culture (Midstream of Yellow River): Royal authority generation. Jade Lǐqì system appeared for the first time in Zhōngyuán Area.

Academy of Social Sciences Archeological Institute YáoShùn堯舜 Period capital discovery presentation, Questions of various fields(2) 2010,8,3. People's Network. http://pic.people.com.cn/ Original text «Jīnghuáshíbào京华时报»

Reaching Táosì Culture the mid term peak period of Táosì Culture. One Táosì mid-term royal mausoleum excavated in 2002 is 5m long, 3.7m wide, 8.4m deep and no tombs are comparable in Yellow River mid and downstream District in the same period. Excavated grave goods are also admirable and pig lower jaw was carved on the wall in front of the remains of the tomb owner and there are a total of 9 pieces, 6 pieces of Yùyuè玉鉞. Yùyuè excavated from the tomb on both sides. Hénú何努 introduces that the lower jaw of a pig symbolizes wealth and Yuè symbolizes royal authority and military authority. Among the current archaeological excavations, nothing has been excavated in a way of combining the above two types.

🌀 Professor Lǐbóqiān李伯謙 (Peking University 震旦古代文明 Research Center)

<Zhōngguógǔdàiwénmíngyǎnjìndeliǎngzhǒngmóshì中國古代文明演進的兩種模式-紅山,良渚,仰韶大墓場隨葬玉器觀察隨想>

Excavation of Shānxī Xiāngfén Táosì Historic Site shows that a early civilization country with one rich contents was founded through the royal mausoleum of numerous Cǎihuì彩繪 pottery Lǐqìi and 6 pieces of Yùyuè grave goods, ruined castle with the area of 2.8millionm², large palace base, meteorological observatory base in the period from 4300 years ago from now to 4000 years ago and putting ancient literature related materials together, scholars tend to recognize that this is the location of Píngyáng平陽, the capital of Yáo堯.

<3> Qíjiā齐家 culture (Xīróng西戎) Culture 4400-3900 years ago: Upstream of Yellow River.

  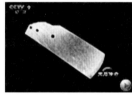 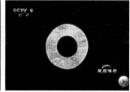

○ Sōngshíyùhuáng松石玉璜, Jade Mask, Jade knife, Yùbì

○ Yùcóng玉琮

🌀 End of the Neolithic Age-Bronze Age Tóngshí铜石 combined period Initial Culture.

Qíjiāpíng齐家坪: Gānsùshěng甘肃省 Guǎnghéxiàn広河県
Pottery development. Early Bronze hóngtóng紅銅, Small bronze artifacts.
Patriarchal society: Male society ruling status. Subordinate status of women.
monogamy. polygamy.

More than 30 kinds of delicate jadeware excavated

Lǐqii: Cóng琮, Bì璧, Huán环, Huáng璜, Yuè钺, Dāo刀, zhāng璋 etc.. weapons. ornaments.

Jade materials: Gānsù, Qīnghǎi 青海(Xingang新疆 Hétiányù和田玉 7:3).

⌬ Yèshūxiàn叶舒宪: Prehistoric Jade Lǐqii and processing technology were transmitted from the East.

<HuánghéshuǐdàoyuyùqìshíQíjiāgǔguó黄河水道与玉器时齐家古国>

■ «Gǔyùshōucángyǔyántǎo古玉收藏与研讨» total 13, 2012,12.

During 2005-2009, fascinated by the academic issues finding the source of Huáxià華夏 Civilization, I explored Gānsù Site over five times and published a small book «Héxī Corridor: Western Myths and Huáxià origin 河西走廊:西部神话与华夏源流» that attempted an explanation of the interrelationships between Zhōngyuán Civilization and Qíjiā gǔguó古國 of 4000 years ago from the similarity of jade culture in 2008. Since I was only interested in elements of material culture spread and transported to Zhōngyuán through Héxī Corridor, that is, wheat, gold, horse, carriage etc. at that time, my evaluation of foreign influencing factors of jadeware origin was not good enough. The current academic opinion is that there was no tradition of producing jade Lǐqii in Mǎjiāyáo馬家窯 Culture, the former of Qíjiā Culture and therefore, there was a phenomenon of using scale production of Qíjiā jadeware by the influence of Qíjiā jadeware. Based on an analysis of the cutting technique of prehistoric Jade materials, Professor Dèngcōng of Chinese University of Hong Kong said that the cutting technique was originated from Dàwènkǒu Culture of Shāndōng and was gradually propagated to Qíjiā Culture of Northwest through Shímǎo Culture of Northern Shǎnxī and Zhōngyuán Lóngshān Culture. In other words, prehistoric Jade Lǐqii and the processing technology were transmitted from the East.

〈4〉Yīnxū殷墟 (Yīnxū Museum) : Yùlóng玉龍

  ○ Smithsonian Museum Freer Gallery H:3.2cm. H:3.1cm H:4.3cm

♞ **Excavated from Yīnxū: Jade animals** (Yùhè玉鶴. Yùé玉鵝. Yùtángláng玉螳螂.

Yùcán玉蚕, Yùniǎo玉鳥, Yùxiàng玉象)

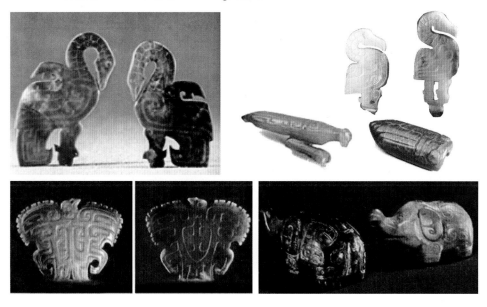

❀ Yùfèng玉鳳 (Yīnxū Museum)" Yùmǎ玉馬, Yùxióng玉熊, Yùhǔ玉虎 (National Museum of China).

❀ Yīnyángyùrén陰陽玉人: Excavated from Yīn殷 Fùhǎomù妇好墓 (National Museum of China).

○ 12.5cm Late Yīn 14th Century B.C.-11th Century B.C.
○ 1976, Excavated from Yīn Wǔdīng武丁 Fùhǎomù (National Museum of China)

❀ Yīn Fùhǎomù: Excavated from Hóngshān Culture Yùgōuxíngqì玉勾形器

○ Excavated from Inner Mongolia Bālínyòuqí巴林右旗 2.5x7cm. China
■ «Guǎngzhōurìbào廣州日報» 2009.11.16. Inner Mongolia Bālínyòuqí Museum

○ Excavated from Fùhǎomù Yùgōuxíngqì.

In the 1970s of the 20th century, Shāng商 Dynasty Fùhǎomù was excavated from Hénán河南 Anyáng安陽. Fùhǎo婦好 is Shāng king Wǔdīng武丁's
wife and bronze, pottery and jadeware were excavated from the tomb in large
quantities of jadeware, several pieces of Yùgōuxíngqì did not receive special
attention because its machining was precise and was regarded as jadeware of
the Shāng Dynasty with other jadeware excavated from the tomb at that time.
As Hóngshān Culture Yùgōuxíngqì was immediately excavated in the 1980s,
people came to realize that Yùgōuxíngqì from Fùhǎomù was originally the remains of Hóngshān Culture. It also means that kings, dukes and nobles during
the Shāng Dynasty already began to collect jadeware of Hóngshān Culture. It
means to have taken two thousand years until these jadeware was handed down
from Hóngshān Culture Period to the Shāng Dynasty.

■ «Hóngshānyùqìshōucángyǔgǎnshǎng紅山玉器收藏與感賞» p.15, p.70, Shanghai University Press, 2004,1.

⊛ Yīn殷-Zhōu周 Dynasty replacement: Bǎoyù寶玉(14000), Pèiyù佩玉
(100,080,000) «Yìzhōushū逸周書-世俘解»

In the suburbs, one evening of the Year of the Rat, King Zhòu紂 of the Shāng
Dynasty put thick Tiānzhìyùyǎn天智玉琰 五 around his body and burned
himself. Usually people said that 4,000 jade was burned, King Wǔ武 saved a
thousand captives, 4,000 Ruìyù瑞玉 and Tiānzhìyù天智玉 was not burned in
the midst of fire. King Wǔ武 regarded Tiānzhìyù as treasure. Usually, King Wǔ
武 obtained 14000 Bǎoyù, 100,080,000 Pèiyù of Shāng.

❀ Guī圭: Yīn

○ Smithsonian Museum Freer Gallery H: 51.0cm H:20.9cm H:17.8cm

❀ Yùxuánjī玉璇璣: Not excavated from tombs since the age of civil wars

○ Xuánjī, astronomical Yíqì儀器, Yábì牙璧.

"Xuánjī" Two letters, «Shàngshū尚書·Shùndiǎn舜典»."Governed political affairs by examining with Xuánjīyùhéng璿璣玉衡"

Interpretation of Xīhàn西漢 Kǒngānguó孔安國

"在, 察也, 璇, 美玉也, 璣衡, 王者正天文之器, 可運轉者."

"zài在 is to observe. Xuán璇 is beautiful jade. jīhéng璣衡 is an object used by a king when governing astronomical phenomena for operation." Looking at Historic Site where jade xuánjī was excavated in chronological order, it appeared in eastern Shāndōng 5000 years ago and jade xuánjī of the Lóngshān Culture period crossed the Bóhǎi渤海 Bay and landed on the eastern coast of Liáoníng 4000 years ago. Before long, it advanced to from Shāndōng to Hénán, Shǎnxī in the west. In the ShāngZhōu period, it spread from Zhōngyuán to south-north and was handed down to Héběi, Húběi etc. The excavation of jade xuánjī cannot be seen in tombs after the Warring States Period.

(3) Yángzǐ River Basin :

〈1〉Hémǔdù河姆渡 Culture (7000–5000 years ago):

Zhèjiāngshěng浙江省, Artificial rice farming ruins.

○ Zhūwéntáobō猪紋陶鉢 11.7cm Hēitáo黑陶

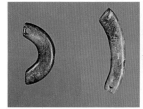  

○ Owned by Zhèjiāngshěng Museum

〈2〉Mǎjiābāng马家浜 Culture (6000–5000 years ago):

○ Shànghǎi Museum Excavated from Shànghǎi Qīngpǔxiàn青浦县.
○ Nánjīng City Museum Excavated from Jiāngsūshěng江蘇省 Chángzhōu常州.
○ Nánjīng City Museum Excavated from Jiāngsūshěng Wúxiàn吴县 cǎoxiéshān草鞋山.

○ jiāngsū Province Museum Excavated from Zhèjiāngshěng Jiāxīng嘉興 Mǎjiābāng. Mano Yùjué excavated from Jiāxīng.

⟨3⟩ Sōngzé松澤 Culture (6000–5300 years ago; Shànghǎi Museum):

The transition period from matriarchal society to patriarchal society.

 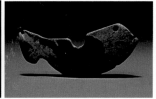

○ Nánjīng City Museum, yùxiàngshì玉项饰, Excavated from Jiāngsū Wúxiàn cǎoxiéshān草鞋山.
○ Shànghǎi Museum, Yùhuáng, Excavated from Shànghǎi Qīngpǔxiàn.
○ Shànghǎi Museum Yùhán玉玲, Excavated from Shànghǎi Qīngpǔxiàn.

 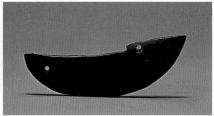

○ Shànghǎi Museum, Yùhuáng, Excavated from Shànghǎi Qīngpǔxiàn.

○ Nánjīng City Museum, Yùhuáng, Excavated from Jiāngsū Wúxiàn cǎoxiéshān.

○ Shànghǎi Museum, yùbi, Excavated from Shànghǎi Qīngpǔxiàn.
○ Nánjīng City Museum, yùhuán (jade ring), Excavated from Jiāngsū Wúxiàn cǎoxiéshān.

⟨4⟩ Běiyīnyángyíng北阴阳营 Culture (6000-5000 years ago):

 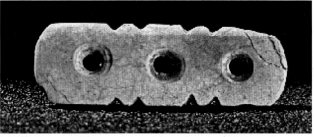

○ Yùjué,Yùhuáng, yùguǎn玉管, Excavated from Nánjīng Běiyīnyángyíng, Nánjīng City Museum,
○ Yùsānkǒngshì玉三孔饰, Excavated from Anhuishěng Háozhōu亳州 yánglóuxiāng杨楼乡, Háozhōu Museum.

⟨5⟩ JiāngHuái江淮 District Culture: Owned by Nánjīng City Museum

 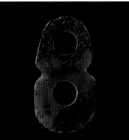 

○ Yùshuāngliánbì玉双联璧, Excavated from Jiāngsū Hǎiānxiàn海安县 Qīngdūn青墩
○ Yùshuāngliánbì, Excavated from Jiāngsū Nánjīng Sānhéxiāng三河乡 Yíngpán shān营盘山.
○ Yùsānjiǎoxíngpèi玉三角形佩, Excavated from Jiāngsū Nánjīng Sānhéxiāng Yíngpánshān

⟨6⟩ Língjiātān凌家滩 Culture (5300-5600 years ago): Huáxià華夏 best dragon.

■ Jade figure statue: Língjiātān Culture <shīluòdetiānshu失落的天書>First volume, Road of discovery «CCTV-9» 2011,2,23.

○ Excavated from Língjiātān No.16 tomb. 4.2cm.
○ Excavated from Yùlóng: Homeland of Chinese dragon culture
○ Càifèngshū蔡鳳書 «National Treasure Excavation Records國寶發掘記» p.22, 齊魯書社, 2004,10

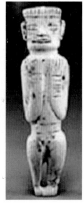

○ 6 pieces of yùrén玉人 excavated. Mongolian doll feature.
○ Similar to Chinese appearance.
○ Chinese civilization unchanged for race, culture 5000 years

❀ Zhāngjìngguó张敬国:

Three kinds of zhānbǔ 占卜 jadeware: Yuguī玉龜 + yùzān玉簪 + yùpiàn玉片.
Língjiātān Historic Site: Anhuī安徽 Hánshān含山 Prefecture Dōngjiǎzhèn 東甲鎮.
The same age as Hóngshān Culture. Earlier than Zhèjiāng Liángzhǔ Culture.
<Língjiātān Jadeware-Aurora of Chinese Civilization>

■ «Gǔyùshōucángyǔyántǎo古玉收藏与研讨» Total 3 2010,4.

* Xǔhóngmíng许洪明 <Gǔyùmíngwényuyǒumíngyùqì古玉铭文与有铭玉器>

■ «wénwùjiàndìnghegǎnshǎng文物鑑定和感赏» 2011, 6.

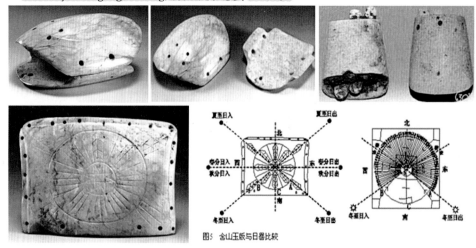

图5 含山玉版与日晷比较

❀ Wǔjiābì武家璧 (Chinese Academy of Sciences Nature and Science Institute): Hánshānyùbǎnyǔrìguǐbǐjiào含山玉版与日晷比较, Identifying winter solstice, summer solstice

■ <Hánshānyùbǎnshàngdetiānwénzhǔnxiàn含山玉版上的天文准线> «Dōngnánwénhuà東南文化» 2nd term in 2006

❀ Jiǎgǔwén甲骨文 冬(=終Jong) shaped jade ornament: Língjiātān Culture

○ Tremolite jade Jiǎgǔwén甲骨文 冬(=終Jong)

❀ Yùyīng玉鷹 Língjiātān Culture: Mexico Mayan civilization Animal Face Pattern jade jewelry-Black skin jade culture shuānglóng雙龍 Yùcóng玉琮.

❀ Professor Zhāngjìngguó張敬国: (Anhuīshěng Cultural Relics Archaeological Institute) <Underground Museum that spent five thousand years of Língjiātān>

Yùyīng玉鷹 (jade eagle) excavated from Língjiātān heads its face to the side and spreads its wings like flying up even now and its beak looks like a hook and eyes expressed as a hole are noticeable. A brave eagle is a symbol of courage and strength but according to the historical research of one expert, this eagle may have been the crest of Shǎohào少昊 family and relatives who were Língjiātānn indigenous people. Noticing the relationship between Yùyīng and ancestral rites, another expert thinks that a circle engraved in center of Yùyīng's body and the octagonal door on the outside represent the sun and the sun's rays and the pig head engraved at the end of both wings of an eagle is a tribute and it seems to contain the meaning that an eagle carrying the tribute flies into the sky and offers it to the heavenly gods and ordinary people's wish for the heavenly gods. Anyway, Yùyīng is the symbol of a village and represents the worship of the sun, birds and pigs and can be considered a symbol of the totem that the Chinese nation combined birds and mammals for the first time in a very long time ago.

■ «RénmínZhōngguó人民中國 Internet Edition» 2010,8. http://www.peoplechina. com.cn/

🕸 **Zhāngjìngguó (Língjiātān Excavation director): Yùyuè玉鉞 (5300-5500 years ago), Securing military authority.**

○ Língjiātān No.23 tomb excavation site. Huáxiàjīngwěiwǎng华夏经纬网 07,6,27.
○ (Original text «JiāngHuáichénbào江淮晨报»)
○ Tomb owner, Shaman with exceptional status. Yùyuè excavated in large quantities, Expressing military takeover.
○ One person military power, divine right, Village chief monopolizing government. Yuguī玉龜, Yùbǎn玉版, Yùcóng玉琮, Yùyuè玉鉞 shaman special
○ jadeware.

⟨7⟩ Liángzhǔ良渚 Culture : Yùcóng玉琮

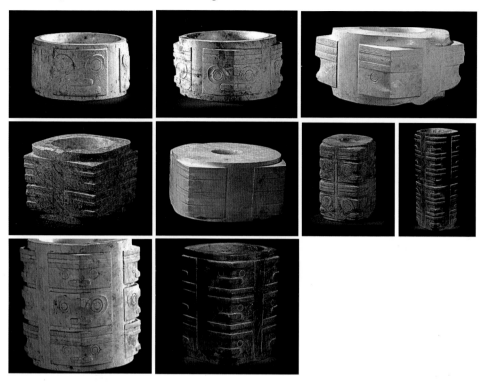

    * Sūnyíngchūn孙迎春 <TànmìLiángzhǔwénhuàyùqìshénrénShòumiànwén 探秘良渚文化玉器神人兽面纹>(下)

■ 《Gǔyùshōucángyǔyántǎo古玉收藏与研讨》 Total12, 2012, 10. (《wénwùjiàndìnghegǎnshǎng文物鑑定和感賞》 2012,10)

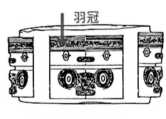

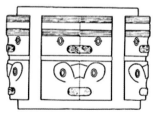

Comparison "Yùhuī 玉徽" Yùcóng and general combination "God statue" and "God man" Yùcóng.

○ Top: Yáoshān瑶山 M2:22 Yùhuī Yùcóng, Simulation
○ Bottom: Fǎnshān反山 M17:1 God statue-God man combination Yùcóng, Simulation

Due to the nature of Yùcóng, sculpture of wide top and narrow bottom shows the growth pole of the family and the growth pole of the family is like one towering gigantic tree, symbolizing that the ancestors have the same root. As the same logic, one node at the bottom of Yùcóng represents the origin of the owner. Because of this, when analyzing the diagram of "god man" and "god statue" combination, we start from the bottom floor and go up in the order. In fact, as a kind of language sign, the diagram of Yùcóng patterns of "god man" and "god statue" combination is understood to have expressed the owner of Yùcóng and lineage and transmission relation of the family.

❀ Yùcóng: Qing清 Dynasty, Smithsonian Museum Freer Gallery.

❀ Yùcóng type Royal Kiln Celadon: Southern Song 12-13th century Royal Kiln.

○ Japan Tokyo National Museum important cultural property.
○ Smithsonian Museum Freer Gallery, Ming明 (16th century-Mid-17th century), Qing清 (18th Century) Jǐngdézhèn景德鎮.

This bottle was modeled on jadeware Cóng琮 and is full of dignified and grave feelings. It was handed down to Owari Tokugawa Family as 'Main tube mizusashi'. It is assumed to be rare Southern Sòng 南宋 royal kiln celadon brought to Japan through the characteristics of glaze and clay.

❀ Jiǎngwèidōng蔣衛東 (Director of Liángzhǔ Museum):
Yùbì玉璧: Altar + Presence of absence of fēiniǎo飛鳥. Owner of both Yùcóng + Yùyuè玉鉞: Liángzhǔ village dominating (divine power + royal authority).
Divine power shaman; Supreme prince.

❀ Liúbīn劉斌 (Zhèjiāng Cultural Relics Archaeological Institute): Shaman dominating village divine power

❀ Móuyǒngkàng牟永抗 (Zhèjiāng Cultural Relics Archaeological Institute):
Shaman (divine power) dominating the whole jadeware making process (Discovery + making + possession)

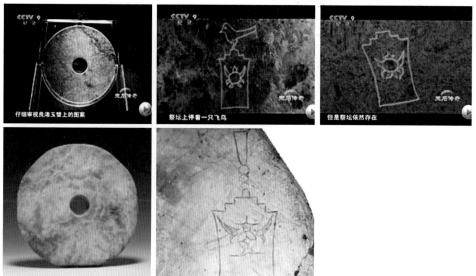

○ Yùbì 13.44cm Taiwan National Palace Museum
○ Divine power (altar) + Royal authority (Fēiniǎo飛鳥)

❀ **Yùyuè**玉鉞: Liángzhǔ Culture. Symbol of royal authority (National Museum of China).

Yùyuè upper part shaman.

Shénrénshòumiànwén神人獸面紋. Lower part Fēiniǎo

❀ **Wángmíngdá**王明達 **(Zhèjiāng Province Cultural Relics Archaeological Institute):** Symbolizing command, military power, life-or-death authority. One piece excavated from one tomb.

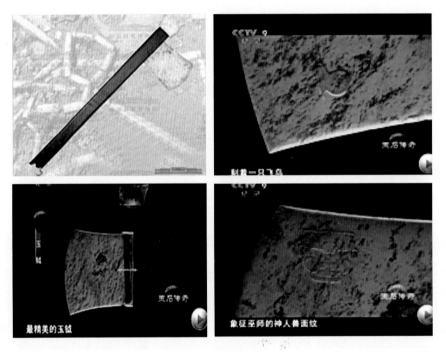

○ Excavated from Zhèjiāngshěng Yúgǎngxiàn余港縣 Yáoshān No.8 tomb in 1987. length 16.3cm.

When using Yùyuè, people used it by tying yuè鉞 in the wood body. While excavated, rotten tree handle traces were found and the handle length was 80cm and there was a guānshì冠飾 ornament at the top of the handle and ornament of Yùyuè at the bottom of the handle. The owner of Yáoshān No.8 tomb was a special person who dominated the military power.

<8> Shíjiāhé石家河 Culture (4500-4000 years ago): Yùrén玉人 Statue.

China Húběishěng Yángzǐ River Midstream Region. Late Neolithic culture. Inheriting Qūjiālǐng屈家嶺 culture in the same region. Large walled city developed from huánháo環濠 jùluò聚落, Primitive capital city (different from Qūjiālǐng Culture).

Shíjiāhé Culture jadeware: Found in adult earthenware coffin. Special primitive religious faith. Many jade tiger Yùhǔtóu玉虎頭 were found in Shíjiāhé Historic Site. This means that Shíjiāhé indigenous people had a custom of worshipping a tiger.

○ Yùrénshòufùhépèi玉人兽复合佩 (8.2cm), Yùmiànréntóuxiàng玉面人頭像

(4) Sìchuān 四川 Region: Gǔshǔ古蜀 Culture.

Jadeware: Sānxīngduī三星堆. Jīnshā金沙 figure related jadeware

○ Yùshénrénmiànxiàng玉神人面像 Jīnshācūn金沙村 3000 years ago Gǔshǔ古蜀.

○ <Jīnshāyízhǐyùqì金沙遺址玉器> Guóbǎodàng'àn «CCTV-4» 2011,11,19.

○ Jade figure statue (14.5cm).

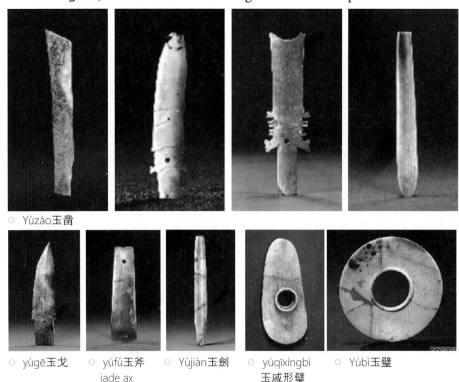

❀ Yùzhāng玉璋: Gǔshǔ Culture: Sānxīngduī Museum http://www.sxd.cn/

○ Yùzáo玉凿

○ yùgē玉戈　　○ yùfǔ玉斧　　○ Yùjiàn玉劍　　○ yùqíxíngbì　　○ Yùbì玉璧
　　　　　　　　 jade ax　　　　　　　　　　　　　　　 玉戚形璧

❀ **Gǔshǔ Culture:** Sānxīngduī Jade stoneware Lìrén立人 175cm found. Dozens of kinds of Bànrénbànshòu半人半獸.

■ <SānxīngduīyùqìshōucángjiāZhāngsīyǒng三星堆玉器收藏家张思勇:wéiguócángbǎo 为国藏宝> 2007,6,3 Xīnhuáshè新华社

Sānxīngduī jade stoneware Ipin owned by Zhāngsāiyǒng was put on the desk. This jade Lìrén and national treasure bronze Ipin in Sānxīngduī Museum were equal in size and molding was also completely the same. The difference is that there is no life-size Sānxīngduī bronze Lìrén holding with two hands but jade Lìrén of Zhāngsāiyǒng holds a pieces of eagle head yīngtóu鷹頭 scepter in the hand. The biggest one among Sānxīngduī jade stoneware Lìrén owned by Zhāngsāiyǒng is a god statue 1.75m tall and 150kg in weight and is dominated by snake, bird, tiger patterns and also has the eagle head scepter in the hand and the shape is mysterious and solemn. Another jade stoneware Lìrén is made of tremolite and the whole sculpture is jade green and very beautiful. According to the words of the industry, if modern man is trying to make this finished product, at least tons of jade gemstone material is required and it is difficult to get even small and large bowls made of tremolite being used currently. Sānxīngduī jadeware owned by Zhāngsāiyǒng personally has already reached hundreds of pieces and most are five kinds of lǐqì, people, animals, Shénwù神物 inscription character sign and already formed early scaling and integration. Among them, animals Sānxīngduī jade stoneware is particularly diverse and abundant. Large ones are elephants, tigers, rhinoceros, Yángzǐ alligators, medium ones are monkeys, cows, horses, sheep and small ones are centipedes, swallowtail butterflies, cicadas, A multitude of animals were personified and a huge variety of dozens of kinds such as Hǔshēnrénmiàn虎身人面, Shéshēnrénmiàn蛇身人面, Niǎoshēnrénmiàn鸟身人面, Yúshēnrénmiàn鱼身人面, Mǎshēnrénmiàn马身人面, even Guōguōshēnrén miàn蝈蝈身人面, Xiēzǐshēnrénmiàn蝎子身人面, Chuānshānjiǎrénmiàn穿山甲人面 can be said to be the world unique "Jade and Stone Zoo."

❀ Ráozōngyí饶宗颐 (1998): Based on the characters we saw, Sānxīngduī Gǔshǔ characters is in a so-called "spell-out" (Picture writing) stage and this stage focuses on pictures (hieroglyphics) and we can see deer shape, ship shape, water shape etc. on the jadeware surface and they have been changed into a single character after a long time. (Yùbǎn玉版 surface, jade Lìrén surface etc.). Finally, a single character was changed into complex characters (Yùměirén玉美人 fish, jade 12 zodiac animals of China statue, yùbǎn surface etc.) and this change process required at least thousands of years even tens of thousands of years and this has been accumulated for ever and ever of Gǔshǔguó people at that time.

❀ Lǐxuéqín李学勤 <Wénzìqǐyuányánjiūhégǔdàiwénmíng文字起源研究和古代文明>

■ «Zhōngguóshūfǎ中國書法» 2nd term in 2001.

For any one point of view, I have told many times in different places and will repeat again this time. I cannot accept ancient characters within China's region saying that there are only the former Chinese characters like YīnZhōu 殷周 characters. Bāshǔ巴蜀 characters found Sìchuān四川 and its vicinity are never Chinese characters. The signs of prehistoric culture and primitive characters are not related to Chinese characters and former Chinese characters and further proof is needed. A few years ago, I announced that Liángzhǔ Culture pottery, a kind of yúnpiàn雲片 type or huǒyàn火焰 type signs on jadeware may not be directly related to the origin of Chinese characters.

🌀 Jīnshā金沙 Historic Site: Insect pattern jadeware. Identified by microscope

■ <Jīnshāyízhǐyùqì金沙遺址玉器>Guóbǎodàngàn «CCTV-4» 2011,11,19.

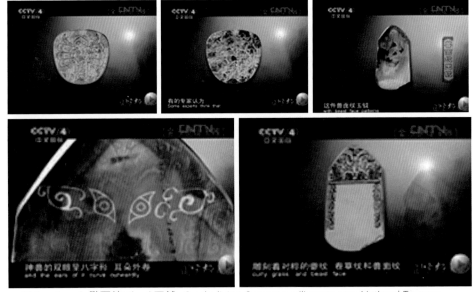

○ Shòumiànwén獸面紋 Yùyuè玉鉞 : Symbolizing Supreme military power. National Treasure

Chapter 2

Jade Totem Society

It means that the old saying 'Serving gods with jade 以玉事神' is the evidence and the main character is a shaman. After all, shaman, sky (god) and yù 玉 (jade) can be regarded as the Trinity. Therefore, it was considered that Jadeware was a creation in the form of ideas and their life was given by the heaven and spiritual animals, landscape and land etc. are exchanged each other like mystical creatures. Clan or tribal societies at that time created Shénqì神器 used in ancestral rites and various objects such as animal totem, nature worship, ancestor worship etc. they worshiped into jade carving, extraordinary three-dimensional space art of the diverse and rich form. Therefore, Black skin Jade Culture and Hóngshān Culture subjects was the 'Jade Totem' society with a conscious system where its subjects took charge of the material culture through funeral customs burying jade belonging to the spiritual culture area in the tomb and had private ownership with an emphasis on the spiritual culture. As the 'Jade Totem society' that expressed all worship targets including ancestral spirits, animals in the form of nature etc. with jade, it can be regarded as a early civilized society with a certain level of social order with jade as its peak.

1 JADE TOTEM

※ **Zhāngdeshuǐ**张得水: (Researcher of Hénán Museum)
<shǐqiányùyuwūguānxìzhi tàntǎo史前玉与巫关系之探讨>

Jade culture in prehistoric times was not developed on the average and there are differences depending on the area. These differences are very closely related to the culture and tradition of different districts. Hóngshān Culture and Liángzhǔ Culture clearly reflect the tradition of Yùbǔ玉卜 religion. Its projected representations are jade funeral (yǐyùwéizàng以玉爲葬) and jade ancestral ritual (yǐyùwéijì以玉爲祭). Anhuī Hánshān Língjiātān凌家灘 Historic Site is a place that integrates these two elements and excavation of both Yùguī and rectangular Yùbǎn explains that two kinds of religious phenomena of Yùbǔ玉卜 and Guībǔ龜卜 (telling fortunes by burning tortoise shell) are present at the same time and Dàwènkǒu大汶口 Culture expresses the religious tradition of Guībǔ relatively much. In Zhōngyuán District, Bǔgǔ卜骨 has been universally found in the mid and late Lóngshān Culture. Generally, Yùbǔ, Guībǔ and Bǔgǔ represent different Shamanism respectively and different cultures are specifically reflected in the religious form.

■ «Zhōngguóyùwénhuàyùxuélùncóng中國玉文化玉學論叢» 紫禁城出版社, 2002,4.

※ **Chinese professor Yèshūxiàn**叶舒宪:<lángtúténg, háishixióngtúténg? guānyú Zhōnghuázǔxiāntúténgdebiànxīyufǎnsī狼图腾,还是熊图腾? 关于中华祖先图腾的辨析与反思>

In Prehistoric Culture on the meadow in Mongolia, Hóngshān various cultures represented by Chìfēng are the most remarkable. The period is 8000-4000 years ago and leads from Xīnglóngwā Culture to Xiàjiādiàn Lower Culture and jadeware culture has lasted for 4000 years. What if examining the totem of mankind under today's northern grassland ecology. That is, every jadeware of Hóngshān Culture belongs to it.

■ «ZhōngguóShèhuìKēxuéyuànyuànbào中国社会科学院院报» 2006,8,2.

❀ **Chinese professor Yánwénmíng嚴文明 (Peking University):** <zǎoqīzhōngguóshì zěnyàngde? 早期中國是怎樣的?>

Since the shape of zhūlóng猪龍 or xiónglóng熊龍 is very special and unified among Hóngshān Culture jadeware, most disputants accept it as the totem of Hóngshān people. This shows that Hóngshān Culture people had unified religious faith. When combined with a certain power system, such faith can produce a huge capacity. This point is impossible in traditional clan villages. Because of this, it can be said to be reasonable that a certain country regime occurred already in the Hóngshān Culture period.

■ «Guāngmíngrìbào光明日報» 2010,1,14.

In«Hànshū漢書» lǜlìzhìxià律曆志下, it was recorded that Tánzǐ郯子 came in the Zhāogōng昭公 17th of Spring and Autumn period and had a talk with Zhāogōng and in old days, the emperor used Yúnshī雲師 as Yúnmíng 雲名, Yándì炎帝 used Huǒshī火師 as Huǒmíng火名, Gònggōngshì共工氏 used Shuǐshī水師 as Shuǐmíng水名, Tàihàoshì太昊氏 used Lóngshī龍師 as Lóngmíng龍名 and Shǎohào少昊 Zhí縶 used Niǎoshī鳥師 (public office) as Niǎomíng鳥名 (bird name).

[1] Development of totem shape

❀ **Professor Oh,jejung:** <gǔdàiZhōngguóshénhuàtúténgxíngzhuàngyǎnbiànch ūtàn古代中國神話圖騰形狀演變初探>

Hegel identified that Rénshǒu人首 (human head) symbolizes the spirit and Shòushén獸身 (animal body) symbolizes the material and Bànrénbànshòu半人半獸 means that the spirit breaks the material. This shows the center of the combination of man and beast, soul. (Omitted) The possibility of appearing the earliest in the divine development process was animal gods (Including single animal god and complex animal god, primitive totem god) and connected to Bànrénbànshòu gods and gods of Rénshén人神 same shape later (This is also divided into two stairs, two stairs of gods and goddesses).

■ «Zhōngguórénwénkēxué中國人文科學» Vol.23, 2001,12. Korea.

◉ **Jeong, Jae-seo:** Rénmiànniǎo人面鳥, Bànrénbànshòu (Outcome of the human concept undifferentiated from nature).

◉ **Chényìmín陳逸民:** Niúshǒurénshēn牛首人身 (Sun god), Rénshēnniútí人身牛蹄 (Chīyóu 蚩尤).

■ «Hēipíyùfēngyúnlù黑皮玉風雲錄» p.151.

◉ **Lǐjǐngjiāng李景江:** Bànrénbànshòu God

■ «Shānhǎijīng山海經» 62/86,

Accounting for 70%. <shìlùntúténgShényuBànrénbànshòuShén試論圖騰神與半人半獸神> 86 Bànrénbànshòu Gods in«Shānhǎijīng» were analyzed and as a result, 26 gods of combining the part of pigs, horses, cows, sheep, dogs, chickens and part of people accounted for 30% and 62 gods of combining the part of wild animals and part of people accounted for 70%. And 64 RénmiànRéntóu人面人頭 and 5 Niǎotóu鳥頭, Lóngtóu龍頭), Shòutóu獸頭 accounted for 74% and 7%, respectively.

■ «Mínjiānwénxuélùntán民間文學論壇» 2nd period in 1987(Total 25) pp.23-25.

(1) Nature worship:

Sun, moon-Yùbì玉璧, gōuyún-type jade jewelry勾雲形玉佩, rainbow-Yùhuáng玉璜, star-Octagonal star shaped jadeware八角星形 玉器.

❀ «Zhuāngzǐ莊子» lièyùkòu列禦寇; 吾以天地為棺槨, 以日月為連璧, 星辰為珠璣.

Heaven and earth are used as a coffin, the sun and moon are used as Yùbì and star is used as beads.

❀ **Sun, moon:** Yùbì (jade disk with a hole in the center).
Hóngshān Culture – Liángzhǔ Culture

❀ **Cloud:** Gōuyún-type jade jewelry (Quánzhàng權杖).

gōuyún-type jade jewelry勾雲形玉佩 -«左传»,«Hànshū漢書» Yúnshī雲師 -Jiǎgǔwén甲骨文 我 origin

《左传》Zhāogōng昭公 17th year: "昔者黄帝氏以云起, 故为云师而云名."

In the old days, Huángdìshì黄帝氏 arose from clouds so it is called as Yúnshī 雲師, Yúnmíng雲名."

❀ **Rainbow:** Yùhuáng玉璜.

○ Jiǎgǔwén甲骨文 Hóng虹 : The dragon head is facing out. Completely the same as Yùhuáng excavated from Dōngshānzuǐ.

○ Excavated from Hóngshān Culture Dōngshānzuǐ東山嘴.

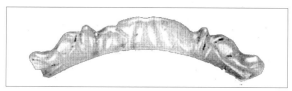

○ Shuānglóngyùhuáng雙龍玉璜 Length 4.1cm.

❀ **Star:** Bājiǎoxīngxíng八角星形 jadeware (Bìyùduōtóuqì碧玉多頭器). A symbol of power. Hóngshān Culture(5500-5000 years ago), The most important Lǐqì禮器.

○ Áohàn cultural relics purification Bìyùduōtóuqì (Lǐqì) Diameter 11cm. Áohànqí 敖漢旗 Museum

(2) Animal Totem

Jade animals: Jade culture (Snakes, birds, bears, pigs, cattle, sheep, turtles, tiger, fish, insects etc.)

1. Snake Totem (Rénshǒushéshēn人首蛇身):

Sun god, Moon god Gāojùlì高句麗(Goguryeo) tomb murals, China Fúxī伏羲, Nǚwā女娲.

Black Skin Jade HóngshānCulture

«Shanhaijing 山海經», «Dìwángshìjì 帝王世紀»

Gāojùlì (Goguryeo) tomb murals

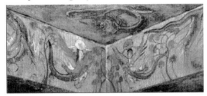

🌀 **Natural animals worship stage:** Snake, Tàihào太昊.

🌀 **Deification 1st step:** Yùlóng玉龍, Fúxī伏羲.
Gāojùlì (Goguryeo) No.5 Tombs No.4, 5 Grave -«Shanhaijing山海經» - Pan Hóngshān Culture jadeware – Yùlóng.

🌀 **China Beijing Palace Museum:** Tribal totem. Hóngshān Culture Early clan art major work.

大玉龙

大玉龙，曲长60cm，直径2.2-2.4cm。新石器时代红山文化。

其玉科为淡绿色老岫岩玉。龙体较粗大，卷曲，呈倒 "C形，长吻微翘起，有圆鼻孔二，双目微椭形凸起，头顶至颈背有长鬣后披，末端翘起，额及颔下有阴刻菱形网纹。龙躯光素扁圆，背部有一钻孔，可系绳穿挂。

此玉龙因其吻前伸，前端凸且翘，因此又有人称之为玉猪龙。这是早期氏族艺术的代表作，属红山文化。其造型夸张、奇特，兼具写实与抽象手法，结构呈简洁，却满盈着生命力，质朴而粗犷，可能是某部族的图腾。

(摹绘人：杨捷)

Professor Lee, Hyeong-gu <The Root of Korean Culture>

■ «jīngxiāngxīnwén京鄉新聞» 1989,2,3. Korea.

❋ **Zhūnǎichéng朱乃誠** (Chinese Academy of Social Sciences Archeological Institute中国社会科学院): Sānxīngtālā三星他拉 Yùlóng is not Hóngshān Culture but the relic of Xiàjiādiàn Lower Culture (4000 years ago-3500 years ago).

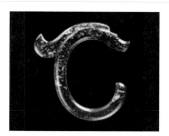

○ Collected from Wēngniútèqí翁牛特旗 Sānxīngtālā 1971,8. Best in the world. National Museum of China.

○ Claimed to be excavated from Dōngguǎibànggōu東拐棒溝 WēngniútèqíMuseum

Sānxīngtālā Yùlóng and Hóngshān Culture ShòumiànjuéxíngYùshì獸面玦形玉飾 have no direct change relationship. (Omitted). Sānxīngtālā Yùlóng is not Hóngshān Culture jadeware.

■ <HóngshānwénhuàShòumiànjuéxíngYùshìyánjiū紅山文化獸面玦形玉飾研究> «Kǎogǔxuébào考古學報» 1st period in 2008.

❧ **Chényìmín**: Yúqiáng禹強, Chinese ancient legend Hǎishén海神. Fēngshén風神.«Shanhaijing山海經» Hǎiwàibějīng海外北經 "北方禺強 人面鳥身, 珥 兩青蛇. 踐兩青蛇." According to«Shanhaijing» Hǎiwàibějīng, "Two blue snakes in Northern Yúqiáng, human face, bird body, ears, stepping on two blue snakes. As for báihuà白話, it means Two blue snakes hung on Northern Yúqiáng, human face, bird body, ears, stepping on two blue snakes with feet." Among Chinese old documents, Yúqiáng is often called as Yújiāng禹疆 and there are many legends about him. According to one opinion, he rules the North Sea as Hǎishén and his shape is also made as a body resembling a fish but Yúqiáng is also called as Fēngshén because he has man's hands and feet and rides a dragon with two heads and is "Xuánmíng玄冥" according to «shuōwénjiězì說文解字» and takes the place of Zhuānxū顓頊 and has the human face and bird body shape and hangs each blue snake on two ears and steps on two blue snakes with his feet and rules the north.

■ «Hēipíyùfēngyúnlù黑皮玉風雲錄» p.159, Shanghai University Press, 2011,5.

❧ **Cháhǎi查海 indigenous people totem:**

Snake totem clan + Toad totem clan = Village configuration.

The tubular Táoguǎn陶管 in the pattern of snake biting a toad 8000 years ago was found in Fùxīn阜新 Cháhǎi查海 Historic Site in the 1980s of the 20th century. This is the earliest snake shape among things found so far. This arti-fact is already a primitive art work and also totem worship work. This Táoguǎn seems to express that the Cháhǎi communit is a village composed of two clans of toads and snakes and Cháhǎi indigenous people already expected very pow-erful reproductive potential of toads and expected an animal with strong power like snakes to protect their clan.

■ <China's first snake civilization 8000 years ago>«Dàliánrìbào大連日報» 2013, 2,21.

* «左傳» 昭公17年"太昊以龙纪,故为龙师而龙名."
«Zuǒzhuàn» zhāogōng 17th year "Tàihào based on a dragon, called Lóngshī 龍師 as a dragon."

❀ «Hànshū漢書» lǜlìzhìxià律曆志下:

世經春秋昭公十七年'郯子來朝'; 太昊氏以龍紀,故為龍師而龍名.

«Hànshū漢書» : According to 'Tánzǐ郯子 came in' the Zhāogōng昭公 17th year of the Spring and Autumn period; Tàihàoshì used a dragon as a standard, he used Lóngshī龍師 and named it as a dragon.

❀ «Gāngjiànyìzhīlù纲鉴易知录»

太昊伏羲氏立春官为青龙氏,夏官为赤龙氏,秋官为白龙氏,冬官为黑龙氏,中官为黄龙氏". 太昊部落以龙为图腾,龙图腾具有青,赤,白,黑,黄五种颜色.

«Gāngjiànyìzhīlù»

For Tàihào Fúxīshì, Blue Dragon shì was established as chūnguān春官, Red Dragon shì as xiàguān夏官, White Dragon shì as qiūguān秋官, Black Dragon shì as dōngguān冬官 and Yellow Dragon shì as zhōngguān中官." Tàihào village used dragons in five colors of Blue, red, white, black, yellow as totem.

❀ Héxīngliàng何星亮 (Ethnology, anthropology researcher of Chinese Academy of Social Sciences):

In China, dragon culture went through a four-step development process: A totem worship step, step of combining dragon worship and lord worship, step of combining Indian dragon worship and Chinese dragon worship. In the totem worship step, some villages in Chinese ancient times worshipped a dragon as totem and used it as the ancestor and marker of their villages. Based on history literature materials and related legends, a dragon (original form is a snake) was originally the totem of Fúxī Clan and became the totem of Tàihào Village later and Tàihào Village is one of the most important origins of dragon totem worship.

■ <Zhōngguólóngwénhuàderénwénjīngshén中國龍文化的人文精神>«Rénmínrìbào 人民日報» 2012,2,24.

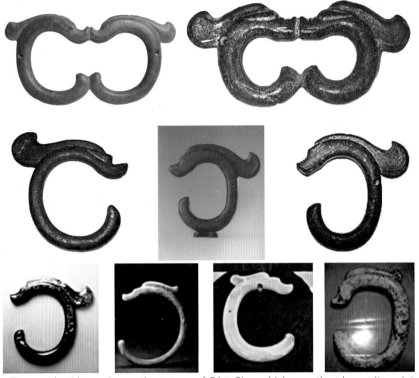

○ Finally, a snake (dragon) was the totem of Fúxī Clan which was the clan unit society and Yùlóng玉龍 seems to have appeared as the symbol of a group in the Tàihào village era, the tribe unit society.

❀ **Deification 2nd step:** Rénmiànshéshēn人面蛇身 (human face and snake body) Fúxī伏羲, Nǚwā女娲 Painting, sun; Three-legged crow. Moon; Toads, rabbits.

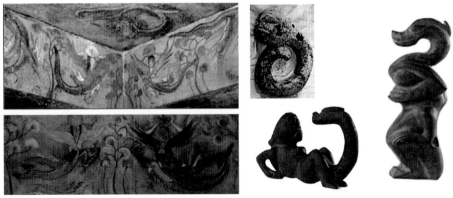

○ Fúxī dragon (Rénmiànshéshēn人面蛇身)

■ Chényìmín«Hóngshānyùqìtújiàn紅山玉器圖鑑» p.176, Shanghai Culture Publisher, 2006,2.

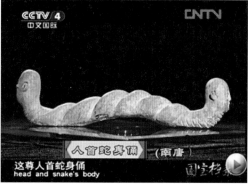

○ Rénshǒushéshēnyōng人首蛇身俑<Guóbǎodàng'àn國寶檔案>
■ «CCTV-4» 2011,9,5.

Nántáng南唐 (Five Dynasties and Ten Kingdoms period) First emperor Lǐbiàn李昇 (888-943) Tomb.

■ Gōngshūduó龔書鐸,Liúdélín劉德麟«chuánshuōshídài-XiàShāngXīZhōu傳說時代-夏商西周» p.22, Jílín吉林 Publishing Ltd., 2006,6.

Literature records on Rénmiànshéshēn人面蛇身 (Chinese side Fúxī伏羲, Nǚwā女娲. Korean side Sun god, Moon god) appearing in such Gāojùlì (Goguryeo) tomb murals are«Shānhǎijīng» 北山經; 其神皆人面蛇身, 北山經 北次二經; 其神皆蛇身人面, 大荒北經; 章尾山 有神,人面蛇身而赤. Finally, the grounds for the mythological background of Gāojùlì (Goguryeo) tomb murals can be primarily identified through the records of«Shānhǎijīng» and be secondarily seen relatively easily through Yùlóng of Hóngshān Culture and Black Skin Jade Culture.

(2) Bear Totem 熊圖騰

Records related to the bear totem are«Shānhǎijīng» 中山經; 熊山.有穴焉,熊之穴,恒出神人.夏啟而冬閉; 是穴也,冬啟乃必有兵. (Xióngshān. There is a cave of bears here and Shénrén神人 comes in and out of it all the time. It opens in summer and closes in winter and if this cave opens in winter, a war breaks out without exception.)

❀ **Zhàobǎogōu趙寶溝 Culture:** Stone bear, Typical memorial ritual vessels (7000 years ago)

○ 14.5cm
■ «Nèiměnggǔchénbào内蒙古晨报» 2013,10,23.

❀ **Yùxiónglóng玉熊龍 (bear-shaped dragon made of jade):** Wéiyùwèizàng唯玉爲葬 (holding a funeral only with jade). Niúhéliáng 2nd point No. 1 tombs No. 4 grave (5500-7500 years ago) Stone Mound Tomb.

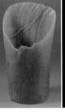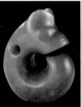

○ Yùgū玉箍8.6cm. Yùzhūlóng玉猪龍 7.2cm,10.3cm

❀ **Féngshí馮時 (Chinese Academy of Social Sciences Archeological Institute):**
«Huáinánzǐ淮南子» God of the North Star is male and female and the male heads to the left and female to the right and are turning back each other. This phenomenon and two pigs placed on the chest of the tomb owner, one point is blue and the other is white and completely matches this direction indicating a boar and sow, respectively and expresses a kind of yīnyáng jiāotài陰陽交泰 thought.

■ «tànsuǒfāxiàn探索發現» 五千年文明見證-牛河梁揭秘(下)«CCTV-10» 2014,08,17.

❀ **Natural animal worship:** Actual bear shape.

Bear foot, bear tooth: Liáoníngshěng Jiànpíngxiàn建平县 Niúhéliáng 16th point No.4 Tomb.
○ Bear tooth Bear foot

🕸 Deification 1st step : Yùxióng玉熊 (Realistic expression).

 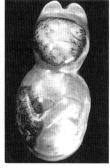 

🕸 Deification 2nd step: Yùxiónglóng玉熊龍 (Shòushǒusānkǒngyùqì獸首三孔玉器)

○ Excavated from Chìfēngshì Bālínyòuqí巴林右旗. Shuāngxióngshǒusānkǒngyùqì雙熊首三孔玉器,

 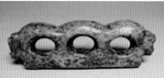 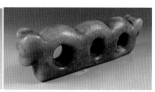

○ Owned by Bālínyòuqí巴林右旗 Museum

🕸 Woo, Sil-ha <Symbolic meaning of Hóngshān Culture Yùzhūlóng, Shuāngshǒuhuángxíngqì (Animal shape jadeware with double beast-heads), Shuāngxióngshǒusānkǒngyùqì and 'Huànrì幻日 (Sundog)' Phenomenon>

■ «East Asian Archaeological Studies» Vol.24,2011,4. East Asian Archaeological Studies. Korea.

✿ Yùxiónglóng玉熊龍: Bear Totem tribe

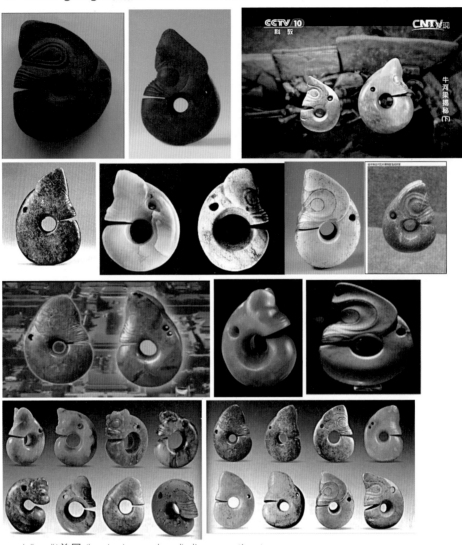

○ shǒuwěi首尾 (beginning and end) disconnection type
○ shǒuwěi首尾 connection type

○ Língjiātān Culture (Yángzǐ River) Yùlóng

○ Yīnxū殷 Yùxiónglóng玉熊龍　○ Guóguó虢國　○ Hánchéng韓城(Xīzhōu西周)

○ Yīn juéxíng (connection type) Yùlóng 玦形玉龍
○ Huánxíng (ring type) Yùlóng 環形玉龍, Smithsonian Freer Gallery FREER SACKLER THE SMITHSONIAN'S MUSEUMS OF ASIAN ART

✿ **Chinese professor Guōdàshùn郭大順:**

Yùxiónglóng玉熊龍, The most representative jadeware of Hóngshān Culture.

"An animal god worshipped by Hóngshān people must be Zhǔshén主神 (Great Spirit) among several gods and Hóngshān people were the clan who worshipped bears." "It can be directly called as "Xiónglóng熊龍" because it does not resemble a pig and resembles a bear. Yùxiónglóng is the most representative jadeware among Hóngshān Culture jadeware and in addition, the technique used in the making has the highest degree of difficulty, explaining Hóngshān Culture people are also the clan worshipping bears."

Zhōnghuárénmíngònghéguó中華人民共和國 GuówùyuànQiáowùbàngōngshì zhǔbàn國務院僑務辦公室主辦 www.gqb.gov.cn

✿ **Chinese professor Zhūnǎichéng朱乃誠:** First symbolic bear

<HóngshānwénhuàShòumiànxíngjuéxíngYùshìyánjiū獸面玦形紅山文化獸面形玦形玉飾研究>

3360 B.C.-2267 B.C. As "C"-shaped dragons, only Sānxīngtālā三星他拉 Yùlóng of Liáohé District and Huánggǔtún黃谷屯 Yùlóng are seen at present. Hóngshān Culture ShòumiànxíngjuéxíngYùshì is a kind of special malformation produced in the process where jade habits are gradually thriving in the late Hóngshān Culture and their period is between 3360 B.C and 2267 B.C and the first symbol is a bear.

■ «kǎogǔxuébào考古學報» 1st period in 2008.

❀ **Professor Lee, Hyeong-gu:** Crucial clue of Hóngshān people bear worship fact

"Xiónglóng carved with jade like this is the most among Hóngshān Culture jadeware and was reported to be about 20 cases. Xiónglóng is considered to be one of 4 types of Hóngshān culture jadeware with Horseshoe-shaped pillow, Cloud-shaped Yùpèi玉佩, square-shape Yùbì玉璧 etc." "This fact shows that Hóngshān people held a memorial service for bears as well as goddess. This is a crucial clue showing the fact that Hóngshān people worshiped a bear." Human bones enshrined in this grave are estimated to be the priest exchanging with heaven because the legs are crossed. Jade placed on the chest embodied a bear. Xiónglóng the most commonly found among jadeware of Hóngshān Culture, what is the relationship between the country founded by Hóngshān people who worshipped bears in their grounds and Gojoseon古朝鮮 (Gǔcháoxiǎn).

❀ **Chinese professor Yèshūxiàn叶舒宪** <lángtúténg,háishixióngtúténg?guānyú Zhōnghuázǔxiāntúténgdebiànxīyufǎnsī狼图腾,还是熊图腾?关于中华祖先 图腾的辨析与反思>

Bear Totem: Forming the foundation of prehistoric totem. Worship of animal god Great Spirit.

In April 2006, some scholars such as the author (Yèshūxiàn professor) and professor Chéngǎnglóng陳崗龍 at Beijing University Oriental Institute and professor Délìgéěr德力格尔, Chifēng Institute Director and professor Xúzǐfēng

徐子锋, Deputy director of Chìfēng Institute Hóngshān Culture International Research Center investigated Hóngshān Culture Area of Eastern Inner Mongolia and Western Liáoníng and carried out the basic analysis by collecting related archaeological cultural relics materials in each archaeological site, qíxiàn旗县 Museum and cultural relics sector: A bear forms one basis of China Northern prehistoric totem and shows that it is already revealed relatively clearly.

■ «ZhōngguóShèhuìKēxuéyuànyuànbào中国社会科学院院报» 2006,8,2.

❀ Liúguóxiáng劉國祥 (Chinese Academy of Social Sciences Inner Mongolia Archeological Institute): Hóngshān Gǔguó古国

After going through Hóngshān Gǔguó-centered unified design and processing, this formative Yùzhūlóng玉猪龍 was given to each village chief within the Gǔguó Area by the leader of Gǔguó and the chief could represent a symbol of his identity, power and honor by wearing this Yùzhūlóng. This Hóngshān Gǔguó has a certain type of a country(国) and there was a loose federation relationship between the villages

■ «Běijīngkējìbào北京科技報» 2007,9,5.

❀ Deification Step 3 : Bànrénbànshòu半人半獸

○ Black Skin Jade(58cm) Neolithic period (About 10000-4000 years ago)
■ «Shǐhǎiyízhēn史海遺珍» p.11, Chinese Museum, 2015,4.

Late Han後漢 WǔshìCítáng武氏祠堂 (AD147) zhuānzhù塼築 Shrine posterior stone chamber 3rd stone 3rd floor Relief sculpture part. Shāndōngshěng Jiāxiáng嘉祥 Zǐyunshān紫雲山.

A bear-shaped figure holds ancient weapons in the head, hands and feet and takes powerful and dynamic appearance and a tiger-shaped figure shows the appearance of pulling out a child with his mouth.

❀ **Deification Step 4:** Figure appearance (+Sun god. birds, pigs and people)

❀ **Yùxiónglóng玉熊龍:** Tribal chief appearance (+figure)

⊛ **Xióngguān**熊冠 **yùdiāoshénxiàng**玉彫神像: British Cambridge University Fitzwilliam Museum.

Xúlín徐琳 <**SānzūnHóngshānYùrénxiàngjiěxī**三尊"红山玉人"像解析>

○ Niúhéliáng 16th point Yùrén.
○ Beijing Palace Museum, Yùzuòrénxiàng玉坐人像.
○ Owned by Cambridge University Museum, yùdiāoshénxiàng, yùdiāoshénxiàng Parietal part. British Cambridge University Fitzwilliam Museum.
■ «shōucángjiā收藏家» 4th Period in 2010 (Original:«Zhōngguókēxuébào中国社会科学報»)

A bear occupies a very important position in the Hóngshān Society and the lower jawbone has been excavated before in No. 2 and No. 4 Stone Mound Tombs of Hóngshān Culture, explaining that the origin of the convention of worshipping a bear has been long. Bear worship is also the convention unique to several ethnic groups in Northeast. Hóngshān Culture regarded a bear as a main worship object and goes very well with the distinct features of regions where jadeware was excavated. But I understand that the thing set on the head of Yùzuòrén owned by Cambridge University Museum is not just Xióngguàn but bear leather with a bear head is put around. The bear head was created into the shape of an official hat and the boundary line between the human face and bear hat can be seen clearly in the front face area of the jade person. Seeing from the back, the bear head and the skirt of the body are connected but the whole bear leather is put around the body. Therefore, the subject of this jadeware is still a human being and it can be said to be a person with one bearskin around his body. The figure body is still a naked jade person like that excavated from Niúhéliáng and an Gùgōng (Palace Museum) collection. One detail to note here is that Yùzuòrén of Cambridge University is bare foot and steps on one round object and it cannot be found what this round object is but given that it appeared here, it was never made carelessly and there must be a particular meaning.

(3) Bird totem : Yùniǎo玉鳥

❀ **Yùniǎo**: Shénniǎo神鳥 (God bird). Heaven and earth communication skills.

Why did birds attract the attention of the indigenous people in Inner Mongolia grassland of prehistoric times? Birds can fly freely in the sky. Primitive human beings thought that birds have the ability to communicate with heaven and earth because they regarded such evolved instinct of birds as a kind of miraculous capacity. Finally, believing God lives above the sky and people live on the ground, primitive mankind thought birds are the animals that can talk to God because they can fly in the sky. As shown above, the mission of communicating between humans and God was given to birds and birds were deified in the mind of primitive mankind due to their characteristic of flying. When carving the bird shape, they expressed a bird's wings and tail with particular attention and a raised tail, mighty wings among bird figures on the head of this goddess statue attract the most attention. Some of primitive humanity often thought that birds can see and hear everything in the sky and the source of this ability lies in the wings and tail of birds.

At the same time, mankind also thought that people's souls and bodies can be separated. After a man died, the soul flew out from the human body and flew to the sky like a bird and birds also became the incarnation of the human soul and furthermore, as the incarnation of ancestral spirits, eventually, birds became an assistant of tōngshén通神 of a shaman. In such a restriction of consciousness, it is no wonder that primitive mankind carved the shape of a bird when creating jadeware. As shown above, when carving an idol worshiped by the village, indigenous people of prehistoric culture could make Shénqì神器 (god vessels) of putting a bird on the head in order to communicate the linkage with the gods of heaven and communicate the connection with ancestors.

❀ **Four direction Gods**: 《Shānhǎijīng山海經》 Specific tribe ancestors.
東方 句芒, 鳥身人面, 乘兩龍. (Hǎiwàidōngjīng海外東經)
Eastern Gōumáng, Niǎoshēnrénmiàn, chéngliǎnglóng.
西方 蓐收, 左耳有蛇, 乘兩龍. (Hǎiwàixījīng海外西經)

Western Rùshōu, zuǒ'ěryǒushé, chéngliǎnglóng.

南方 祝融, 獸身人面, 乘兩龍. (Hǎiwàinánjīng海外南經)

Southern Zhùróng, Shòushēnrénmiàn, chéngliǎnglóng.

北方 禺彊, 人面鳥身, 珥兩青蛇, 踐兩青蛇. (Hǎiwàiběijīng海外北經)

Northern Yújiāng, Rénmiànniǎoshēn, ěrliǎngQīngshé, jiànliǎngQīngshé.

❀ Fēngshén風神 Yúqiáng: Emperor's Grandson,

   «Shānhǎijīng山海經» Dàhuāngdōngjīng大荒東經

"The emperor gave birth to Yú禺 and Yú禺 gave birth to Yújīng禺京. This Yújīng is Yújiāng."

❀ Natural animal worship: Bird life-size shape.

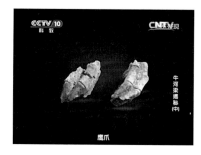

Eagle Claw Yīngzhǎo鷹爪 : Liáoníngshěng Jiànpíngxiàn Niúhéliáng 16th point No.4 Tomb.

❀ Deification Step 1 : Yùniǎo玉鳥 (Realistic expression).

   Shǎohào少昊 Bird totem tribe:

❀ «Shíyíjì拾遺記» Shǎohào少昊; kèyùwéijiū 刻玉為鳩 (Carved jade pigeon)

帝子與皇娥泛於海上, 以桂枝為表, 結熏茅為旌, 刻玉為鳩, 置於表端.

In«Shíyíjì» Vol.1 Shǎohào, when Huángé皇娥, Shǎohào's mother Huángé was enjoying in the blue ocean riding a raft in the daytime in her girlhood, she made a dove shape with jade and decorated the flagpole. Later, Huángé gave birth to Shǎohào and called a pen name as "Fèngniǎoshì鳳鳥氏". This is the best example of using jade as totem.

❧ «Zuǒzhuàn左傳» zhāogōng昭公17年:

"郯子来朝,公与之宴.昭子问焉曰:'少昊以鸟名官,何故也?'郯子曰:'吾祖也,我知之,…我高祖少昊挚之立也,凤鸟适至,故纪于鸟,为鸟师而鸟名.凤鸟氏,历正也;玄鸟氏,司分者也;伯赵氏,司至得也;青鸟氏,司启者也;丹鸟氏,司闭者也;祝鸠氏,司徒也;鴡鸠氏,司马也;鸤鸠氏,司空也;爽鸠氏,司冠也;鹘鸠氏,司事也;五鸠,鸠民者也;五雉,为五工正.利器用,正度量,夷民者也.九扈,为九农正,扈民无淫者也".

❧ «Zuǒzhuàn左傳» zhāogōng昭公17th year:

"Tánzǐ entered and had a party with me. Zhāozǐ asked 'Why was Shǎohào named after a bird name?' Tánzǐ said: 'When our ancestor gāozǔ Shǎohào Zhí 繁 found a country, a phoenix flew in time so the bird used as Niǎoshī鳥師 and was newly named'. Fèngniǎoshì鳳鳥氏, governs lìzhèng歷正; Xuánniǎo 玄鳥(black bird), sīfēn司分; Bózhàoshì伯赵氏, sīzhìdé司至得; Qīngniǎoshì 青鸟氏, sīqǐ司启; Dānniǎoshì丹鸟氏, sībì司闭; Zhùjiūshì祝鸠氏, sītú司徒; Danjiūshì鴡鸠氏, sīmǎ司马; shījiūshì鸤鸠氏, sīkōng司空; Shuǎngjiūshì 爽鸠氏, sīguàn司冠; Gǔjiūshì 鹘鸠氏, sīshì司事; Wǔjiū五鸠, jiū mín鸠民; Wǔzhì五雉, set Wǔgōng五工 to rights. To benefit qìyòng器用, straighten out dùliàng度量, make people comfortable yímín夷民. jiǔhù九扈, set jiǔnóng九 农 to rights, hùmín扈民 are not obscene."

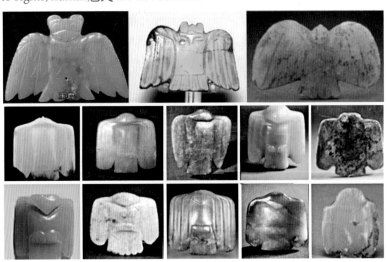

⚛ **Yùyīng玉鷹**: Shanghai Museum. Beijing Palace Museum (Hóngshān Culture, Found relatively much, Eagle related)

○ Liáoníng Fùxīn阜新 Hútóugōu胡頭溝 (200km from the east of Niúhéliáng)
○ "Yùxiāo玉鴞 (Jade owl)

⚛ **Yùniǎo玉鳥**: Black Skin Jade Culture

○ Horned Bat God/H18*18. Bat Male God/H19*15.5

⚛ **Inscription Yùbì玉璧**: A symbol of power, Black Skin Jade Culture, Liángzhǔ Culture, Common inner world.

Yùjiàn玉劍, Yùyuè玉鉞: Divine right, Altar. Royal authority.

○ Yùbì 13.44cm. Taiwan National Palace Museum Priesthood (altar+Royal authority (Fēiniǎo飛鳥)

○ Inscription Yùniǎo, Yùfǔ玉斧 (jade ax): Black Skin Jade Culture, Liángzhǔ Culture Yùyuè. A symbol of power.

🌀 **Jiǎngwèidōng蔣衛東 (Director of Liángzhǔ Museum):** Describing memorial activities on the Wūshī巫師 altar. Fēiniǎo飛鳥 on the altar.

Owner of Yùcóng玉琮+Yùyuè玉鉞: Dominating Liángzhǔ village, Priesthood and royal authority. Supreme sovereignty wángzhě王者.

🌀 **Liúbīn劉斌 (Zhèjiāngshěng浙江省 Cultural Relics Archeological Institute):** Divine right Wūshī巫師 dominating the village.

Móuyǒngkàng牟永抗 (Zhèjiāngshěng Cultural Relics Archeological Institute): Wū巫 Priesthood domination yǐyùshìshén以玉事神

○ Yùniǎo inscription jade dagger: Certain production style.

🌀 **Deification Step 2:** Yùniǎoxíngjué玉鳥形玦 (Yùlóng). Excavated from Chìfēngshì Bālínyòuqí巴林右旗 Nàsītái那斯台.

○ Niǎoxíngjué 5.5cm.1979, Owned by Bālínyòuqí Museum

○ A Bird on the Pig Back/H15*17, p.101. Rabbit and Eagle/H15.5,

■ «Hēipíyù黑皮玉» p.97.p.88.

❀ Shòushǒuniǎoshēn獸首鳥身: Gāojùlì (Goguryeo) tomb murals.

○ jílì吉利: Is Shòushǒuniǎoshēn and makes a pair with wealth and also has the meaning of a lucky omen.

○ Fùguì富貴: Is Shòushǒuniǎoshēn and contains the auspicious meaning

❀ deification Step 3 : Bànrénbànshòu 半人半獸 (Rénmiànniǎo人面鳥); Gāojùlì (Goguryeo) tomb murals,«Shānhǎijīng»

山海經

黑皮玉文化 紅山文化

高句麗 古墳壁畫

❀ Rénmiànniǎo人面鳥 (Réntóuniǎoshēn人頭鳥身; human head and bird body):

Qiānqiū千秋 Cheonchu,Wànsuì萬歲 Manse (Gāojùlì Déxīnglǐ德興里 tomb murals)

Qiānqiū千秋: As the appearance of Réntóuniǎoshēn, it has the auspicious meaning of praying for longevity

Wànsuì萬歲: As Réntóuniǎoshēn, it makes a pair with Qiānqiū and also has the meaning of praying for longevity

Rénmiànniǎo (Réntóuniǎoshēn): Yǔrén羽人 (Feather man)«Shānhǎijīng».

Gāojùlì (Goguryeo) No.5 Tombs, Déxīnglǐ, Wǔyǒngzhǒng舞踊塚 (Dancers Tomb), Sānshìzhǒng三室塚 -«Shānhǎijīng» - Black Skin Jade Culture

❀ **Réntóuniǎoshēn人頭鳥身**: human head and bird body.

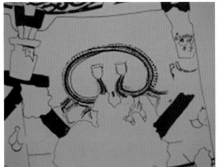 

○ They are Qiānqiū (Cheonchu)·Wànsuì(Manse) drawn in Déxīnglǐ Ancient tomb, Sānshìzhǒng·unknown Rénmiànniǎo人面鳥 of Wǔyǒngzhǒng murals.

❀ **Jeong, Jae-seo:**

Their shapes are all derived from«Shānhǎijīng». The fact that«Shānhǎijīng» is originally Wūshū巫書 and clearly reflects the bird totem, the important contents of Dōngyí東夷 myth is also confirmed in the image of bird flying implemented through this book by Yǒuyì有翼 (winged) animals such as Fēiniǎo 飛鳥·Fēiyú飛魚·Fēishòu飛獸 etc. appearing innumerably. Among them, in addition to winged Yǔrén羽人 shape, the shape of Rénmiànniǎo is the representative expression of Niǎorényìtǐ鳥人一體 myth in «Shānhǎijīng»." Déxīnglǐ Mural Tomb is a tomb with Jìniánmíng紀年銘 of 408 located in Déxīnglǐ, Gangseo江西 Area, Nánpǔshì南浦市, Píng'ānnándào平安南道.

■ «Angtti-Oedipus's Mythology For new Establishment of Chinese mythology» pp.278-280. Changbi. 2010,9. Korea.

@ **Black Skin Jade Culture Rénmiànniǎoshēn人面鳥身: Yúqiáng«Shānhǎijīng».**

○ Yúqiáng禺強 :«Shānhǎijīng» Hǎiwàiběijīng海外北經 "北方禺強 人面鳥身"
○ Chényìmín«Hēipíyùfēngyúnlù» p.159, Shanghai University Press, 2011,5.
○ Rénshǒuniǎoshēn人首鳥身, Shāng商.
○ Gōngshūduó龔書鐸 Liúdélín劉德麟
■ **«Chuánshuōshídài-XiàShāngXīZhōu傳說時代夏商周» p.133, Jílín Publishing Ltd., 2006,6**

@ **Deification Step 4: Yùniǎo玉鳥 +Figure statue.**

○ Chényìmín«Hēipíyùfēngyúnlù» «Hóngshānyùqì紅山玉器»

@ **Liúguóxiáng劉國祥: Three kinds of jadeware (5000 years ago). Appeared as kingship.**

Tomb owner statusWūshī巫師, sānzhǒngyùqì三種玉器 three kinds of jade-ware = Yùrén玉人 + Gūxíngqì箍形器 + Yùfèng玉鳳.
Bear Tooth

  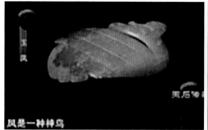 

○ Bear Tooth

■ <tànsuǒfāxiàn探索發現>五千年文明見證-牛河梁揭秘(中)《CCTV-10》 2014,08,16.

(4) Cattle totem : Shénnóng神農 Yándì炎帝 (Gāojùlì Goguryeo tomb murals Niúshǒurénshēn牛首人身)

《拾遺記》 卷一 炎帝神農

築圓丘以祀朝日, 飾瑤階以揖夜光.

有石璘之玉, 號曰'夜明', 以闇投水, 浮而不滅.

《Shiyiji》 Vol.1 Yándì炎帝 Shénnóng神農

When building the altar and performing ancestral rites to the morning sun, we decorated the jade staircase and bowed to the light of darkness. There is shílín's jade called 'Yèmíng' and you become immortal if it rises when you throw it in the water when dark.

《漢書》 律曆志下 :

世經春秋昭公十七年「郯子來朝」, 傳曰昭子問少昊氏鳥名何故, 對曰:

「吾祖也, 我知之矣.昔者, 黃帝氏以雲紀, 故為雲師而雲名;炎帝氏以火紀, 故為火師而火名;共工氏以水紀, 故為水師而水名;太昊氏以龍紀, 故為龍師而龍名.我高祖少昊摯之立也, 鳳鳥適至, 故紀於鳥, 為鳥師而鳥名」

《Hànshū漢書》 lǜlìzhìxià :

It was recorded that Tánzǐ郯子 came in the Zhāogōng昭公 17th of Spring and Autumn period and had a talk with Zhāogōng and in old days, the emperor used Yúnshī雲師 as Yúnmíng雲名, Yándì炎帝 used Huǒshī火師 as Huǒmíng火名, Gònggōngshì共工氏 used Shuǐshī水師 as Shuǐmíng水名, Tàihàoshì太昊氏 used Lóngshī龍師 as Lóngmíng龍名 and Shǎohào少昊 Zhí 摯 used Niǎoshī鳥師 as Niǎomíng鳥名.

❀ **Natural animal worship: Cattle**

  * Deification Step 1: Yùniú玉牛 (jade cattle).

  * Deification Step 2: Yándì (Niúshǒurénshēn)) Power expansion of tribal groups.

  * Deification Step 3: Yùshénrén玉神人.

Black Skin Jade Culture Hóngshān Culture

Diwángshìjì 帝王世紀
Shǐjizhèngyì 史記正義

Insinwoosu
(rénshēnniúshǒu)
(human body, cow head)

Gāojùlì Goguryeo tomb murals

❀ **Professor Jeong, Jae-seo:** Shaping Yándì, Gāojùlì (Goguryeo) tomb murals the most faithfully.

"The mythical figure of «Shānhǎijīng» embodied the most faithfully in Gāojùlì (Goguryeo) tomb murals is Yándì, the god of agriculture and medicine. Yándì is a god considered important by Gāojùlì (Goguryeo) nation enough to appear in No.5 Tombs No.4 Grave, No.5 Grave murals three times and especially, the Yándì shape of Rénshēnniúshǒu人身牛首 (Human body and cow head) of holding ears of rice in the right hand and grass or medicinal herbs in the left hand in No.5 Tombs No.5 Grave murals implements the appearance of Yándì, the god of agriculture and medicine the most faithfully."

"It would be okay to see Shénxiàng神像 of Rénshēnniúshǒu appearing side by side in two ancient tombs as Yándì Shénnóngshì神農氏. Because the nature of a farming god can be clearly identified from the appearance of holding ears of rice in the right hand especially in the case of No.5 Tombs No.5 Grave.

■ «Angtti-Oedipus's Mythology» p.155-6,284, Changbi, 2010, 9. Korea.

However, there are no direct records on the shape of Yándì and records on Yándì's descendants and wife in «Shānhǎijīng» Běishānjīng北山经, Dàhuāngxījīng大荒西经, Hǎinèijīng海内经. Rather, the following records of«Dìwángshìjì帝王世紀» are cited for the first time in«Shǐjizhèngyì史記正義», «Shǐjì史記» commentary of Táng唐 Zhāngshǒujié張守節,«帝王世紀» 曰:神農氏,姜姓也. 母曰妊姒,有喬氏之女,登爲少典妃. 游華陽,有神龍首,感生炎帝. 人身牛首, 長於姜水. 有聖德, 以火德王, 故號炎帝. According to«Dìwángshìjì» : Shénnóngshì is Jiāngxìng姜姓 and first name is Rènsì, is a daughter of Qiáoshì and became a princes of Shǎodiǎn. She met Shénlóng神龍 while wandering in Huàyáng and gave birth to Yándì. He has the cow head and human body (Rénshēnniúshǒu人身牛首) and was raised in Jiāngshuǐ. He became a king by building holiness with fire and therefore, was called Yándì.

☸ Lǚyīngzhōng呂應鐘 <Bànrénbànshòu半人半獸> One person is Shénnóng, the other person is Chīyóu蚩尤.

Shénnóng is Yándì and a great Southern emperor ruling south. From "Yándì is the sun." in the«Báihǔtōng白虎通» fifth line, Yándì is the sun god. «Dìwángshìjì» "Yándì Shénnóngshì is Rénshēnniúshǒu. Chīyóu is the later generation of Yándì and according to «Lùshǐhòujì路史後紀», "The last name of Bǎnquánshì 阪泉氏 Chīyóu is Jiāngxìng and the descendent of Yándì" Yándì is the god of Niútóurénshēn牛頭人身 (Cow head and human body) and his future generations are also Niútóurénshēn.

■ «Táiwānshíbào台灣時報» September 12, 1981.

✿ Niúshǒurénshēn牛首人身: Sun god, Black Skin Jade Culture official airing.

■ <ShìbókànguóbǎoHóngshāngǔyù世博看国宝红山古玉>国宝档案《CCTV-4》 2010.8.17.

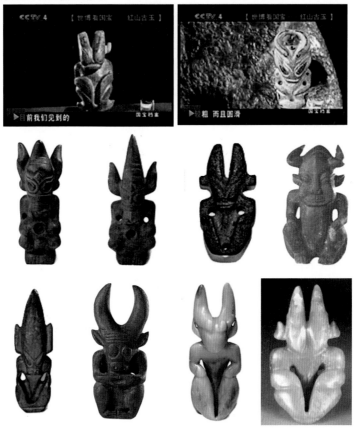

✿ **Professor Xiàdéwǔ夏德武**: Niúshǒurénshēn Sun god, Accounting for about 30% of Hóngshān Black Skin Jade carving

■ Jadeware Art Collector Association, Jadeware Collection Committee Zhǔbiān«Zhōngguóshénmìdehēipíyùdiāo中國神秘的黑皮玉雕» Preface,Wànguó Academic Publishing, 2009.

The most remarkable expression among formative arts of Pan Hóngshān Culture black skin jade carving is commonly called "Sun god" black skin jade carving. This kind of black skin jade carving expression is a combination of "Niúshǒu牛首 and Rénshēn人身" of a kind of supernatural phenomenon. This kind of black skin jade carving accounts for about 30% of Hóngshān Black skin jade carving objectively. Substantially, the formation of Rénshòu人獸 combination shows the shape of totem ancestors of the ancient ethnic society.

❀ Qiáoqiān喬遷, China:

"In ancient China, there are many sex myths between God and man(人神). 'Shǎodiǎnfēi少典妃 contacted with Shénlóng神龍 and gave birth to Yándì and the body was human and the head was cow.' of Yándì Clan.'

■ «yìshùshēngmìngyuqíngshén藝術生命與情神» Héběi Educationpublisher,2006,10.

❀ **Shénnóng Yándì tribe:** Other cows, Bird totem. Tribe bonding. Figure: Appearance of leaders of tribal groups

❀ Deification Step 3: Yùshénrén玉神人.

○ Yùrén excavated from Niúhéliáng 16th point.
○ Beijing Palace Museum, Yùzuòrénxiàng玉坐人像.
○ Owned by Cambridge University Museum, yùdiāoshénxiàng, yùdiāoshénxiàng Parietal part.

❀ Xúlín徐琳 <SānzūnHóngshānYùrénxiàngjiěxī三尊"红山玉人"像解析>
■ «shōucángjiā收藏家» 4th Period in 2010 (Original:«Zhōngguókēxuébào中国社会科學報»)

❀ Taiwanese professor Jiāngměiyīng江美英: Owend by museum unexcavated Yùshénrén materials.

■ <ZhōngguóxīnshíqìshídàiYùrénxíngwénchuàngyìshèjì-中國新石器時代玉人形紋創意設計-藝術, 文化,社會跨域思索> 2009,12.

(5) Pig totem:

* Natural animal worship: Pig totem worship.
* Deification 1st step: Yùzhūlóng (See Bear Totem, Yùxiónglóng)

⊛ **Deification 2nd step** : Zhūshǒurénshēn猪首人身 (Shǐwéishì豕韦氏, Fēngxīshì封豨氏).
Xīnglóngwā興隆窪 Culture (About 8200 years ago-7200 years ago)

Aohànqí Xīnglóngwā Rénzhū人豬 Couple's Tomb Historic Site
Aohànqí Bǎoguótǔxiāng宝國吐鄉, dragon shape (Pig Skull+Stone Mound)
The tomb owner is a leader class figure and it has the meaning of totem worship because two pigs are buried to the right.
XīnglóngwāwénhuàRénzhūhézàngJūshìmù 兴隆洼文化人猪合葬居室墓

■ ZhōngguóAohànwǎng中国敖汉网 2010,6,18. http://www.aohan.gov.cn/

(6) Turtle (Guī龟) totem: Emperor Xuānyuánshì軒轅氏 related.

«Shānhǎijīng» Hǎinèidōngjīng海內東經
Tàihào太昊 Fúxī-Nǚwā: Léizé雷澤's Great Spirit lightning Léishén雷神.
Guīshēnréntóu龟身人頭 (Turtle body and human head)

🌀 **Professor Léiguǎngzhēn**雷廣臻: Tiānyuán天黿 Shénguī神龜 fúhào符號 found, Claiming Huángdì黃帝 culture evidence.
Niúhéliáng 1st point, 5th point No.1 Tomb already robbed tomb

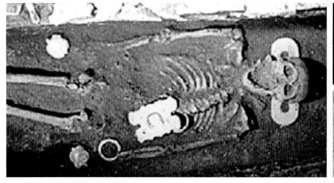  

Léiguǎnzhēn emphasized that Huángdì Culture fúhào Tiānyuán Shénguī engraved on Hóngshān Culture historical site slate was found and this not only suggests that ancient people already began to show the origin of a tribe by using carved stone shapes or letters 5000 years ago but provides one new evidence to Hungshan Culture, that is, Emperor culture.

■ «Liáoníngrìbào遼寧日報» 2011,12,28.

(7) Sheep totem:

Yángshǒurénshēn 羊首人身 (Sheep head and human body). Gǔqiāngzú古
羌族.

(8) Deer totem: Lùshǒurénshēn鹿首人身

○ Chényìmín«Hóngshānyùqìtújiàn紅山玉器圖鑑» p.135,143.Shànghǎiwénhuà chūbǎn shè.
2006,2.

(9) Other Animals Totem:

❁ Rénmiànyúshēn人面魚身 (human face, fish body): Dīrénguó氐人国.

○ Right: Rénshǒuyúshēnyǒng人首魚身俑 (Táng唐,táoyǒng陶俑) 48cm, Excavated from Jiāngsū江蘇 Nánjīng南京 in 1950.

❁ Jeong, Jae-seo : Língyúrénmiàn陵魚人面, Dīrén氐人,Rénmiànyúshēn

○ «Shānhǎijīng»

❁ Hǎinèiběijīng: 陵魚人面, 手足, 魚身, 在海中.

"Língyú has the human face, arms and legs and the body is fish and lives in the sea."

Dàhuāngxījīng: Rénmiànyúshēn

"There is Rénmiànyúshēn in Hùrénzhīguó互人之國. Among Yándì's grandsons, there is Língjiá靈恝 and Língjiá gave birth to Hùrén互人 and could go up and down to heaven."

■ «Angtti-Oedipus's Mythology» p.124. Changbi. 2011. Korea.

❁ Dog totem: Dog head goddess statue wearing a scepter on the head. Tiger? dog?

⊛ **Horse totem:** Mǎtóu馬頭(horse head) Statue with Mǎshǒurénshēn馬首人身(Horse head and human body) Statue on the head.

⊛ **Frog totem:** Nǚwāshì女媧氏 with a frog on the head

The goddess statue with a frog on the head is Hóngshān Culture sex worship and idol of reproduction worship. The head part of this carving is very big and one frog is put on the head and the statue body stands bent and has protruding breasts and this kind of carving with unusually large female genitals has a very clear and sincere purpose, substantially reflecting sex and reproduction worship of primitive village people and the frog right on the head is the best explanation of the reproduction worship. Particularly vigorous reproductive performance of a green frog already received the attention of prehistoric men. Chényìmín «Hóngshānyùqìtújiàn紅山玉器圖鑑» p.129,130. Shanghai Culture Publisher, 2006,2.

※ Earthworm :

As described above, in order to grasp the big picture of 'Jade totem' society of Black Skin Jade Culture and Hungshan Culture, we systematically analyzed jadeware of Black Skin Jade Culture and Hóngshān Culture difficult even for 21st century modern people to understand by first using morphological classification (snakes, cows, dogs, bears, pigs, etc.) of jade carving as one axis and using the development stage of the universal consciousness world of Neolithic ancients as the other axis of nature (animal) worship-Divine right society (Step 1, step 2, step 3)-Royal authority society. And the divine right society step 1 is to realistically represent the shape of animals in its natural state such as birds, bears, turtles, sheep etc. into Yùniǎo玉鳥, Yùxióng玉熊, Yùguī玉龜 through jade and is assumed to be a state of combining the animal worship of clan society step and Jade totem consciousness. And in divine right society step 2, Yùlóng and Yùshòuxíngjué 玉獸形玦(including Yùxiónglóng玉熊龍, Yùzhūlóng玉猪龍 of China Beijing Palace Museum are based on the explanation of "Dàyùlóng大玉龍 may be the totem of a certain tribe. "Yùshòuxíngjué is a kind of deified expression for animals reflecting relatively wide range of animal worship."

In«Běijīngkējìbào北京科技報» (2007,9,5), Chinese Liúguóxiáng (Inner Mongolia Archeological Institute) argues, "After going through Hóngshān Gǔguó古國-centered unified design and processing, this formative Yùzhūlóng was given to each village chief within the Gǔguó Area by the leader of Gǔguó and the chief could represent a symbol of his identity, power and honor by wearing this

Yùzhūlóng. This Hóngshān Gǔguó has a certain type of a country (guó國) and there was a loose federation relationship between the villages." Such appearance of Yùlóng must symbolize the historical fact that the society at that time was already entering the early country stage through the clan society or tribal society stage. Finally, the fact that extremely similar type of jadeware is found in a geographically quite far away place is just relic confirmation for political domination relations by divine right or royal authority. Therefore, divine right society step 3 is the period corresponding to the transitional development process of the totem consciousness society and the main characters of legends and myths that have been handed down for generations such as unnatural shapes called Bànrénbànshòu半人半獸 (half man and half beast) or Shòushǒushòushēn獸首獸身 (Different animal head, body) could be expressed into the real world of three-dimensional space called jade carving. In fact, it can be seen to a breakthrough step where the consciousness world of jade culture subjects found the contact point with the real world. Because the main characters of legends and myths who appeared at that time are presently progressive enough to directly or indirectly influence Our Humanities world belonging to East Asian society as well as three countries of Korea, China, Japan in any form even in modern times. Step 4 shows that figure-centered royal authority appeared beyond the mythic stage.

Jade Totem Society

Animal worship	Cow	Bird	Snake	Bear	Pig	Turtle	Sheep	Other
Divine right society step 1 Jade animals		Yùniǎo		Yùxióng		Yuguī	Yùyáng	
Divine right society step 2 yùlóng		Yùniǎo lóng	Yùlóng	Yùxióng lóng	Yùzhū lóng			
Divine right society step 3 Bànrén bànshòu Shòu shǒu shòu shēn	Niúshǒu rénshēn	Yǔrén	Rénshǒu shéshēn	Xióngshǒu rénshēn	Zhūshǒu rénshēn		Yángshǒu rénshēn	
Royal authoritysociety Yùshén rén								

2 ANIMAL TOTEM

Bànrénbànshòu 半人半獸

Regardless of any nation or country on earth, reverence of ancient mankind for natural objects, especially animals provides a basis of the primitive totem birth and awe for a specific natural environment or animal has been even changed into the object of overcoming. Myths and totem shapes appearing in these series of processes fully reflect the transition process of collective social consciousness of primitive mankind and the birth of a myth was ideologically based on wànwùyǒulínglùn萬物有靈論 (Theory that all things have spirit) and totem ideas they had worshiped. Therefore, myths were changed from a simple structure to organized configuration in accordance with the discipline of self-development and had the vitality according to the historical continuity through more planning (political and religious) embellishment. As shown above, the totem shape of the initial myth of sacrosanctity reflecting changes in the collective consciousness world was changed step by step from a simple form to appearance of Bànrénbànshòu (half man and half beast) and even to the form of Rénjiànshén人間神 (human god). This is a symbol of vitality of the myth and expression of human thinking development at the same time.

In his book «Angtti-Oedipus's Mythology», a Korean professor Jeong, Jae-seo said, "In Chinese mythology, the shape of Bànrénbànshòu is also the appearance of good and omnipotent God. All great gods such as Huángdì黄帝 .Yándì炎帝.Shǎohào少昊.Fúxī伏羲.Nǚwā女娲 showing the appearance of Bànrénbànshòu form a striking contrast with great gods of Greek and Roman mythology almost expressed as handsome men.beautiful women. Bànrénbànshòu, it symbolizes the unity with a sacred totem animal, furthermore, sense of unity with holy nature."

In other words, the leading characters appearing in Chinese mythology have the Bànrénbànshòu shape. In particular, the society of neolithic Black Skin Jade Culture and Hóngshān Culture used jade as a symbol of clan or tribal groups for the main characters of myths and legends such as Tàihào太昊 Fúxī伏羲 (Rénshǒushéshēn人首蛇身), Shénnóng神農Yándì炎帝 (Niúshǒurénshēn牛首人身), Chīyóu蚩尤 (Chiu;Niúshǒurénshēn牛首人身) etc. The first animal totem is a realistic representation of the object of worship and a snake indicated a snake and a tiger indicated a tiger. And gradually, the shape was changed to Bànrénbànshòu such as Rénshǒushéshēn, Rénshǒuniǎoshēn人首鳥身 (human head and bird body), Gǒushǒurénshēn狗首人身 (Dog head and human body) etc. in the Neolithic Age and these types of gods appeared a lot in the late Neolithic Age. However, we should pay attention to the fact that 86 Bànrénbànshòu gods are recorded in «Shanhaijing».

[1] Snake totem : Rrénmiànshéshēn人面蛇身 (human face and snake body)

«Shanhaijing山海經» Běishānjīng北山經;

自單狐之山至于隄山,凡二十五山,五千四百九十里,其神皆人面蛇身.
"There are a total of 25 mountains from Mt. Dānhú to Dīshān and the distance amounts to 5490 lǐs and all the gods here have the human head and snake body"

❀ Yùlóng玉龍, Yùshòuxíngjué玉獸形玦: Main characters of myths and legends

'Shǎodiǎnfēi少典妃 of a Yándì炎帝 clan contacted with Shénlóng and gave birth to Yándì and his body was a human and head was a cow'

■ Qiáoqiān喬遷 «yìshùshēngmìngyuqíngshén藝術生命與情神» p.58,HéběiEducation Publisher. 2006,10.

○ (left) Fúxī Dragon: Rénshǒushéshēn. Fúxī shape first Chúxíng雛形. Owned by Liáoníng private. Chényìmín陳逸民

■ «Hóngshānyùqìtújiàn紅山玉器圖鑑» p.176, Shanghai Culture Publisher, 2066,2.

※ **Rénshǒushéshēn人頭蛇身 (=Rénmiànshéshēn人面蛇身): Sun god. Moon god. Jí'ān集安 Gāojùlì高句麗 (Goguryeo) tomb murals No.5 Tombs No.4 Grave, No.5 Grave. China: Fúxī, Nǚwā.**

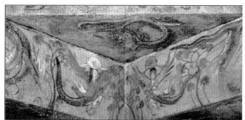

※ **«Shanhaijing» Hǎiwàibějīng海外北經**

Xiàngliǔ相柳, Zhúyīn燭陰: Rénmiànshéshēn人面蛇身.

■ Jeong,Jae-seo «Angtti-Oedipus's Mythology» pp.243, 244. Changbi,2010,9.

@ Rénmiànshéshēn: Carved Stone of China in Hàn漢 Dynasty. Fúxī and Nǚwā Painting. Xīwángmǔ西王母(God of Growth) Dōngwángfù東王父.

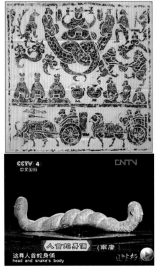

○ Rénshǒushéshēnyōng人首蛇身俑 (Excavated from Nán-táng南唐(937~975) Lǐbiàn李昇 (888-943) royal tomb)
■ «CCTV-4» <Guóbǎodàng'àn國寶檔案> 2011,9,5.

@ Héxīngliàng何星亮 (Ethnology, anthropology researcher of Chinese Academy of Social Sciences) : <Zhōngguólóngwénhuàderénwénjīngshén中國龍文化的人文精神>

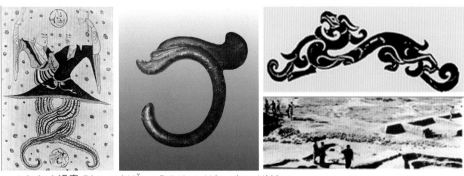

○ Juànhuà絹畫 Fúxī and Nǚwā Painting. Hóngshān Yùlóng
○ Qín秦 and Hàn漢 dragon pattern. Liáoníng Fùxīn Cháhǎi Historic Site Yùlóng

The dragon culture origin is identified multifactorially, saying, "In China, dragon culture went through a four-step development process. A totem worship step, step of combining dragon worship and lord worship, step of combining Indian dragon worship and Chinese dragon worship. In the totem worship step, some villages in Chinese ancient times worshipped a dragon as totem and used it as the ancestor and marker of their villages. Based on history literature materials and related legends, a dragon (original form is a snake) was originally the totem of Fúxī Clan and became the totem of Tàihào太昊 Village later and Tàihào太昊 Village is one of the most important origins of dragon totem worship."

■ 《Rénmínrìbào人民日報》 2012,2,24.

However, the most interesting fact is that the Chinese side calls Sun god, Moon god in Gāojùlì (Goguryeo) tomb murals No.5 Tombs No.4 Grave, No.5 Grave as Fúxī, Nǚwāi and first comparing them with Fúxī and Nǚwā Painting of the Chinese Hàn Dynasty morphologically, Sun god and Moon god face each other in Gāojùlì (Goguryeo) tomb murals and Chinese Fúxī and Nǚwā Painting face each other but not only there are not significant differences except intertwined bodies but main components such as sun, moon, humans, snakes, three-legged crow, gold toad etc. appearing in Gāojùlì (Goguryeo) tomb and Fúxī and Nǚwā Painting are almost the same. But the fact we must not pay attention is that unlike Hóngshān Culture and Black Skin Jade Culture of the Northeastern area of current Chinese continent, that is, Liáohé遼河 Area, dragon made of jade and Bànrénbànshòu artifacts have not been found officially in Zhōngyuán 中原 Neolithic culture historic site represented by the Yellow River civilization. Therefore, it is necessary to note jade culture and historical facts that can also never deny the overall association with Gāojùlì (Goguryeo) as well as mythical affinity with Sun god (Tàihào Fúxīi), Moon god (Nǚwā) directly related to dragon (snake) totem appearing in Gāojùlì (Goguryeo) tomb murals and humanities spirit of Chinese dragon culture as above.

[2] Cattle totem:
Sun god(Shòushǒurénshēn獸首人身 type)

In 《Shanhaijing》, a record desribing the cattle totem is as follows:
Běishānjīng北山經; 有獸焉,其狀如牛,而赤身,人面,馬足,名曰窫窳,其音如嬰兒,是食人.

"Some beasts look like a cow and their body is red and they have human face and feet of a horse. Their name is Alyǔ and they sound like a child and eat human".

Xīshānjīng西山經 Xīcièrjīng西次二經; 其七神皆 人面牛身.

"The 7 gods all have the human face and cow body".

Chinese Qiáoqiān said, In his book «Yìshùyǔshēngmìngyujīngshén藝術生命與精神» "In ancient China, there are many sex myths between God and man (人神). For example, 'A swallow came down and gave birth to Shāng商' of Shāng(Yīn殷) Clan, 'A blue rainbow covered her and she became pregnant and gave birth to Páoxī庖犧(=Fúxī) after 12 years. of Fúxī Clan: 'Shǎodiǎnfēi少典妃 contacted with Shénlóng and gave birth to Yándì炎帝 and the body was human and the head was cow.' of Yándì Clan: 'Fùbǎo附寶 saw large lightning surrounding the Big Dipper and got pregnant.' of Huángdì黃帝 Clan"

❀ **Gāojùlì (Goguryeo) Jí'ān tomb murals Sānshìzhǒng 三室塚, No.5 Tombs No.4 Grave, No.5 Grave: Yándì炎帝(Sun god)**

■ The «Cháoxiǎnrìbào朝鮮日報» Jí'ān集安 Area local shooting in 1993.

❀ **Black Skin Jade Culture Sun god: Official airing.**

■ <Shìbókànguóbǎo Hóngshāngǔyù> 国宝档案 «CCTV» 4. 2010.8.17.

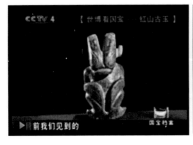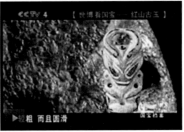

❀ Black Skin Jade Culture Center circle made with two hands. Symbolizing the sun?

     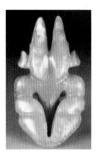

* The relevance between Shénnóng神農 Yándì炎帝 and mythical topics of Gāojùlì (Goguryeo) tomb murals is a fact that cannot be denied and hence, Jeong, Jae-seo said in «Angtti-Oedipus's Mythology», "The mythical figure of «Shanhaijing» embodied the most faithfully in Gāojùlì (Goguryeo) tomb murals is Yándì, the god of agriculture and medicine. Yándì is a god considered important by Gāojùlì (Goguryeo) nation enough to appear in No.5 Tombs No.4 Grave, No.5 Grave murals three times and especially, the Yándì shape of Rénshēnniúshǒu人身牛首 (Human body and cow head) of holding ears of rice in the right hand and grass or medicinal herbs in the left hand in No.5 Tombs No.5 Grave murals implements the appearance of Yándì, the god of agriculture and medicine the most faithfully."

❀ Niúshǒurénshēn牛首人身: One person is Shénnóng神農, the other person is Chīyóu蚩尤.

Shénnóng is Yándì and a great Southern emperor ruling south.

From "Yándì is the sun." in the «Báihǔtōng白虎通» fifth line, Yándì is the sun god. «Dìwángshìjì帝王世紀» "Yándì Shénnóngshì is Rénshēnniúshǒu. Chīyóu is the later generation of Yándì and according to «Lùshǐhòujì路史後紀», "The last name of Bǎnquánshì阪泉氏 Chīyóu is Jiāngxìng姜姓 and the descendent of Yándì" Yándì is the god of Niútóurénshēn牛頭人身 (Cow head and human body) and his future generations are also Niútóurénshēn.

■ «Táiwānshíbào台灣時報» September 12, 1981.

⌬ **Taiwan Jiāngměiyīng**江美英: **Yùshénrén**玉神人 (Owned by museums worldwide, Non-excavated artifacts)

新石器時代紅山文化神人 : 均爲博物館收藏未見出土 資料				
北京故宫博物館 高14.6　6公分	劍橋大學博物館 高12 公分	Ernest Erickson 高10.8公分	Cleveland Museum of Art 高13.5公分	北京故宫博物館 長27.7　11.7

○ <ZhōngguóxīnshíqìshídàiYùrénxíngwénchuàngyìshèjì中國新石器時代玉人形紋創意設計-藝術,文化,社會跨域思索>

With respect to Black skin jade carving of such Niúshǒurénshēn (Sun god) shape, a Chinese professor Xiàdéwǔ夏德武 explains in «Zhōngguóshénmìde hēipíyùdiāo中國神秘的黑皮玉雕», "The most remarkable expression among formative arts of Pan Hóngshān Culture black skin jade carving is commonly called "Sun god" black skin jade carving. This kind of black skin jade carving expression is a combination of "Cow head (niúshǒu牛首) and rénshēn人身" of a kind of supernatural phenomenon. This kind of black skin jade carving accounts for about 30% of Hóngshān black skin jade carving objectively. Substantially, the formation of Rénshòu人獸 combination shows the shape of totem ancestors of the ancient ethnic society." It can be finally seen that Yándì God appearing three times in Gāojùlì (Goguryeo) tomb murals consistently penetrates the historical period and East Asian mythology including China such as «Shanhaijing», Black Skin Jade Culture (Hóngshān Culture) jade carving as well as the relevance with ancestral myths of Gāojùlì (Goguryeo).

[3] Bird totem: Yùniǎo(玉鳥=Shénniǎo神鳥)
Heaven and earth communication skills.

Why did birds attract the attention of the indigenous people in Inner Mongolia grassland of prehistoric times? Birds can fly freely in the sky. Primitive human beings thought that birds have the ability to communicate with heaven and earth because they regarded such evolved instinct of birds as a kind of miraculous capacity. Finally, believing God lives above the sky and people live on the ground, primitive mankind thought birds are the animals that can talk to God because they can fly in the sky. As shown above, the mission of communicating between humans and God was given to birds and birds were deified in the consciousness world of primitive mankind due to their characteristic of flying.

At the same time, mankind also thought that people's souls and bodies can be separated. After a man died, the soul flew out from the human body and flew to the sky like a bird and birds also became the incarnation of the human soul and furthermore, as the incarnation of ancestral spirits, eventually, birds became an assistant of Tōngshén通神 of a shaman. In such a restriction of consciousness, it is no wonder that primitive mankind carved the shape of a bird when creating jadeware. As shown above, when carving an idol worshiped by the village, indigenous people of prehistoric culture could make Shénqì神器 (god vessels) of putting a bird on the head in order to communicate the linkage with the gods of heaven and communicate the connection with ancestors.

(1) Yùniǎo玉鳥

❀ **Yùyīng玉鷹 (jade eagle)**: Shanghai Museum.Beijing Palace Museum(Hóngshān Culture, Found relatively much, Eagle related)

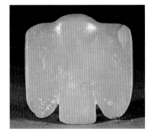

❀ **Liúguóxiáng劉國祥**: Three kinds of jadeware (5000 years ago). Appeared as a price status. Tomb owner status Wūshī巫師,

three kinds of jadeware = Yùrén玉人 + Gūxíngqì箍形器 + Yùfèng玉鳳
Excavated from Liáoníngshěng Jiànpíngxiàn Niúhéliáng 16th point No. 4
Tomb in 1984 (Bear foot, Bear Tooth, Eagle Claw).

  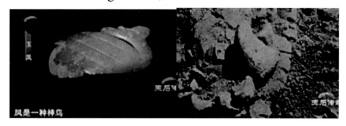

When compared with the records of «Shānhǎijīng», Nánshānjīng南山經 and
Dàhuāngdōngjīng大荒東經 generally known as a geography book, Yùfèng excavated here provides a crucial clue that identify the base of Dōngyí東夷 Tribe
bird totem as well as the direction of North-South, East-West that can conclude
a geographical space.

According to the records of Nánshānjīng南山經,

"丹水出焉,而南流注于渤海.有鳥焉,其狀如雞,五采而文,名曰鳳皇,首文
曰德,翼文曰義,背文曰禮,膺文曰仁,腹文曰信.是鳥也,飲食自然,自歌自舞,見
則天下安寧."

Dānshuǐ comes from here and flows into Bóhǎi in the south. Some birds
here look like chicken and have a pattern in five colors and are called Phoenix.
The head pattern of these birds indicates Dé, wing pattern Yì, back pattern Lǐ,
chest pattern Rén and belly pattern indicates Xìn. Eating and drinking of this
bird is suitable for the discipline of nature and it sings and dances by itself and
the whole world becomes comfortable.

According to the records of Dàhuāngdōngjīng大荒東經,

"東海之外大壑,少昊之國.少昊孺帝顓頊於此,棄其琴瑟."
There is Dàhè outside the East Sea and it is Shǎohàoguó. Shǎohào raised
king Zhuānxū here and left qínsè at that time"

Recently, a vice researcher of Xúchūnlíng徐春苓 Tiānjīnshì天津市 Museum in China stated, "The whole area of Shāndōng, Jiāngsū, Zhèjiāng through

Southern Yānshān燕山 from ancient Northeast is a place where the bird totem clan of Dōngyí Tribe used to live. Shǎohào family and relatives among bird totem clans, an eagle totem clan is the totem worship object of Shǎohào Tribe using an eagle as totem or Zúhuī族徽 (A pattern symbolizing a tribe) of the clan." Especially in «Hóngshānwénhuàyùqìyánjiū红山文化玉器研究», Chinese Yánxiángfù颜祥富 said, "In the early Chinese primitive society, there was a step called jade totem that the ancestors of the Chinese nation previously expressed jade sculpture containing a certain implied meaning as the marker of the nation. In the historical literature, there are numerous records about this aspect, for example, in «Shíyíjì拾遗记» 卷一Shǎohào, when Huángé皇娥, Shǎohào's mother Huángé was enjoying in the blue ocean riding a raft in the daytime in her girlhood, she made a dove shape with jade and decorated the flagpole. Later, Huángé gave birth to Shǎohào and called a pen name as "Fèngniǎoshì鳳鳥氏."

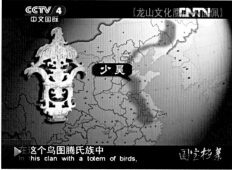

○ Dōngyíi Tribe Shǎohào: <Lóngshān Culture 龍山文化 Yīngjuérénmiànpèi鷹攫人面佩> Guóbǎodàng'àn国宝档案 «CCTV-4» 2012,5,7.

🐦 Yùniǎo玉鳥: Liáoníng Fùxīn Hútóugōu (200km from the east of Niúhéliáng).

Right above layer of Hóngshān occupation layer: Mandolin-shaped bronze dagger Representative relics of Korean Peninsula Bóhǎi Coast

○ Excavated from Fùxīnshì Hútóugōu Historic Site "Yùniǎo"Yùxiāo玉鸮 (Jade owl)

❀ **Black Skin Jade Culture Yùniǎo: +Sun god. +Yùxiónglóng玉熊龍 (bear-shaped dragon made of jade).**

○ «Hēipíyù黑皮玉» Dragon and Bird, p.93.

○ «Hēipíyù黑皮玉» A Bird on the Pig Back,p.101. Rabbit and Eagle, p.97.p.88.

❀ **Yùniǎo:**

○ «Hēipíyù黑皮玉» Horned Bat God. Bat Male God.p.91. p.83

❀ **Yùniǎo**: A Bird Sitting on the Altar. Liángzhǔ Culture inscription Yùbì玉璧 (No priesthood altar bird)

○ «Hēipíyù黑皮玉» p.84. Yùbì (jade disk with a hole in the center) 13.44cm.
○ Taiwan National Palace Museum Priesthood (altar)+Royal authority (Fēiniǎo飛鳥)

❀ **Inscription Yùniǎo Yùfǔ (jade ax)**: Liángzhǔ Culture Yùyuè玉鉞. Common.

 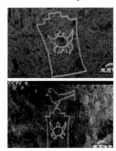 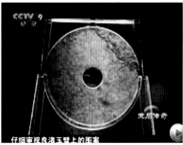

❀ **Jiǎngwèidōng蔣衛東 (Director of Liángzhǔ Museum)**: Describing memorial activities on the Wūshī巫師 altar. Fēiniǎo飛鳥 on the altar.
Owner of Yùcóng玉琮 + Yùyuè玉鉞: Appearance of supreme sovereignty dominating Liángzhǔ village.

❀ **Liúbīn劉斌 (Zhèjiāngshěng Cultural Relics Archeological Institute)**: Divine right (shénquán) Wūshī巫師 dominating the village.

❀ **Móuyǒngkàng牟永抗 (Zhèjiāngshěng Cultural Relics Archeological Institute)**: 'Serving gods with jade 以玉事神' is so called Wū巫 Priesthood domination.

❧ Yùniǎo inscription jade dagger: Certain production style.

❧ Yùshòuxíngjué玉獸形玦(Yùlóng玉龍): Excavated from Chìfēngshì Bālínyòuqí
Nàsītái那斯台.

○ Niǎoxíngjué鳥形玦(Yùniǎolóng玉鳥龍)5.5cm.1979, Owned by Bālínyòuqí Museum

❧ Black Skin Jade Culture Yùniǎo: Shénniǎo神鳥 (=Gods of heaven).

(2) Rénmiànniǎo人面鳥 (human face, bird body):

Gāojùlì (Goguryeo) Déxīnglǐ tomb murals. Sānshìzhǒng三室塚,
Wǔyǒngzhǒng舞踊塚 mural paintings.

❀ **Black Skin Jade Culture:** Yúqiáng禹強, Yǔrén羽人 (Feather man)

○ Black skin jade carving at the bottom and Yúqiáng of «Shānhǎijīng» Hǎiwàibějīng海外北經 are associated in Chényìmín «Hēipíyùfēngyúnlù 黑皮玉風雲錄».

❀ **«Shānhǎijīng» Rénmiànniǎo:** Tribe ancestors specifying four direction Gods.

Four direction Gods 四方神

«Shānhǎijīng山海經» Specific tribe ancestors.

東方 句芒, 鳥身人面, 乘兩龍. (Hǎiwàidōngjīng海外東經)

Eastern Gōumáng, Niǎoshēnrénmiàn, chéngliǎnglóng.

西方 蓐收, 左耳有蛇, 乘兩龍. (Hǎiwàixījīng海外西經)

Western Rùshōu, zuǒ'ěryǒushé, chéngliǎnglóng.

南方 祝融, 獸身人面, 乘兩龍. (Hǎiwàinánjīng海外南經)

Southern Zhùróng, Shòushēnrénmiàn, chéngliǎnglóng.

北方 禺彊, 人面鳥身, 珥兩青蛇, 踐兩青蛇. (Hǎiwàibějīng海外北經)

Northern Yújiāng, Rénmiànniǎoshēn, ěrliǎngQīngshé, jiànliǎngQīngshé.

Among these four direction gods, the god of the north Yúqiáng is recorded as "禺強得之,立乎北極" in «Zhuāngzǐ莊子» Dàzōngshī大宗師. In addition, an interesting fact is that Rénmiànniǎoshēn人面鳥身 (human face, bird body) Yúqiáng appearing in Black Skin Jade Culture is handed down even to modern 21st century as well as the Warring States period (350 B.C.-250 B.C.) through «Shānhǎijīng». This means that jade totem society and culture of FànHóngshānwénhuà泛红山文化 (including Black Skin Jade Culture) with a focus on Neolithic Liáohé遼河 Area are still alive in the consciousness world and ideological system of the East Asia international community. Generally, the shape of Yǒuyì有翼 animals such as Fēiniǎo翡鳥·Fēiyú飛魚·Fēishòu飛獸 etc. related to numerous new totem clearly reflecting bird totem, the important contents of Dōngyí東夷 Myth appears as Yǔrén羽人 shape, the winged human shape such as Yǔmín羽民·Huāntóu讙頭 etc. in «Shānhǎijīng» known as Wūshū巫書 of Dōngyí Tribe. In particular, these are described as follows in

«Shānhǎijīng» Hǎiwàinánjīng海外南經:

羽民國在其東南, 其爲人長頭, 身生羽.

There is Yǔmínguó in the southeast and people have the long face and wings in the body.

讙頭國在其東南, 其爲人人面有翼, 鳥喙, 方捕魚.

There is Huāntóuguó in the south and the people have wings in their face and bird's beak and are catching fish now.

우민국(羽民國)　힁두국(讙頭國)　주(鴸)　욕(顒)　산어(酸與)

«Shānhǎijīng» Hǎiwàinánjīng海外南經, Yǔmín·Huāntóu,
«Shānhǎijīng» Nánshānjīng南山經 Náncièrjīng南次二經, Ju鴸, Náncìsānjīng
南次三經 Yóng顒, «Shānhǎijīng» Běishānjīng北山經 Suānyǔ酸與.

On the other hand, there is a record worth noting as follows in «Shānhǎijīng» Hǎinèijīng海內經 generally known as 'Cháoxiānjì朝鮮記'.

帝俊生晏龍, 晏龍是爲琴瑟.

Dìjùn帝俊 gave birth to Yànlóng晏龍 and Yànlóng made Qínsè.

As described above, Rénmiànniǎoshēn人面鳥身 engraved in Luódiànzǐtánpípá螺鈿紫檀琵琶 being held in Zhèngcāngyuàn正倉院 as a cherished thing of Shèngwǔ聖武 Emperor in Japan across the Sea and shape of Rénmiànniǎoshēn appearing innumerably in Gāojùlì tomb murals, Dìjùn 帝俊 who was the god of a bird totem tribe of «Shānhǎijīng» may be the shape of Bànrénbànshòu半人半獸 God common in East Asian mythology related to music rather than mere outward relation.

○ Japan Zhèngcāngyuàn Luódiànzǐtánpípá (Enlarging the original part)
○ Zhèngcāngyuàn treasure Full length 99.6cm. After all, morphologically, it is the Bànrénbànshòu shape of bird totem but it is the god of music or seems to related to God of Gēwǔ歌舞. We look forward to future studies.

❂ Jiǎgǔwén甲骨文 (Shell-and-bone characters): Same person as Dìjùn帝俊≒Sun(Shùn舜) (Ancestral god, Niǎotóurénshēn鳥頭人身 of Yīn殷)

Generally, «Shānhǎijīng» is known as Wūshū巫書 of Dōngyí Tribe but Hǎinèijīng海內經 among them is also famous for 'Cháoxiānjì朝鮮記' But why does the representative spirit of «Shānhǎijīng» Dìjùn帝俊 have the Niǎotóurénshēn shape of bird totem? In the pronunciation, Dìjùn is not only estimated to be the same person as Shùn but appears in the shape of Hóushén猴神 or Niǎotóurénshēn in Jiǎgǔwén as the ancestral god of Yīn and the Shéntǐ神體 is Xuánniǎo玄鳥 or Cūnniǎo踆鳥 related to the founding myth of Yīn and is also Sānzúwū三足烏 (three-legged crow) in the sun. In <xiānqínliǎnghànDōnghǎishénhuàyánjiū先秦兩漢東海神話研究>,Taiwanese Fùshìxīn傅仕欣 (Chung-Ang University) argues, "Despite several discussions of scholars, only according to record of «Shānhǎijīng», Dìjùn's activities and most countries of their descendants were in the East; Dìjùn's family and relatives used birds as their totem and this is one of the characteristics of Dōngyí Tribe and therefore, Dìjùn was the supreme great god of the East and king of kings worshiped by ancient Dōngyí Tribe."

■ (傅仕欣, Taiwan Central University Chinese Literature Research Institute, Thesis, 2011,6)

❂ Rénmiànniǎoshēn人面鳥身 (=Rénmiànniǎo人面鳥): Gāojùlì (Goguryeo) Déxīnglǐ tomb murals. Sānshìzhǒng, Wǔyǒngzhǒng mural paintings.

○ Hèniǎo賀鳥 Qiānqiū千秋 Wànsuì萬歲

○ Sānshìzhǒng Wǔyǒngzhǒng

Déxīnglǐ德興里 Mural Tomb is a tomb with Jìniánmíng紀年銘 of 408 located in Déxīnglǐ, Jiāngxī江西 Area, Nánpǔshì南浦市, Píng'ānnándào平安南道. Hèniǎo is drawn right above the Déxīnglǐ tomb anterior chamber north ceiling anterior chamber epitaph. It has the human face and bird body, stretched its neck and tail and stretched out its wings. It carries a pot on its back and inscription of 'Hèniǎozhixiàngxuédàobùchéngbēijiǎoyàokǒu賀鳥之像學道不成背角藥口' is written next to it. In addition to the Rénmiànniǎoshēn shape of Bànrénbànshòu explaind in the above, Jílì吉利 (makes a pair with wealth and also has the meaning of an auspicious sign) of expressing a deified animal and bird body in stead of human face as a complex body Shòushǒuniǎoshēn獸首鳥身 (beast head and bird body) and Fùguì富貴 (containing auspicious meaning) appear in Gāojùlì (Goguryeo) Déxīnglǐ tomb murals. In «Angtti-Oedipus's Mythology», a Korean professor Jeong, Jae-seo said, "They are Qiānqiū·Wànsuì drawn in Déxīnglǐ Ancient tomb, Sānshìzhǒng·unknown Rénmiànniǎo of Wǔyǒngzhǒng murals. Their shapes are all derived from «Shānhǎijīng». The fact that «Shānhǎijīng» is originally Wūshū and clearly reflects the bird totem, the important contents of Dōngyí myth is also confirmed in the image of bird flying implemented through this book by Yǒuyì有翼 (winged) animals such as Fēiniǎo·Fēiyú·Fēishòu etc. appearing innumerably. Among them, in addition to winged Yǔrén shape, the shape of Rénmiànniǎo is the representative expression of Niǎorényìtǐ鳥人一體 myth in «Shānhǎijīng»."

※ Rénshǒushòushēn人首獸身 (human head and animal body):
Déxīnglǐ ancient tomb, Dìzhóu地軸.
Tiānwángdìshénzhǒng天王地神塚 Dìshén地神.

Gāojùlì (Goguryeo) Déxīnglǐ tomb murals were filled with a variety of shénxiān神仙 with miraculous powers and auspicious animal paintings. A four-legged animal with two human heads drawn in the north ceiling dǐngzhù頂住 is the appearance of Dìzhóu地軸. A big star was drawn in the upper part of the north ceiling dǐngzhù center and the Big Dipper in the above and 9 mysterious animals were portrayed under these stars and Dìzhóu was drawn in just below the Big Dipper. In the left, there is the inscription of 'Dìzhóuyìshēnliǎngtóu地軸一身兩頭'. He wore a hat with two thin straps on the head and there is hair in the part of connecting the legs and body on the left.

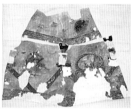

○ Anterior chamber north ceiling Dìzhóu (Déxīnglǐ Ancient tomb north ceiling Dìzhóu. Inscription 'Dìzhóuyìshēnliǎngtóu地軸一身兩頭')
○ And also in Tiānwángdìshénzhǒng, the heavenly king riding Ruìniǎo瑞鳥 is drawn on the left of the bottom screen and Earth God with the snake body and four legs on the right. The inscription of 'Tiānwáng天王' 'Dìshén地神' is written in the above each shape.

❈ Réntóushòu人頭獸: Xīngxing猩猩: Ānyuè安岳 Tomb No.1

○ Gāojùlì(Goguryeo) Déxīnglǐ tomb murals, 'Xīngxing' with human head and animal body.
○ Gāojùlì(Goguryeo) Ānyuè Tomb No.1(End of 4th century-Early 5th century, Ānyuèjùn安岳郡 Huánghǎinándào黃海南道)
○ A beast with human head drawn on the mùshì墓室 dōngbì東壁 ceiling dǐngzhù. Gesture rushing with the top of the head forward.

❀ Niǎotóurénshēn鳥頭人身: Hawk (Horus; Egyptian Sun god).

○ Ramesses II (BC 1279-1213). Horus Egyptian Sun god. Hawk head.

[4] Bear totem: Xióngshǒurénshēn熊首人身

A record related to bear totem is as follows:

«Shānhǎijīng» Zhōngshānjīng中山經 ; 熊山.有穴焉,熊之穴,恒出神人.夏啟而冬閉;是穴也,冬啟乃必有兵.

Xióngshān. There is a cave of bears here and Shénrén comes in and out of it all the time. It opens in summer and closes in winter and if this cave opens in winter, a war breaks out without exception.

(1) Bear molding bear foot, teeth:

Cháoyángshì朝陽市 Niúhéliáng牛河梁 16th point No. 4 tomb.

Professor Liúguóxiáng劉國祥: Three kinds of jadeware (5000 years ago). Appeared as kingship王者. Tomb owner status Wūshī巫師, sānzhǒngyùqì三種玉器 three kinds of jadeware = Yùrén玉人 + Gūxíngqì箍形器 + Yùfèng玉鳳

○ Bear Tooth

(2) Yùxiónglóng玉熊龍:

Wéiyùwèizàng唯玉爲葬 (holding a funeral only with jade). Niúhéliáng 2nd point No. 1 tombs No. 4 grave(5500-7500 years ago) Stone Mound Tomb.

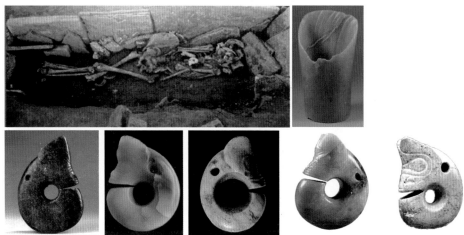

○ Excavated from Bālínyòuqí Nàsītái那斯台.
○ Excavated from Bālínzuǒqí jiānshānzǐ尖山子. Owned by Bālínzuǒqí Museum.

❀ Yùxiónglóng玉熊龍 : Shòushǒusānkǒngyùqì獸首三孔玉器

Excavated from Chìfēngshì Bālínyòuqí Nàsītái.

○ Shòushǒusānkǒngyùqì: Three-holes Jade ware with beast-heads, Shuāngxióngshǒusānkǒngyùqì 雙熊首三孔玉器, Partially enlarged

○ Owned by Bālínyòuqí Museum

☸ **Woo, Sil-ha:** <Symbolic meaning of Hóngshān Culture Yùzhūlóng玉猪龍, Shuāngshǒuhuángxíngqì双首璜形器 (Animal shape jadeware with double beast-heads), Shuāngxióngshǒusānkǒngyùqì雙熊首三孔玉器 and 'Huànrì幻日 (Sundog)' Phenomenon> «East Asian Archaeological Studies» Vol.24,2011,4. East Asian Archaeological Studies. Korea.

☸ **Yùxiónglóng** : Dual carving(Combined with cicadas, animals, Yùcóng etc.)

○ Legged dragons and cicadas. Bird and pig dragon «Hēipíyù黑皮玉» p.101 Yùzhūlóng to-paz. 16.5cm.

■ Shāngxiāngtāo商湘濤 «Zhōngguógǔyùjiàncáng中國古玉鑒藏» p.20,Shanghai Culture Publisher,2006,8.

(3) Bear crown Yùdiāoshénxiàng 熊冠 玉彫神像:
British Cambridge University Fitzwilliam Museum.

☸ **Xúlín**徐琳: <SānzūnHóngshānYùrénxiàngjiěxī三尊"红山玉人"像解析> Niúhéliáng 16th point Yùrén. Beijing Palace Museum, Yùzuòrénxiàng玉坐人像.

Owned by Cambridge University Museum, yùdiāoshénxiàng, yùdiāoshénxiàng Parietal part.

■ «shōucángjiā收藏家» 4th Period in 2010 (Original: «Zhōngguókēxuébào中国社会科學報»)

A bear occupies a very important position in the Hóngshān Society and the lower jawbone has been excavated before in No. 2 and No. 4 Stone Mound Tombs of Hóngshān Culture, explaining that the origin of the convention of worshipping a bear has been long. Bear worship is also the convention unique to several ethnic groups in Northeast. Hóngshān Culture regarded a bear as a main worship object and goes very well with the distinct features of regions where jadeware was excavated. But I understand that the thing set on the head of Yùzuòrén owned by Cambridge University Museum is not just Xióngguàn 熊冠 but bear leather with a bear head is put around. The bear head was created into the shape of an official hat and the boundary line between the human face and bear hat can be seen clearly in the front face area of the jade person. Seeing from the back, the bear head and the skirt of the body are connected but the whole bear leather is put around the body. Therefore, the subject of this jade-ware is still a human being and it can be said to be a person with one bearskin around his body. The figure body is still a naked jade person like that excavated from Niúhéliáng and an Gùgōng (Beijing Palace Museum) collection. One detail to note here is that Yùzuòrén of Cambridge University is bare foot and steps on one round object and it cannot be found what this round object is but given that it appeared here, it was never made carelessly and there must be a particular meaning.

✿ Black Skin Jade Culture Xióngshǒurénshēn熊首人身

○ Xióngshǒurénshēn (Height 58cm).

○ Bànrénbànshòu半人半獸: Xióngshǒurénshēn熊首人身, Hǔshǒurénshēn虎首人身 the Later Hàn後漢 WǔshìCítáng武氏祠堂: 2100 years ago 147, zhuānzhù塼築 Shrine. Shāndōngshěng Jiāxiángxiàn嘉祥縣 Zǐyunshān紫雲山.

○ A bear-shaped figure holds ancient weapons in the head, hands and feet and takes powerful and dynamic appearance and a tiger-shaped figure shows the appearance of pulling out a child with his mouth.

✿ Chányú單于 of the Xiōngnú匈奴 was born from sexual intercourse with a bear:

«Hòuhànshū後漢書» Xiōngnúzhuàn匈奴傳, Chányú單于 of the Xiōngnú was born from sexual intercourse with a bear. As shown above, numerous historical figures in prehistoric times are all the result of sexual intercourse between humans and animals.

(4) Appearance of tribal chief:

Yùxiónglóng + Shénrén神人. Sun god. Pig god

☙ **Chinese professor Guōdàshùn郭大順**: Yùxiónglóng, The most representative jadeware of Hóngshān Culture. Hóngshān people, Worship of bear animal god Great Spirit.

"An animal god worshipped by Hóngshān people must be Zhǔshén主神 (Great Spirit) among several gods and Hóngshān people were the clan who worshipped bears." "It can be directly called as "Xiónglóng熊龍" because it does not resemble a pig and resembles a bear. Yùxiónglóng is the most representative jadeware among Hóngshān Culture jadeware and in addition, the technique used in the making has the highest degree of difficulty, explaining Hóngshān Culture people are also the clan worshipping bears."

Zhōnghuárénmíngònghéguó中華人民共和國

■ GuówùyuànQiáowùbàngōngshìzhǔbàn國務院僑務辦公室主辦 www.gqb.gov.cn

❧ **Chinese professor Zhūnǎichéng朱乃誠: First symbolic bear**

<HóngshānwénhuàShòumiànxíngjuéxíngYùshìyánjiū獸面玦形紅山文化獸面形玦形玉飾研究>

3360 B.C.-2267 B.C. As "C"-shaped dragons, only Sānxīngtālā三星他拉 Yùlóng of Liáohé District and Huánggǔtún黃谷屯 Yùlóng are seen at present. Hóngshān Culture ShòumiànxíngjuéxíngYùshì is a kind of special malformation produced in the process where jade habits are gradually thriving in the late Hóngshān Culture and their period is between 3360 B.C and 2267 B.C and the first symbol is a bear.

■ «Kǎogǔxuébào考古學報» 1st period in 2008.

❧ **Professor Lee, Hyeong-gu: Crucial clue of Hóngshān people bear worship fact**

"Xiónglóng carved with jade like this is the most among Hóngshān Culture jadeware and was reported to be about 20 cases. Xiónglóng is considered to be one of 4 types of Hóngshān culture jadeware with Horseshoe-shaped pillow, Cloud-shaped Yùpèi玉佩, square-shape Yùbì玉璧 etc." "This fact shows that Hóngshān people held a memorial service for bears as well as goddess. This is a crucial clue showing the fact that Hóngshān people worshiped a bear." Human bones enshrined in this grave are estimated to be the priest exchanging with heaven because the legs are crossed. Jade placed on the chest embodied a bear. Xiónglóng the most commonly found among jadeware of Hóngshān Culture, what is the relationship between the country founded by Hóngshān people who worshipped bears in their grounds and Gojoseon古朝鮮 (Gǔcháoxiǎn).

[5] Pig and other totem

(1) Pig totem:

Zhūshǒurénshēn猪首人身 (Shǐwéishì豕韦氏, Fēngxīshì封豨氏).
«Shānhǎijīng» Zhōngshānjīng中山經 ; Zhōngcìqījīng中次七經
"皆豕身而人面."
all the remaining gods have the human face in the pig body.

(2) Turtle (Guī龟) totem:

Emperor Xuānyuánshì軒轅氏 related.
«Shānhǎijīng» Hǎinèidōngjīng海內東經
Tàihào太昊 Fúxī-Nǚwā: Léizé雷澤's Great Spirit lightning Léishén雷神.
Guīshēnréntóu龟身人頭 (Turtle body and human head)

⚜ **Professor Léiguǎngzhēn雷廣臻: Tiānyuán天黿 Shénguī神龜 fúhào符號 found, Claiming Huángdì黃帝 culture evidence.**

Niúhéliáng 1st point, 5th point No.1 Tomb already robbed tomb.

Léiguǎnzhēn emphasized that Huángdì Culture fúhào Tiānyuán Shénguī engraved on Hóngshān Culture historical site slate was found and this not only suggests that ancient people already began to show the origin of a tribe by using carved stone shapes or letters 5000 years ago but provides one new evidence to Hóngshān Culture, that is, Emperor culture.

■ «Liáoníngrìbào遼寧日報» 2011,12,28.

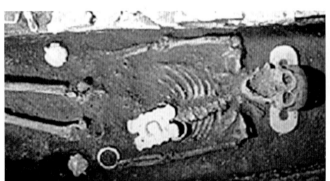 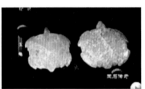 

(3) Sheep totem :

Yángshǒurénshēn羊首人身 (Sheep head and human body). Gǔqiāngzú古羌族.

«山海經» 西次三經 其神狀皆 羊身人面, 東山經 東次三經 其神狀皆人身而羊角.

(4) Deer totem:

Lùshǒurénshēn鹿首人身

■ Chényìmín «Hóngshānyùqìtújiàn紅山玉器圖鑑» p.135,143.上海文化出版社.2006,2.

(5) Fish totem 魚圖騰:

Rénmiànyúshēn人面魚身 (human face, fish body): Dīrénguó氐人国.

○ Rénshǒuyúshēntáoyǒng 人首魚身陶俑 (Táng唐) 48cm, Excavated from Jiāngsū江蘇 Nánjīng南京 in 1950

 Jeong, Jae-seo : Língyúrénmiàn陵魚人面, Dīrén氐人,Rénmiànyúshēn

■ «Shānhǎijīng»

Hǎinèiběijīng海內北經: 陵魚人面, 手足, 魚身, 在海中.

"Língyú has the human face, arms and legs and the body is fish and lives in the sea."

Dàhuāngxījīng大荒西經: Rénmiànyúshēn人面魚身

"There is Rénmiànyúshēn in Hùrénzhīguó互人之國. Among Yándì's grand-sons, there is Língjiá靈恝 and Língjiá gave birth to Hùrén互人 and could go up and down to heaven."

■ «Angtti-Oedipus's Mythology» p.124. Changbi. 2011. Korea.

(6) Dog totem:

Dog head goddess statue wearing a scepter on the head.

Tiger? dog?

«Shānhǎijīng» Běishānjīng北山經 ; 獄法之山---有獸焉,其狀如犬而人面.

"Yùfǎshān---A beast looks like a dog and has the human face."

(7) Horse totem:

Mǎshēnrénmiàn馬身人面 (Horse body and human head)

«Shānhǎijīng» Xīshānjīng西山經 Xīcìèrjīng西次二經;

其十神者, 皆人面而馬身.

"The 10 gods have all human face and horse body."

○ Mǎtóu馬頭 (horse head)
Statue with sun god.

■ <Hànjiāzhìzūn漢家至尊-HànhuàtàpiànzhōngdeXīwángmǔyuDōngwánggōng漢畫拓片中的西王母與東王公> «CCTV-4» 2005,3,1.

(8) Frog totem:

Nǚwāshì女娲氏 with a frog on the head

○ The goddess statue with a frog on the head is Hóngshān Culture sex worship and idol of reproduction worship. The head part of this carving is very big and one frog is put on the head and the statue body stands bent and has protruding breasts and this kind of carving with unusually large female genitals has a very clear and sincere purpose, substantially reflecting sex and reproduction worship of primitive village people and the frog right on the head is the best explanation of the reproduction worship. Particularly vigorous reproductive performance of a green frog already received the attention of prehistoric men.

■ Chényìmín «Hóngshānyùqìtújiàn紅山玉器圖鑑» p.129,130.上海文化出版社.2006,2.

(9) Réntóushòu人頭獸 Xīngxing猩猩:

Rénmiànshòushēn人面獸身

Gāojùlì (Goguryeo) Déxīnglǐ tomb murals, 'Xīngxing' with human head and animal body.

«Shānhǎijīng»

Dōngshānjīng東山經 Dōngcìsānjīng東次三經; 其神狀皆獸身人面.

All the shapes of the god are the body of the beast and human face.

Zhōngshānjīng中山經 Zhōngcìsìjīng中次四經; 其神狀皆人面獸身.

All the shapes of the god are the body of the beast and human face.

○ 'Xīngxing' with the human face and beast body.
○ Gāojùlì (Goguryeo) Ānyuè Tomb No.1 (End of 4th century-Early 5th century, Ānyuèjùn安岳郡 Huánghǎinándào黃海南道)
○ A beast with human head drawn on the mùshì墓室 dōngbì東壁 ceiling dǐngzhù. Gesture rushing with the top of the head forward.

(10) Elephant totem 象圖騰:

Xiàngshǒurénshēn象首人身 (Elephant head and human body)

- Black skin jade Xiàngshǒurénshēn 5.2cm
- Wèijìn魏晋 "象首人身" 画像石
- ShāndōngfāxiànZhōngguóGuónèihǎnjiànde"Xiàngshǒurénshēn"huàxiàngshí

■ <山东发现中国国内罕见的"象首人身"画像石> «Wéifāngwǎnbào潍坊晚报» 2008,12,25.

(11) Shímǎo石峁 Yùrén玉人:

Shǎnxīshěng陝西省 Shénmùxiàn神木縣 Shímǎo石峁
Historic Site (Late Neolithic Age)

■ <Shímǎo石峁 Historic Site, YīmùguóYùrénzhimí一目国玉人之谜> 国宝档案 «CCTV-4» 2014,10,30.

Dàiyīngxīn戴應新 (Shǎnxīshěng kǎogǔ考古researcher)
«Shānhǎijīng» Claiming Yīmùguó一目國 possibility in 三十六國.

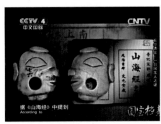

- As described above, the mythical topics of Bànrénbànshòu statue such as Rénmiànniǎo人面鳥, Shénnóng神農 Yándì炎帝 of Niúshǒurénshēn牛首人身 appearing in Gāojùlì (Goguryeo) tomb murals were available in «Shānhǎijīng» and in the case of ShímǎoYùrén石峁玉人 excavated from Shímǎo Historic Site of China Shǎnxīshěng, Late Neolithic Age, the literature basis can be also found in Dàhuāngběijīng大荒北经, Hǎinèiběijīng海内北经 and Yīmùguó appearing in «Shānhǎijīng» Hǎiwàiběijīng海外北經.

3 YÙSHÉNRÉN玉神人

[1] Yùshénrén (Jade god man): Figure statue

(Life-size comparison 10 :1, Unit cm)

Hēipíyù	Hóng shān	Língjiā tān	Liáng zhǔ	Shíjiāhé	Táosì	Qíjiā	Gǔshǔ
70	18.5	10以下	10以下	10以下		10以下	14.5

❀ Hēipíyù(黑皮玉)wénhuà tribal society

(1) Molded goddess statue

○ Hóngshān Culture Figure Statue Distribution Chart.

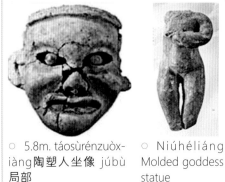

○ 5.8m. táosùrénzuòxiàng陶塑人坐像 júbù局部

○ Niúhéliáng Molded goddess statue

○ Figure sculpture. Cháoyángshì Kāzuǒ喀左 Dōngshānzuǐ东山嘴. 1982. 7.8m.

○ Chìfēng Xīshuǐquán西水泉 Hóngshān Culture táosù陶塑 female bust; Tiánguǎng lín田廣林, a professor at Liáoníng College of Education

○ Figure statue excavated from the west of Niúhéliáng Goddess grave first point main chamber 22.5x23.5cm. nísùrénshǒucánkuài泥塑人手殘块

■ <GuānyúÁohànxīnchūtǔzuòzīrénxíngtáoxiàngdexìngzhì關于敖漢新出土坐姿人形陶像的性質> Above black-and-white image.

❀ **Hóngshān Culture. Liáohé遼河 Civilization:** Who is the force leading a bear totem tribe.

Around 4000 years ago, Hóngshān Culture is followed by Xiàjiādiàn夏家店 Lower Culture. In Xiàjiādiàn Lower Culture, stone fortress with protrusions, mandolin-shaped bronze dagger etc. are found and these are clearly distinguished from those of Zhōngyuán中原. This means that the leading force of Liáohé Civilization is a different group from Zhōnghuá Mínzú. stone fortress with protrusions shows the characteristics of Gāojùlì (Goguryeo) fortresses and mandolin-shaped bronze daggers are not found in Zhōngyuán but in Liáohé Basin and the Korean Peninsula. Xiàjiādiàn Lower Culture is evaluated to be a complete national stage and what is the country that may have been in the Liáohé Basin around 2000 years B.C. When searching all historic books, there is no country other than Gǔcháoxiǎn古朝鮮 (Gojoseon). The interesting thing is that the jawbone of a bear and feet of a bear made of mud were also excavated together from the Goddess grave of Hóngshān Culture Niúhéliáng. In addition, human bones seen as the chief priest had Yùlóng玉龍 symbolizing the face of a bear in the chest. This is the evidence that Hóngshān People were the bear totem tribe worshiping a bear with goddess.

⚙ Féizhēnyǒng裵眞永 <The form of political organization of Shāngdài商代 in Beijing Region viewed through Jiǎgǔ甲骨-Jīnwén金文>

■ «Chinese History Study» Vol. 47 2007,4. Korea.

The representative culture of Yànshān燕山 Northern and Southern regions was Xiàjiādiàn Lower Culture. In Late Shāng商 to Liáoxī District of Northern Yànshān, Wèiyíngzǐwénhuà魏營子文化 occurred after Yàoyùmiào苭玉廟 type of Xiàjiādiàn Lower Culture around Dàlínghé大凌河 and Xiǎolínghé小凌河 basin. Wèiyíngzǐwénhuà and Zhāngjiāyuánshàngcéngwénhuà張家園上層文化 are the original types of culture that newly emerged within the Xiàjiādiàn Lower Culture distribution range and estimated to be closely related given that the age is the same and the regions are nearby. The cultural influence of Shāng商 can be seen not to have reached this region in that the culture of Xiàjiādiàn Lower Culture genealogy has formed in Liáoxī Region during the Shāng-Zhōu Period. In this sense, even if the presence of a power group is confirmed in this region during the Shāng-Zhōu, it is thought that this force may have not existed as a state or country with Shāngwénhuà商文化 in the Shāng Dynasty.

☸ **Appearance of jade, dragon shape (8000 years ago).**: Civilization early stage

Focus on Hóngshān Culture ancestral rites (Entering a civilized society: 5000 years ago) :

Gǔguó古國-Fāngguó方國(Xiàjiādiàn Lower Culture)-Dìguó帝國(QínHàn 秦漢)

<Liáohé Basin: One place of Chinese civilization birthplaces>

According to A person in charge of State Cultural Relics Bureau, only the emergence of the shape of dragon and jadeware as early as 8000 years ago from now can be said to have already entered the beginning stage of civilization at that time and Niúhéliáng Hóngshān Culture memorial service center located in a Liáoxī mountainous district symbolizes Gǔguó (Old country) of 5,000 years ago and then, went through Fāngguó Era represented by Xiàjiādiàn Lower Culture and was finally unified into one, multi-ethnic QínHàn Empire. "As the origin and development process of civilization from old country-country-state, Liáohé River Basin is the vivid embodiment of pluralistic Chinese civilization".

■ 《Rénmínrìbào人民日報》 2009,8,7.

(2) Táorén陶人: Ancestor worship, ancestral god

■ 《tànsuǒfāxiàn探索發現》 Áohàn敖漢-hànzuònóngyètànyuán旱作農業探源旱作農業探源(下) 《CCTV-10》 2014,06,09.

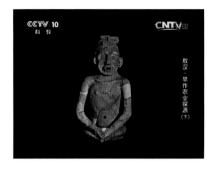 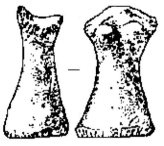

☸ **Director of Wángwēi王巍 Chinese Academy of Social Sciences Archeological Institute**: Governing style of Hóngshān Culture Period.

Artificial cultivation, seeds sowing, increased harvest, feeding and breeding livestock (pigs)

Population growth: Ruler sacralization, combination of kingship and divine right.

❀ Áohànqí: Hánguó韓國 Zhōngqīngběidào忠淸北道 size. Region with more relics, ruins than those in the whole Korean Peninsula. The area of Áohànqí is 8300km² and ruins excavated from this Áohànqí are much more than those excavated or found in the whole Korean Peninsula. Neolithic ruins found throughout North and South Korea are about 300 places and relics were excavated in about 60 places. Bronze historic sites are about 600 places and findspots are less than about 200 places. But Neolithic historic sites investigated in Áohànqí are more than 1000 places and Bronze Age historic sites are more than about 2000 places. The population of Áohànqí is only 600,000 so 'there is still much land unearthed yet.' Most regions are the farmland or grassland and hence, if digging for development, chances are high that more relics will come out.

There is 'Xītái西臺 Historic Site' in a place approximately 1km away to the northwest from Xītái西臺 Village of ChìfēngShì Áohànqí Wángjiāyíngzǐxiāng王家營子鄉. In the Xītái Historic Site, relics of Xīnglóngwā Culture and Hóngshān Culture, Xiǎohéyán Culture, Xiàjiādiàn Lower Culture, Xiàjiādiàn Upper Culture and China's Warring States Period are said to have been excavated in large quantities. Except for Zhàobǎogōu Culture, all cultural relics that rose from Chìfēng Region were discovered.

This fact means that people have lived here for a long time. But with the end of relics of the age of civil wars, the 5th century~3rd century B.C., relics after that have not been discovered and this means that people who lived here left. People may have left a base where they have lived for a long time because of war or natural disasters, diseases or due to climate change.

(3) Shírén石人 : Tiánguǎnglín (Liáoníng College of Education)
<GuānyúÁohàn xīnchūtǔzuòzīrénxíngtáoxiàngdexìngzhì關于敖漢新出土坐姿人形陶像的性質>

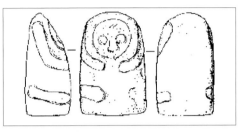  

○ Xīnglóngwā Culture zuòzī坐姿 Stone Statue. Xīnglóngwā second point táosùjījùnǔrénxiàng 陶塑箕踞女人像 5.2cm.

○ Hóngshān Culture zuòzī坐姿 Stone Statue Owned by Chìfēng Museum

🐚 **Shírén石人**: Ancestor pagod worshiped during Hóngshān Culture ancestral rites.

○ Excavated in Aohànqí Sìjiāzǐzhèn四家子鎮 Cǎomàoshān草帽山. Area near the altar was buried.

🐚 **Shídiāonǔrénxiàng石彫女人像 (Stone goddess statue)**: Zhàobǎogōu Culture (6000-6500 years ago).

Aohànqí Hòutāizǐ后台子 historic site (Héběishěng Luánpíngxiàn灤平縣 from Beijing170km)<Shídiāonǔrénxiàng石彫女人像> 國寶檔案

■ 《CCTV-4》 2011,3,1.

✹ Stone figure (shíréndiāoxiàng)

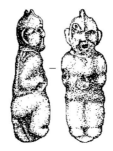

○ 19.4cm. Collected in 1980. Excavated in Bālínyòuqí巴林右旗 Nàsītái那斯台
○ Báiyīnchánghàn白音長汗AF19 Nàsītái Gāozuòshírénxiàng高坐石人像.

✹ Aohànqí: Aohàn means "Lǎodà老大 (elder)" in Mongolian.

■ «tànsuǒfāxiàn探索發現» Aohàn敖漢-hànzuònóngyètànyuán旱作農業探源(上) «CCTV-10» 2014,06,07.

Liúguóxiáng Chinese Academy of Social Sciences Archeological Institute: 8500 years ago-4000 years ago

○ "Five suns" in the sky is a phenomenon commonly seen in Aohànqí and there was also a strange phenomenon of being bright for eight days in Aohànqí.

✹ Tiányànguó田彦國 (敖漢史前文化博物館): The historic site of Chéngzǐshān 城子山 Mountain Fortress, the central area of Xiàjiādiàn Lower Culture.

○ The largest ritual mountain fortress of 4000 years ago

(4) Petroglyphs portrait(human face).

Chìfēngshì human face petroglyphs - Tumen River bone figure statue - Yùshān蔚山 Petroglyphs - Black Skin Jade Culture Figure Statue

❀ Inner Mongolia Chìfēngshì Wēngniútèqí human face petroglyphs

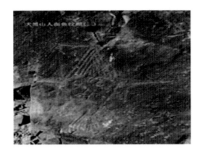

○ Wújiǎcái吴甲才 (Finder Inner Mongolia Petroglyphs Protection Research Society):
○ Petroglyphs characters are certainly a kind of unforeseen event or related to a certain intention expected by Wūshī巫師.

(5) Yùshénrén玉神人 (Jade god man):

Wūrén巫人(shaman) ancestor. Great shaman. Shénwū神巫.

Appeared in the late Neolithic Age Animal gods: Sacralization of animal totem targets of dragon, phoenix etc. (including single, composite god animals, native totem gods)

Bànrénbànshòu God: God of Rénshén人神 (man god) same shape.

Hegel: A human head symbolizes the spirit and beast body symbolizes a material. Identified the meaning of Bànrénbànshòu (half man and half beast) is that the spirit breaks a material. A portion of the human body could be raised to the divine status.

«Shānhǎijīng» Records of 86 Bànrénbànshòu Gods.

❀ Xúlín <SānzūnHóngshānYùrénxiàngjiěxī三尊"红山玉人"像解析>: These three points of Yùrén expressed a group of people, that is, the shape of the shaman during the Hóngshān period and expressed under different conditions when a shaman performs shénshì神事.

⚛ Zhōuxiǎojīng周曉晶 <Hóngshānwénhuàdòngwùxínghérénxíngyùqìyánjiū 紅山文化動物形和人形玉器研究>

"Yùrén is to carve a Wūrén statue. The tomb owner is to lead live shamans, wear jade carvings of the shamans of dead ancestors and wish the protection and cooperation to the soul of the shamans to perform Shénshì神事."

⚛ Yángbǎidá楊伯達 <wū.yù.shénjiǎnlùn 巫·玉·神简论> 2006,11,8.

Jade god man: Secured the right to ancestral rites, started priesthood ruling. Zhuānxū顓頊 "Juédìtōngtiān绝地通天". Great shaman burial tombs among Hóngshān Culture, Liángzhǔ Culture tombs are never those of Wūxí巫覡 (shaman) of general Shénshì and resembled the "Juédìtōngtiān绝地通天" of Dì帝 Zhuānxū顓頊 written in the literature as Shénwū or great shaman who dominated a federation of villages or seized 5 power at once such as politics, economy, tribe, military and Shénshì of the chief organization or prime period of Wūxí power after that.

"Juédìtōngtiān" of Zhuānxū: Appearance of chief priest. According to «Shǐjì 史記» Wǔdìběnjì五帝本紀, as a grandchild of the Ancient Chinese emperor, Zhuānxū hated that civilians are related to God so he ordered great-grandchildren Zhòng重, Lí黎, to block the way leading to heaven and made a difference between God and human beings. This means that only the limited class seized the right to ancestral rites and Zhuānxū is the leader of the priesthood ruling in that sense.

Mutual integrated action of Wū, Yù, Shén

Through the individual analysis of Wū, Yù, Shén, the vertical mutual relation of three parties as one (WūYùShén mutual relevance) could be found without difficulty. Wūxí (shaman) controlled the relationship of the three parties essentially. According to the process changing from the late prehistoric matriarchal clan community to the patriarchal society, Wūxí exploited the prerogatives such as religion, politics, military etc. and achieved one essence of key governance and social monumental image.

Chinese Cultural Relics Society Jadeware Research Committee
中國文物學會 玉器研究委員會 http://www.chinajades.cc/

🐚 Yùshénrén玉神人(Jade god man): Stick type. praying.

🐚 Xióngguān熊冠 Yùshénrén玉神人: Yùdiāoshénxiàng玉彫神像

○ Jade persons excavated from Niúhéliáng 16 points.
○ Beijing Palace Museum Yùzuòrénxiàng玉坐人像.
○ Owned by Cambridge University Fitzwilliam Museum. Appearance from behind yùdiāoshénxiàng. Crown of the head.
■ Xúlín徐琳 <SānzūnHóngshānYùrénxiàngjiěxī三尊"红山玉人"像解析> 010,2,16.
■ «shōucángjiā收藏家» 4th Period in 2010(Original: «Zhōngguókēxuébào中国社会科学报»)

A bear occupies a very important position in the Hóngshān Society and the lower jawbone has been excavated before in No. 2 and No. 4 Stone Mound Tombs of Hóngshān Culture, explaining that the origin of the convention of worshipping a bear has been long. Bear worship is also the convention unique to several ethnic groups in Northeast. Hóngshān Culture regarded a bear as a main worship object and goes very well with the distinct features of regions where jadeware was excavated. But I understand that the thing set on the head of Yùzuòrén玉坐人 owned by Cambridge University Museum is not just Xióngguàn but bear leather with a bear head is put around. The bear head was created into the shape of an official hat and the boundary line between the human face and bear hat can be seen clearly in the front face area of the jade person. Seeing from the back, the bear head and the skirt of the body are connected but the whole bear leather is put around the body. Therefore, the subject of this jadeware is still a human being and it can be said to be a person with one bearskin around his body. The figure body is still a naked jade person like that excavated from Niúhéliáng and an old palace collection.

🦋 **Yùshénrén**: Official report of Black Skin Jade Culture.

▪ <Shìbókànguóbǎo世博看国宝-HóngshānGǔyù红山古玉> «CCTV-4» 2010.8.17. Léicóngyún雷從云, Researcher of National Museum of China.

 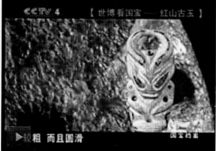

🦋 **Migration Period**: Hóngshān Culture Chìfēngshì Petroglyphs-Korean type Petroglyphs–American, Mexican Region.

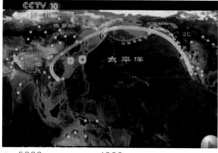 

- ○ 5000 years ago-4000 years ago
- ○ 3000 years ago-1000 years ago: En-masse migration of the Korean people
- ○ A Chinese professor Sòngyàoliáng宋耀良 (Harvard University)
- ○ A Korean professor Son, Seong-tae (Pai Chai University, Korea)
- ▪ <Riddle of Human Face Petroglyphs> «CCTV-10» 2011,5,5.

❀ **Human Face Petroglyphs:** Hóngshān Culture Chìfēngshì Petroglyphs - Korean type Petroglyphs – American, Mexican Region.

○ Korean type Petroglyphs ruins distribution map Korean Studies Promotion Service 2008,9.

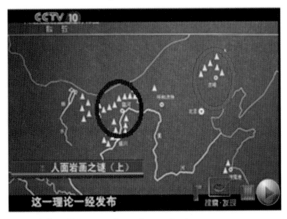

○ <Riddle of Human Face Petroglyphs>
■ «CCTV-10» 2011,5,5.

❀ **Yùshénrén:** Hóngshān Culture Chìfēngshì Petroglyphs - Korean type Petroglyphs Figure Shape.

Tumen River bone Figure Statue - Niúhéliáng goddess statue - Yùshān蔚山 Petroglyphs human face statue

Bone Figure Statue excavated from Tumen River Basin Stone Cist. Owned by Seoul National University Museum, Korea.

Yùshān蔚山 Petroglyphs Rénmiànxiàng人面像 and replica face size.14.5cm

■ Lee, Hyeong-gu «The Secrets of Korean Ancient History» pp.128-129

🌀 **Yùshénrén:**

🌀 **Yùguān**玉冠 (jade crown) **Nǔshénrén**女神人(female god man): Tribal chief.

🌀 **Yùniǎo**玉鳥 (jade bird) **Nǔshénrén:** New totem tribe, Main characters of myths and legends. This goddess statue with a bird on the head reminds us of this mythical legend and there is an old story among old documents 《Shíyíjì拾遺記》:

Shǎohào is King Jīndé金德 and his mother is Huángé皇娥 and wove hemp cloth after hanging outside the palace or went around during the day on a raft,--there was a child prodigy when passing Sāngcāngmáng桑蒼茫 Port and he was good-looking and the son of Báidì白帝, that is, the essence of Tàibái太白 and enjoyed the feast with Huángé down on the waterfront--The disciple and Huángé were floating on the sea with a cassia bark tree branch as a sign and formed fragrant grass as a flag and made a pigeon with jade玉鳩 and put it to support the sign. The pigeon said it knew time--and Huángé gave birth to Soho and named him as Qióngsāngshì窮桑氏 or Sāngqiūshì桑丘氏--There is WǔFèng五鳳 in times so they gathered in Dìtíng帝庭 according to the color of the province and that is why it is called Fèngniǎoshì鳳鳥氏.

■ 《Cháoxiǎnrìbào朝鮮日報》 2009.1.31.Korea.

❀ Pregnant women

❀ **Yùguān**玉冠 **Nánshénrén**男神人**(Male god man):** Male Yùshénrén with the crown on the head.

Jade bird crown god man: Chief of bird totem tribe.

○ «Hēipíyù黑皮玉» H38.8, H30, H19

❀ **Yùzhūguān**玉猪冠 **Nánshénrén:** Chief of pig totem tribe.

○ «Hēipíyù黑皮玉» A man dreaming of a pig/H 24 p.39

❀ **Niúshǒurénshēn牛首人身 and Yùshénrén:** Chief of cattle totem tribe.

○ Cattle and Yùshénrén/H24.5   ○ Niúshǒurénshēn and baby cow with human face/H26

❀ **Yùshénrén and Yùguī玉龜(Jade Turtle Crown God man):** Chief of turtle totem tribe.

○ Professor Léiguǎnzhēn: <HóngshānwénhuàhéHuángdìwénhuàdeguānxi紅山文化和黃帝文化的關係>
○ Guōmòruò郭末若 said this Xuānyuán轩辕 is Tiānyuán天黿 and both Xuānyuán and Tiānyuán point to a turtle and prescribed it as Shénguī神龟 and intepreted it as the primitive totem of Huángdìshì黄帝氏 Tribe.

■ «Chángyáng朝陽日報» 2010,4,22.

❀ **Yùguān玉冠(Jade Crown) Nánshénrén:** Tribal chief.

○ «Hēipíyù黑皮玉» Senior with big ears with a skullcap/H18.8. p. 71, p.68

❀ «Shānhǎijīng山海經» Yǔrén羽人(Feather man)

○ «Hēipíyù黑皮玉» H25. Cicada God/H24. p.121

❀ Male god wearing a round crown.

❀ Twin-horn crown male god. Big crown male god.

○ «Hēipíyù黑皮玉» Twin-horn crown/H20 p.44

○ «Hēipíyù黑皮玉» A man wearing a big crown/H21.6 p.66

❀ Yùxiónglóngguān玉熊龍冠 male god:

Male god wearing Yùshòuxíngjué玉獸形玦(Side).

❀ Yùnánshénrén 玉男神人

❀ Yùshénrén玉神人: Praying boy and girl.

❀ Yùrénshòushénxiàng玉人獸神像(Jade man beast god statue):

Hóngshān Culture-Black Skin Jade Culture-Liángzhǔ Culture.

BěijīngGùgōngbówùyuàn北京故宫博物院: Hóngshān Culture Yùrén-shòushénxiàng

○ Hóngshān Culture 27.7cm.
○ Black Skin Jade Culture

Liángzhǔ Culture Shénrénshòumiànwén神人獸面紋 (God man beast face pattern)

Turquoise jade, a dirt stain is stuck on jadeware. It is the complex of one partially opened man and one beast and consists of a man at the top and beast at the bottom. Shénrén神人 wore a cloud type high crown on the head with cloud ornaments on both sides of the body and ears, eyes, mouth, nose and eyebrows are clear and the triangular nose protrudes and the shoulder part and back of the clothes it is wearing are decorated with the net pattern. Shénrén gathers both hands in front of the chest to hold a stick-shaped object with hands and steps on the arrow-shaped horn shape with bare foot. There is one beast similar to a bear under the horn and the shape is to lie face down for yielding, holding out two front paws. The back of the jade carving is the other side of the front pattern and is decorated with the net pattern and cloud shape pattern of the ditch form.

This Yùrénshòushénxiàng was transferred from Tiānjīn天津 to Běijīng北京 in the early 1960s of the 20th century and owned by National Palace Museum in 1963. Recently, it was provided to appraise standard jadeware through a large quantity of Hóngshān Culture jadeware placed in front of people according to the archaeological excavation of Hóngshān Culture in the Northeastern province. More and more evidence shows that this Yùrénshòushénxiàng is Hóngshān Culture jadeware because the characteristics of detailed patterns do not deviate from the scope of Hóngshān Culture and it is owned by a museum relatively quickly. But, the complexity of the jade statue composition has never been seen and it was jadeware of the highest grade among the existing Hóngshān Culture statues.

(4) Yìtóuduōmiàn一頭多面 (one head and many faces):

Black Skin Jade Culture- «Shānhǎijīng» - Yīn殷

❀ **Yìtóuliǎngmiàn一頭兩面 Shénrén (God man with one head and both heads):** NánnǚyìtóushuāngmiànYùshénrén男女一頭雙面玉神人 20cm

@ Yìtóusìmiàn一頭四面(One head and four faces)shénrén: Huángdì黃帝 myth related.

○ «Hēipíyù黑皮玉» H20
■ Lǐsuǒqing李鎮濤: Huángdì, Yìtóusìmiàn «Zhōngguólìshǐwèijiězhīmí中國◻史未解之謎» p.12.

Huángdì is the god of lightning among mythical legends and became the emperor of the center later. He is said to be able to see every direction of North, South, East and West at the same time because he has four faces.

@ Yìtóuduōmiàn一頭多面:

«Shānhǎijīng» Hǎiwàinánjīng, Sānshǒuguó三首國
Yīn殷 Male and female one head and both faces (Excavated from Fùhǎomù 妇好墓.1976). 12.5x1cm

○ Yīnyángrén陰陽人(YīnyángyìtóushuāngmiànYùshénrén陰陽一頭双面玉神人)

@ **Hermes with two faces.**

○ Vatican Museum: Myth of Janus with one head and both faces.

○ Cambridge University Fitzwilliam Museum, Cambridge.
http://www-cm.fitzmuseum.cam.ac.uk/

○ Pergamon Museum in Berlin, Germany. Bust of Seneca (Work of 3rd century)«Hankyoreh» 2011,8,20. Korea.

○ 'January' refers to January in English and was originated from Latin Januarius. In Roman mythology, Janus is the god of gates or the god of beginnings and endings and is described as a being with two faces heading the opposite direction.

(5) Comparison of Jade Figure Statues:

Hóngshān Culture, Língjiātān Culture, Liángzhǔ Culture, Shíjiāhé Culture.

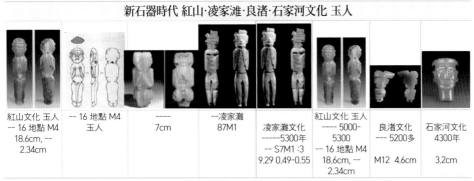

新石器時代 紅山·凌家灘·良渚·石家河文化 玉人

紅山文化 玉人 -- 16 地點 M4 18.6cm, -- 2.34cm	-- 16 地點 M4 玉人	---- 7cm	--凌家灘 87M1	凌家灘文化 -----5300年 -- S7M1 :3 9.29 0.49-0.55	紅山文化 玉人 ---- 5000- 5300 -- 16 地點 M4 18.6cm, -- 2.34cm	良渚文化 -- 5200多 M12 4.6cm	石家河文化 4300年 3.2cm

○ jiāngměiyīng江美英 <ZhōngguóxīnshíqìshídàiYùrénxíngwénchuàngyìshèjì中國新石器時代玉人形紋創意設計-藝術,文化,社會跨域思索>

Hóngshān Culture Yùrén is 18.6cm in height, 2.34cm in thickness and is the biggest and evenly thick when compared to Língjiātān Culture 7.7cm-10cm, Liángzhǔ 5.5cm, Shíjiāhé Yùrénshòu average 2-4cm among currently excavated Neolithic Yùréns. Jade materials are also the most excellent among Yùrén in the Neolithic Age. This is the tomb of the Hóngshān Culture highest position at that time and great Phoenix etc. excavated together are also admirable objects excavated for the first time.

❧ Gǔfāng古方: Jade Figure Statue, only about 10 pieces found.

■ <Yùdiāorénrwù玉雕人物> 2007,7,17.

China sculpture figure statues have a long history and sculpture figure statues have been found among some prehistoric ruins in Yellow River Basin and Yángzǐ River Basin as early as 7000 years ago from now. The materials of prehistoric sculpture figure statues include pottery, bones, stones, jade etc. and for example, the earliest stone figure statue was excavated from the Inner Mongolia Áohànqí Xīnglóngwā historic site 8000 years ago from now. Figure statues made of jade are relatively few and only about 10 pieces have been found so far.

■ «Zhōngguówénwùxuéhuìyùqìyánjiūwěiyuánhuì中國文物學會玉器研究委員會»

❧ Zhānghóngmíng張宏明: Taiwan Bēinán卑南 Culture (4000-2000 years ago)

■ «Zhōngguógǔyùzhípíng中國古玉值評» p.22, YuǎnfāngChūbǎnshè遠方出版社.

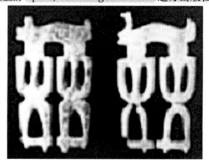

○ 6.6x3.3 6.8x2.8 Taiwan Bǐngdōngqiúlā屏東裘拉 6.5cm

❀ Yīn殷: Jade god man.

❀ Mexico La Venta zhūshāyùrén硃砂玉人(Praying holding a mirror).

○ Excavated from Mexico La Venta, BC900–400.
○ Ax-shaped Yùshénrén with holding two hands in the chest (B.C 300 years ago – A.D.300)

(6) Sex worship: Phallicism -Sexual intercourse worship

1. Sex figure statue:

Human – Animal(人与兽), human-bird(人与鸟), human-insect(人与昆虫),

The Prehistoric mankind had no precise awareness of reproduction and the reproductive capacity of women is gifted and matriarchal society formation was taken for granted in the early days of human society. This is because legends regarding women as ancestors are only shown and those regarding men as ancestors are not shown among humanity ethnic origin legends. Black Skin Jade Culture (Includig Hóngshān Culture) people at that time had infinite reverence for sex, sexual organs, sexual intercourse and those were transformed into active worship while intertwined with each other. Therefore, figure statues among jade carvings in the Black Skin Jade Culture period express the reproductive ability given to humans by God and women's physical beauty. The sexual intercourse of men and women was the extremely important social target. Numerous sculptures in the Neolithic art express the reproductive ability given to humans by God and other divine power. The sexual intercourse of god and man was a relatively important art theme. A female shaman was often a practitioner of these rituals.

■ Manuscript <Neolithic Culture Jadeware and Figure Type Yùrén> «Institute for Traditional Korean Cultural Studies» 2011,11,07.

* They had infinite reverence for sex, sexual organs, sexual intercourse and those were transformed into active worship while intertwined with each other. Sex worship and phallicism, reproduction worship are all connected internally because the result of sexual intercourse is reproduction and includes the pursuit of joy brought by sex in the part of sex worship and on the other hand, the pursuit of reproduction also occurs while relying on sex or reproductive organs. Naturally regardless of reproduction worship, phallicism, all the sex worship is also associated with gods of primitive times. God granted the reproductive ability and reproductive organs granted by God brought the function of reproduction and pleasure.

■ Qiáoqiān «Yìshùyǔshēngmìngjīngshen» p.57.

❀ Reproduction worship Petroglyphs : Hóngshān Culture-Xiǎohéyán Culture.

■ «Zhōngguóxīnwénwǎng中國新聞網» 2013,10,3.

Six types of reproduction worship Petroglyphs were found in Inner Mongolia Chìfēngshì Wēngniútèqí Dàhēishān大黑山. According to the measuring results, they belong to the late Hóngshān Culture to the Xiǎohéyán Culture period.

According to «Hòuhànshū後漢書» Xiōngnúzhuàn匈奴傳, Chányú單于 of the Xiōngnú was born from sexual intercourse with a bear. As shown above, numerous historical figures in prehistoric times are all the result of sexual intercourse between humans and animals. To be a ruler, they always borrowed the power of a dragon to establish their authority and dragons were also worshipped universally because they could get a more illustrious status for this reason and had a huge impact on the ancient politics and culture in the Northeastern society. Animals appearing among Petroglyphs with the theme of sexual intercourse between humans and animals probably express the target of a kind of totem worship. Totem animals in the idea of ancient people were the first ideological beings of the first ancestors.

❀ **Female genital organ worship:**

○ Eagle female genital organ

❀ **Jade disk with a hole in the center:** Female genital organ worship: Chényìmín

■ «Hóngshānyùqì紅山玉器» pp.127-8, Shanghai University Press, 2004,4.

  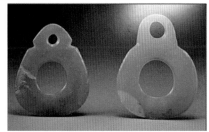

○ Shuāngliánbì双聯璧 excavated from Hēilóngjiāng Yàbùlì亞布力

○ Niúhéliáng eight-shaped jade disk with a hole in the center (Shuāngliánbì)

🌀 Phallicism: Penis

🌀 Bronze Penis Tóngzǔ銅祖:

Excavated from Xīhàn西漢 Jiāngdūwáng江都王 Liúfēi劉非 Men's tomb.

■ «tànsuǒfāxiàn探索發現» 龍塘下的王陵(二) CCTV-10 2015,4,3.

🌀 Professor Chényìmín: Phallicism, Male genital organ(Primitive religion)

■ <Hēipíyùyùqì-Rénlèiyuǎngǔwénmíngdetúténg黑皮玉器-人類遠古文明的圖騰>

The society that created this shape is the nomadic village period and the representation of projected sexual organs among figure statues belonging to the matriarchal society stage is a factual record about the prosperity and magnificent and desperate hope of these villages and black skin jadeware of numerous female shapes also supports this inference.

○ Black Bālínshí巴林石. Height 10cm.
■ «Hēipíyùfēngyúnlù黑皮玉風雲錄» p.70, Shanghai University Press, 2011,5.

❀ Hieroglyphic shell-and-bone character Ssi(shì): Penis worship.

A penis idiograph refers to a man's penis(從人, 爲男根意)

❀ ChineseQiáoqiān: hieroglyphic Jiǎgǔwén甲骨文 祖, 且, 匕.

■ «yìshùshēngmìngyujīngshen藝術生命與精神» p.56

It is cited, "Guōmòruò郭末若 ascertained the relationship between "zǔbǐ" and reproduction worship from a graphonomic perspective in <Shìzǔbǐ釋祖妣> («甲骨文研究» People's Publishing House,1952). According to him, "bǐ妣" originally "bǐ匕"is the hieroglyphic character of a female genital organ and "qiě且", the shape of "zǔ祖" is the hieroglyphic character of penis. He said that bǐzǔ妣祖 worship since ancient times reflected one important historical fact, that is, female genitals and penis worship in Chinese ancient times and it was proved that this was developed from the worship of female and male ancestors."

❀ Sex worship: Myth main characters (Origin of woman + snake tale).

○ 《Hēipíyù黑皮玉》 pp.131-132

○ XìngchóngbàiYùshéntánshù 性崇拜玉神壇樹

4 JADE CULTURAL CHARACTERS

[1] Character: Main jade culture in the Neolithic Age.

Hēipíyù	Hóngshān	Xiǎohéyán	Liángzhǔ	Língjiātān	Táosì

(1) Jade totem:

The role character origin relationship of identification, division, symbol and marking of a group.

Niǎoshòuchóngyú鳥獸蟲魚 → graphic character

→ Zúhuī族徽 (A pattern symbolizing a tribe) (jadeware, bronzeware)

→ Names of Guózú 國族 (Blood relatives of the King)

❀ Guōmòruò <Yīnyímíngzhōngtúxíngwénzì殷彝銘中圖形文字之一解>:
Zúhuī, Future character development relationship.

The names of ancient Guózú of graphic characters are usually so-called descendants of totem or changed. The graphic characters were considered to have the characteristics of the character. Usually, the graphic characters of Niǎoshòuchóngyú are always ancient ethnic totem or the descendant and non-Niǎoshòuchóngyú form was changed from totem and is beyond Zúhuī of the primitive area as almost already fairly advanced culture.

The concept of totem is close to Zúhuī and looking at the actual situation from the inscription use of Zúhuī, it is appropriate to interpret it as totem. However, Guō matched Jiǎgǔwén甲骨文 characters with character shapes and for example, Zúhuīs of jīnwén金文 Tiānyuán天黿, Yàchǒu亞醜, Yàqí亞其 are characters certain as a name telling the belonging of the name. Actually, judging based on current research of Jiǎgǔwén (shell-and-bone characters) Jīnwén from character shapes, the sound and meaning of numerous Zúhuīs are revealed when clearly reading all of them. Of about 200 currently understood Zúhuī, these examples are about 80 and this is impossible if there is no development relationship between the shape of Zúhuī and future generation characters.

⊛ Lǚyīngzhōng呂應鐘 <Bànrénbànshòu>
■ «Táiwānshíbào臺灣时报» 1981, 9,12.

A totem marker or totem writing uses a totem shape as the sign and symbol of a group. It is the sign and symbol of a social organization for the first time in the Chinese history and has the role of identification and division. A totem marker and the origin of Chinese characters are correlated.

⊛ Yángbǎidá <Wū·Yù·Shénjiǎnlùn巫·玉·神简论> 2006,11,8.

Looking at the structure of Jiǎgǔwén Wū巫, a close relationship with jade can be seen. Yīnxū殷墟 Jiǎgǔwén Wū was made in the form of crossing paired jade. Mr. Tánglán唐蘭 revealed Wū based on <Zǔchǔwén诅楚文> and it may be the initial hieroglyphics of Shénshì that Wū used jade.
Chinese Cultural Relics Society Jadeware Research Committee

Zhōngguówénwùxuéhuìyùqìyánjiūwěiyuánhuì中國文物學會玉器研究委員會

- http://www.chinajades.cc/

(2) Shard characters:

1. Yellow River Basin:

Shíjiāhé Culture (Yángzǐ River Basin) Táowén陶文 found.

- <Hànzìtànyuán汉字探源> 国宝档案 《CCTV-4》 2011,10,17.

Dàwènkǒu Culture Táowén (C14 age dating, 6300-4600 years ago).
Character: Dàn 旦

○ Character composed of three parts:
○ Top: Sun, Middle: Cloud, Bottom: Mountain.

☸ Dàwènkǒu Culture=Shíjiāhé Culture=Anhuī Méngchéng蒙城 yùchísì尉遲寺

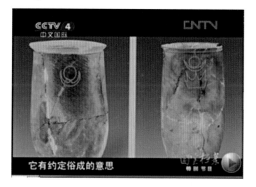

❀ **Lóngshān Culture**: Shāndōng Zōupíng鄒平 Dīnggōng丁公 carved sign shard.

Shāndōng Chānglèxiàn昌樂縣 Gǔkèwén骨刻文 (bone characters): Dōngyí Characters (4500-4000 years ago)

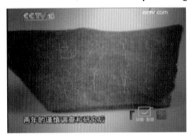 

❀ **Professor Lǐxuéqín李学勤 (QīnghuáDàxué)**: Formal characters.

If looking at the shape of these characters in each area, it can be seen the order is clear because these characters have original order in writing and the right-hander carved them as planned. It cannot be explained in other meanings other than this way.

❀ **Professor Liúfèngjūn刘凤君 (Shāndōng College of Art Archeological Institute)**: Gǔkèwén (Mid and later Shāndōng Lóngshān Culture)

Cattle (shoulder blade, rib), deer bones, elephant bones. About 4000-4500 years ago. Dōngyí Characters (Early Túhuà圖畫 hieroglyph)

❀ **Níngxià寧夏 Hèlánshān賀蘭山**: Character petroglyphs <tànsuǒfāxiàn探索.發現-yuǎngǔdeshēngyīn遠古的聲音>

■ «CCTV-10» 2009,7,3.

 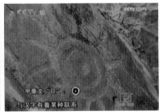 

○ Níngxià Zhōngwèi中衛 Dàmàidì 大麥地

❀ Táosì Culture: Zhūshūpiànhú朱書片壺. Shānxī Province.

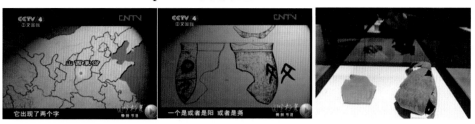

❀ Wángzhènzhōng 王震中 (Chinese Academy of Social Sciences): Characters appeared 5000-4000 years ago. Entered civilized society.

❀ Hénú何駑 Chinese Academy of Social Sciences Shānxī ancient team:

Táosì Culture; Entered civilized society. National Society. Captain Hénú introduced that archaeologically embodying the core sign of civilization formation proves the existence of the state capital. Of course, the capital of a country includes palace section, royal tomb section, castle wall, large ritual construction section, official handicraft production area, normal inhabitant residence area, large warehouse controlled by royal authority etc. and "Shānxī Táosì Historic Site has the above-described functional area elements. Táosì social organization already entered the national stage 4200 years ago." Hénú told reporters that characters, metal matrix and palace are all the spirit of civilization lifestyle and representation of the material aspect and "the component of civilization." He intensively introduced 3 pieces of treasure excavated from Táosì Historic Site. "These three kinds of large evidence have very important significance that proves elevating the Chinese civilization by 500 years".

■ «Shānxīwǎnbào山西晚報» 2010,7,29.

Three kinds of treasures: Cǎihuìlóngpán彩繪龍盤. Hóngtónglíng紅銅鈴 (Bronze technology). Zhūshūpiànhú朱書片壺.

2. Yángzǐ River Basin

🌀 **Liángzhǔ Culture:** Excavated from Wúxiàn吳縣 Chénghú澄湖. Four letters.

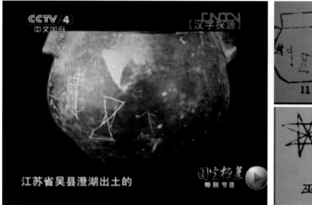
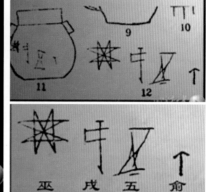

3. Liáohé遼河 Basin

Chìfēngshì Áohànqí Hóngshān Culture: Sìjiāzǐzhèn四家子镇 Cǎomàoshān 草帽山Pyramid. "米"-shaped shard Hóngshān Culture Historic Site 2009,11,1.

■ <Wǔqiānniányǐqiándewénmíng五千年以前的文明> Vol. 5. Rìchūhóngshān日出红山 «CCTV-9» 2011,6,18.

○ Partial residence excavated in 1991, Ash pit.
○ The 2nd point 2001 excavation site, 2nd Tomb.
○ A stone figure statue wearing a crown (Hóngshān Culture). Excavated from Cǎomàoshān. Owned by Áohànqí Museum.

⊛ **Chìfēngshì Áohànqí Hóngshān Culture**: Sìjiāzǐzhèn Pyramid (Stone 30x15m)

▪ <5000-year-old Pyramid Ancient Tomb in Inner Mongolia> «Rénmínrìbào人民日報» 2001,7,9.

According to Guōdàshùn, a famous Chinese archaeologist of Archeological Research Center of Liáoníngshěng, this pyramid ancient tomb was built in Hóngshān Cultivation times 6000-5000 years ago from now. Seven tombs and the ruins of the altar were found at the top of the pyramid and ceramic pieces with a carved Chinese character 米-shaped picture were found in a place where the alter used to be. Archaeologists said that the 米-shaped picture was used when ancient people learned Tiānwén天文 (astronomy). Archaeologists found a pipe made of bones and stone ring in one ancient tomb and found a stone where Nǚrénxiàng (goddess statue) as big as a person is carved was unearthed in another ancient tomb. Archaeologists were surprised to find a phallus as a similar symbol of Lord Shiva of current Hinduism engraved on the walls of a tomb and found a small stone statue with Nǚshén (goddess)s under the symbol similar to Lord Shiva of current Hinduism engraved on the walls.

⊛ **Professor Lee, Hyeong-gu**: Gǔcháoxiǎn (Gojoseon) character pottery Gāobēi高杯 (cup,glass). Public post name, name (Characters connecting two letters).

○ Gǔcháoxiǎn (Gojoseon) Era character earthenware Gāobēi and characters, character rubbing: Possibility of public post name or name.
○ Earthenware with characters from current Liáoníngshěng Lǚdàshì旅大市 Lǚshùnkǒuqū旅順口區 Yǐnjiācūn尹家村 No.12 tomb. Two letters are carved outside the plate portion of foot-shaped Gāobēi.
○ The period is about 5th-4th century BC. Th height of earthenware 16cm,

▪ «The Secrets of Korea Ancient Culture Found in Bóhǎi Coast» p.134.

(3) Sign characters :

<1> Xiǎohéyán Culture sign character earthenware found (4900 years ago).

❀ **Professor Bok, Gi-dae:** Before and after 24th century BC (Chìfēng Area)
<About Xiǎohéyán小河沿 Culture>

	Chìfēng赤峰 Area	except Chìfēng赤峰 Area
about 24th century BC	Xiàjiādiàn Lower Culture	Xiàjiādiàn Lower Culture
	Xiǎohéyán Culture	
30th century BC	Hóngshān Culture	Hóngshān Culture

Regionally, a case of Hóngshān Culture → Xiǎohéyán Culture → Xiàjiādiàn Lower Culture is a phenomenon that appears a lot around Chìfēng Area and a case leading to Hóngshān Culture Xiàjiādiàn Lower Culture is a phenomenon that appears a lot areas outside aforementioned Chìfēng Area.

Sign: Signs have been found in the bowls of Xiǎohéyán Culture. These are not just individual signs but a shape with a distinctive structure.

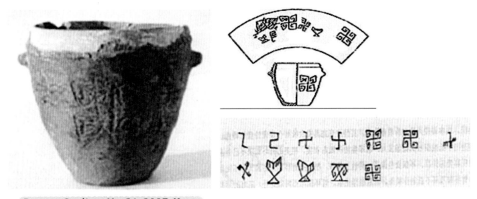

■ «Dangun Studies» No. 21, 2007. Korea.

❀ **Liúbīng (Director of Chìfēngshì Museum):** Early hieroglyphics = Shūhuàtóngyuán書畫同源 (same origin of calligraphy and painting)

It went through Xiàjiādiàn Lower Culture in the first of Shípéngshān石棚山 Primitive túwén圖文 and then, went southward with Shāng ancestors and finally formed Jiǎgǔwén characters and Jīnwén of Shāng Dynasty System after undergoing the evolution of about a thousand years.

Primitive funeral oration Shípéngshān石棚山 30km in the north of Chìfēngshì

"織, 豆, 田; 窯, 窯, 窯, 豆".

🐚 **Chénhuì陳惠**: <Nèiměnggǔwēngniútèshípéngshāntáowénshìshì內蒙古翁牛特石棚山陶文試釋> Inner Mongolia Chìfēngshì Wēngniútèqí Shípéngshān porcelain sign character (Appeared with deer picture) of 4900 years ago
Signs of 7 letters came out only in a piece of earthenware among them and signs include an antiquated style such as 飛, 燕, 己, 乙 etc. in addition to 田, 卍. 卍形 letters:
Báizhái白翟 bùzú部族 zúhuī族徽 Symbol of Báizhái tribe.

■ «Wénwùchūnqiū文物春秋» 1992.

🐚 **Bok, Gi-dae**: Use possibility of primitive characters, character appearance possibility <About Xiǎohéyán小河沿 Culture>

Sign: Their meaning has not been revealed yet. But given that signs of one type appear in different places, it deems to be reasonable to regard them as markers with certain meaning. Among them, the form expressing the mountain and sun can be seen to be similar to that shown in Shāndōngshěng Dàwènkǒu Culture as well as Xiǎohéyán Culture. I think a lot of research is needed in this part in the future. It is the possible appearance of characters that should be studied carefully in this (Xiǎohéyán) Culture. In the above, the author presented several things assumed to be signs. Among these, some things are repeated. And a phenomenon shared with other regions is also shown and this is thought to be a way to communicate in any form. Then, it will be reasonable to assume that primitive characters are highly likely to have started to be used in this culture time. Although research should be continued in the future, if the expression method of a shape appeared in Xiǎohéyán Culture, this will be also a big breakthrough in character research.

■ «Dangun Studies» No. 21, 2007. Korea.

❀ **Japan:** Xiǎohéyán Culture → Xiàjiādiàn Lower Culture, Denial of top bottom duplicate trail discovery.

Jiǎyuánzhēnzhī甲元眞之 Komoto masayuki <Climate Change and Archeology 気候動と考古学>

From Southeastern Inner Mongolia to Western Liáoníngshěng, this period corresponds to the period of changing from Xiǎohéyán Culture to Xiàjiādiàn Lower Culture. However, it is difficult to identify environmental changes from the concrete appearance of the ruins because there are almost no traces that Xiǎohéyán Culture and Xiàjiādiàn Lower Culture are duplicated up and down.

2. Lower Culture: Before and after 24th century B.C. Xiàjiādiàn

Scientific experiment results: Constitutional anthropological analysis. Race classification.

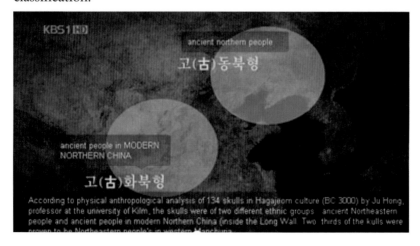

🌀 **Korean Bok, Gi-dae (University of Brain Education Department of Korean Studies):**

More than 60% of ancients in the Liáoxī area are the old Northeast type affinitive with Koreans. "It seems right to think that the ancient culture of the Liáoxī area was established by Korean ancestors and Korean ethic groups."

🌀 **China Jílín University Zhūhóng朱泓:** Xiàjiādiàn Lower Culture remains (134 pieces, 5000 years ago)

We tried the constitutional anthropological analysis of 134 human bones from Xiàjiādiàn Lower Culture. According to the research findings, they were largely divided into two tribes and the old Northeast type around Liáohé civilization was found to account for more than 2/3.

🌀 **Only one Wūrén (shaman) (7500-5500 years ago):** Niúhéliáng牛河梁 first point already robbed tomb

Guōdàshùn:<Hóngshānwénhuàde"wéiyùwéizàng"yuLiáohéwénmíngqǐyuán tèzhēngzàirènshi 紅山文化的"唯玉爲葬"與遼河文明起源特征再認識>

🌀 **Bok, Gi-dae <An Essay on the Relevance between Hóngshān Culture and Xiàjiādiàn Lower Culture>**

Gōuyún-type jade jewelry勾雲形玉佩 (Hóngshān Culture): Originated from Xiàjiādiàn Lower Culture Tāotièwén饕餮紋.

○ Hóngshān Culture and Xiàjiādiàn Lower Culture distribution map

○ Xiàjiādiàn Lower Culture: Hóngshān Culture relevance (Stone Fortress, Yùgū玉箍, Gōuyún-type jade jewelry, Tāotièwén)

○ Hóngshān Culture is the culture with very developed jadeware. Some of this jadeware expressed beasts symbolically. If looking at the form engraved in the center of the object, there is an expression that can be regarded as the face of a beast. These are carved relatively simply. Rather than being solemn, various forms of expressions are shown in the face. If comparing this with the expression shown in colored earthenware of Xiàjiādiàn Lower Culture, it can be seen that the pattern of Xiàjiādiàn Lower Culture has become somewhat solemn. But, the basic framework is very similar in the two cultures. Therefore, given the similarities of two vessels, it can be seen that Tāotièwén of Xiàjiādiàn Lower Culture came from Hóngshān Culture.

⚜ **Xiàjiādiàn Lower Culture:** Sānzuòdiàn三座店 Stone Fortress shard character mature character signs (4000-3400 years ago).

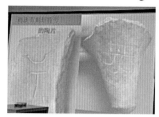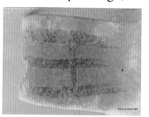

⚜ **Guōzhìzhōng**郭治中 (Inner Mongolia Cultural Relics Archeological Institute) character signs (Hieroglyphic signs)

left image; lower part "丌Gi" Hieroglyphic signs, upper part "柴chái" Hieroglyphic signs. There were mature character signs during the Xiàjiādiàn Lower Culture period.

(4) Yùjiàn玉劍 inscription and character petroglyphs

<1> Character petroglyphs: Made by a tribe chief or great shaman.

* Undoubtedly, petroglyphs character signs were made by the chief of the local tribe or great shaman. An early Wū巫 (shaman) character sign appears repeatedly in many provinces and it was not a kind of simple repetition but a shamanic act coexisting in other regions in the same period. The early Wū character shape is very similar to Yùxuánjī玉璇璣 appearing in Neolithic Hóngshān Culture. It is like providing a window so that later people decrypt the Wū character sign in prehistoric times. Xuánjī璇璣 skeleton is the reproduction of a cross sign and both round head cross and round thing of the head are a kind of lively embodiment.

⚜ **Wújiǎcái**吳甲才 (Inner Mongolia Wēngniútèqí Humanities and History Institute): Xiǎohéyán Culture (5500-4200 years ago)

■ Dàhēishān大黑山 Petroglyphs characters likely to be the China's first characters 2008,9,2.

Wújiǎcái, a researcher of Inner Mongolia Chìfēngshì Wēngniútèqí Humanities and History Institute exhibited Petroglyphs on which primitive character signs found in Wēngniútèqí Dàhēishān are drawn and one of a thousands of petroglyphs in about 40 places from about a hundred mountains after 9 years in the previous meeting. In «Xīnhuáshè新華社», there were about 400 pieces whose top and bottom of were associated with these petroglyphs or primitive character signs are exclusively engraved. Wújiǎcái said that Petroglyphs exhibited this time are the history of 4200 years ago from 5500 years ago from now, leading to Xiǎohéyán Culture period belonging to later Hóngshān Culture.

 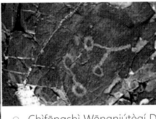 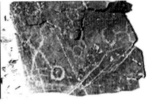

○ Chìfēngshì Wēngniútèqí Dàhēishān Petroglyphs characters

<2> Inscription Yùjiàn (jade dagger): Bird(phoenix) totem. Symbolizing authority.

○ Two letters at both sides of Black skin jade culture Yùjiàn. Lower part "冬＝終" Yīn殷 Jiǎgǔwén甲骨文 "冬 (＝終)"

⊚ Inscription Yùjiàn : Ox handle inscription Yùjiàn (Certain making style).

❀ Phoenix handle inscription Yùjiàn (約20cm X 5cm). Yīn殷 Jiǎgǔwén甲骨文
"dōng冬 (=zhōng終)"

❀ Yángzǐ River Basin Língjiātān Culture. Tremolite jade

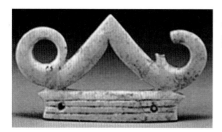

○ Yīn殷 Jiǎgǔwén甲骨文 "冬" - shaped Yùguàn玉冠 (jade crown) decoration

❀ Inscription Yùjiàn: Yīn殷 Jiǎgǔwén = Some characters of Gǔcháoxiǎn古朝鮮
<Tiānfújīng天符經>

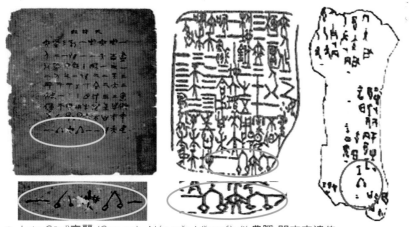

○ Late Gāolì高麗 (Goryeo) «Nóngyǐn Mǐnānfùyíjí 農隱 閔安富遺集»
○ Miàoxiāngshān妙香山 rock inscription rubbing
○ «Joong-Bu Maeil» July 11, 2007, Korea.

✿ Jiānjiǎxíngtóngqì肩甲形銅器 (Rediscovery of Korean Beauty-Prehistoric Relics and Ruins, 2003.6.25, Sol Publisher, Korea)

○ Jiānjiǎxíngtóngqì (Shoulder armor type bronzeware) length 23.8 ㎝, Owned by Tokyo National Museum.

○ Jiānjiǎxíngtóngqì, a relic excavated from Shěnyáng Zhèngjiāwāzǐyíjì 瀋陽 鄭家窪子 遺蹟 No. 6512 Tomb (Partially enlarged)

* This bronzeware was a collection of Xiǎocāngwǔzhīzhù小倉武之助 (Ogura), a Japanese who used to live in Korea before independence but currently, it was donated to and stored in Tokyo National Museum of Japan and designated as a Japanese important art work. The findspot is unsure but is known to be an excavated article of Qìngzhōu慶州 distric. On the back, a total of four ∩-shaped knobs are hung one by one towards the edge. This shape of bronzeware has been excavated as the decoration of a bag containing a small working ax in Shěnyáng, Liáoníngshěng in China, showing a deep relationship with this region.

✿ Professor Liǔdōngqīng柳冬青 (Inner Mongolia Chìfēng University): Possibility of early character appearance in the Hóngshān Culture period.

○ Female Shénshòu神獸 (God beast) Yùgū玉箍
○ Prehistoric Northeastern Hóngshān Culture Gǔyù. Evidence of early characters engraved found.
○ 1. Dàyùlè大玉勒 (add xiàbù下部 土: Collected in Hóngshān Historic Site)
○ Three rows 9 characters: Rì日, Yuè月, Shān山, Yǔ雨, Rén人 etc. 12kg
○ 2. Female Shénshòu Yùgū, Front 4 letters (Picture).
○ 3. Xiǎoyùbì, 3 letters of the same shape.
■ «Hóngshānwénhuà紅山文化» p.172, Inner Mongolia University Press, 2002.

❀ Black Skin Jade Culture sign character Sun god (Tàiyángshén太陽神): Official report.

Léicóngyún雷從云, a researcher of National Museum of China researcher.

■ <ShìbókànguóbǎoHóngshāngǔyù世博看国宝红山古玉> «CCTV-4» 2010.8.17.

(5) Origin of Jadeware and Yīn殷 Jiǎgǔwén甲骨文

❀ Yīn Jiǎgǔwén lóng龍: Yùlóng玉龍.

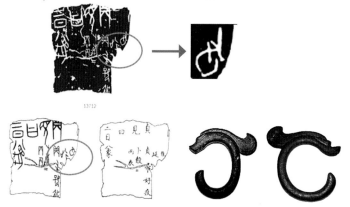

❀ Féngshí馮時, a researcher of Chinese Academy of Social Sciences Archeological Institute: It has the concept of the prince wearing a crown. A kind of connection between human presiding mankind and king of kings presiding kings and all things.

○ Late Yīn Jiǎgǔwén "lóng龍" red part "wáng王",

⊛ **Yīn Jiǎgǔwén Yù玉**: Yùshízhilù玉石之路 2000km (Earlier by one thousand years than Silk Road)

Why did they take faraway Hétiányù和田玉 without taking Xiuyanyù岫岩玉 in Liáoníngshěng.

Yīn Jiǎgǔwén Yù玉: zhēngyù征玉, qǔyù取玉, guǐfāng鬼方 (Westsouthern nomadic tribes).

«Zhōuyì周易» Gāozōng fáguǐfāng sānniánkèzhī 高宗 伐鬼方 三年克之, Gāozōng: Wǔdīng武丁 (BC1250-1192 years ago)

⊛ **Yīn Jiǎgǔwén Yù玉, Wū巫**: Jade totem.

Jiǎgǔwén	Jīnwén	zhuànwén
玉 干	王 王	巫

⊛ **Yángbǎidá <Wū·Yù·Shén jiǎnlùn简论> 2006,11,8.**

Yīn Jiǎgǔwén Yù is "丰" and is written by penetrating 3-4 horizontal lines perpendicularly and is used as today's Yù玉 in the future. "工" is the sound part and shape part as well, indicating a sophisticated tool.

Wū, Jiǎgǔwén 工(a sophisticated tool + seize, hold), To hold a tool with the hand and rap spirit and bless during an ancestral rite.

Jiǎgǔwén甲骨文	Jīnwén金文	zhuànwén篆文
丰 丰	王	王

✺ **Yīn Jiǎgǔwén Nòng**: Influenced by ancestral rites. Jade totem.

- ○ Hieroglyph: An image of holding jadeware with both hands.
- ○ Changed into meaning 'enjoy and touch jade', amusement.

✺ **Yīn Jiǎgǔwén Gōng工** : Sex totem.

Gònggōngshì共工氏. Idiograph: Worship for female genitalia.

✺ **Yīn Jiǎgǔwén Shì氏** : Idiograph: It came from human rén人 and an idiograph of the penis.

✺ **Yīn Jiǎgǔwén Jiāo交** : Hóngshān Culture Burial culture.

✺ **Féngshí (Researcher of Chinese Academy of Social Sciences Archeological Institute)**: Niúhéliáng No. 4 Tomb. Jiǎgǔwén "交". «Yìjīng易經» Jiāo交 means jiāotài. Jiāotài means that the energy of heaven and earth is exchanged and united together.

🏵 **Yīn Jiǎgǔwén Jué玦**: Jade earrings: 8000 years ago Xīnglóngwā Culture, 7000 years ago Hémǔdù河姆渡 Culture found.

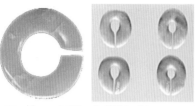 

○ Xīnglóngwā Wényánlǐ Lìshuǐ Japanese Archipelago

Four jade earrings excavated from Xīnglóngwā: Two pieces of right and left ears from a woman's tomb. Two pieces found among grave goods of a man's tomb. One jade earring was found in the waist part of a village chief and the other jade earring in the pig belly. This explains to grant a special delivery function to jade earrings. The above two facts may be the sign of meaning representing the bond between people and pigs. If so, the function of Hieroglyphic signs representing this type of bond is given to jade earrings. Of Jiǎgǔwén, the character Jué explains that these jade earrings are the primitive Hieroglyphic sign of combination, marriage, signing of a treaty. One hand holds the upper left of the jade earring and the other hand holds the lower right. The Jué mouth is heading toward the upper right. Ring-shaped jadeware is a sign that prepares marriage or signing of a treaty. If succeeding in marriage or signing of a treaty, the person made the mark of determination just above Yùhuán玉環. It indicated the constancy of signing of a treaty.

🏵 **Yīn Jiǎgǔwén Hóng虹**: Yùhuáng玉璜.

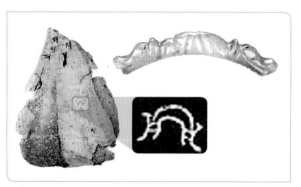

○ Shuānglóngshǒuyùhuáng 双龍首玉璜 excavated from Hóngshān Culture Kāzuǒ 喀左 Dōngshānzuǐ東山嘴 ruins.

■ LiáoníngshěngMuseum.Wénwùkǎogǔyánjiūsuǒ 文物考古研究所 «Liáohéwénmíngzhǎnwénwùjícuì 遼河文明展文物集萃» Shěnyáng, Liáoníngshěng Museum 2006, p.35.

☸ **Yīn Jiǎgǔwén Wǒ我**: Gōuyún (Cloud)-type jade jewelry.

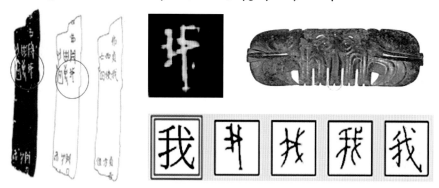

○ Wǒ is a shape resembling an ax with sharp tooth-shaped blade. A kind of an ancient weapon. The original meaning has disappeared as borrowing the meaning of the first person in the future.

☸ **Yīn Jiǎgǔwén Dān單**: Y形 jadeware.

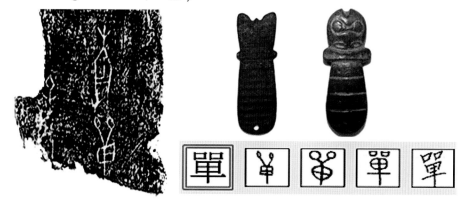

☸ **Yīn Jiǎgǔwén Dì帝**: Square Yùbì玉璧.

甲骨文　金文　小篆　標準字形

○ Symbolizing the contour of a person wearing a crown on the head holding jade with both hands or carrying Yùbì in front of the chest. In the character "Dì", Yùbì in front of the chest is the square shape.

❀ Yīn Jiǎgǔwén Fēng豊, Lǐ禮: Jadeware-related.

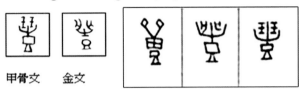

❀ Yīn Jiǎgǔwén, Jīnwén: '豊' is vessels used during protocol events.

○ '禮' Various act norms formed due to customs, habits in the process of social life.

❀ Yīn Jiǎgǔwén: Hóngshān Culture descendants, inheritance of jade culture. In a state of not having the consonants and vowels format, Chinese hieroglyphs were finally evolved from the form of primitive hieroglyphic signs to Jiǎgǔwén. Shāng (Yīn) royal family is the descendants of Hóngshān Culture. Shāng (Yīn) kings and Zhēnrén貞人s inherited jade culture of Hóngshān Culture the most. Jade Culture of Hóngshān is the collective wisdom of ancestors of Hóngshān Culture and intensively reflected the privilege of Wéiyùérzūn唯玉而尊 of chiefs of native villages. Niúhéliáng Historic Site Center is the evidence of clear grade of Wéiyùwèizàng唯玉爲葬.

Wéiyùwèizàng explains 4 kinds of facts:

1. The grading system of one person conceit has already appeared in Hóngshān Culture native villages.

2. Privatization has emerged in Hóngshān Culture native villages and especially jadeware was highly privatized.

3. In Hóngshān Culture native villages, jade was already the best material sign and furthermore, it was a spirit sign.

4. Jade was a symbolic sign with a special meaning and status display of village leader or Wūshī巫師 of Hóngshān Culture.

❀ **Professor Wénxuánkuí文旋奎 «Introduction to Chinese Linguistics中國言語學概論»** : Shūqì書契, sign of promise.
«Zhōuyì周易» xìcí系辞

> "shànggǔjiéshéngérzhì上古結繩而治, hòushìshèngrényìzhīyǐshūqì後世聖人易之以書契"

According to preface of Xǔshèn許愼's «Shuōwénjiězì說文解字»,<zhùyúzhúbó wèizhīshū 著於竹帛謂之書> . And there is a statement <qìkèyě契刻也, kèshíqíshùyě刻識其數也契刻也> in «Shìmíng釋名» written by Liúxī劉熙 of Hòuhàn後漢. According to these old writings, Shūqì書契 meant to inscribe the sign of a promise in bamboo trees.

(6) Mexican Jiǎgǔwén characters inscription Yùguī玉圭

❀ **Professor Son, Seong-tae (Pai Chai University):** n-masse migration of the Korean race (3000-1000 years ago).

Qūyù曲玉 (rounded jade): Early Korean Peninsula Qūyù - Late Korean Peninsula Qūyù - Excavated from Amur River basin – Mexican Qūyù

 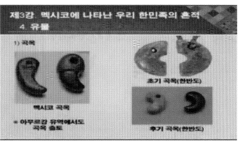

@ **Mexican Jiǎgǔwén Yùguī and 16 men figure statue: La Venta, Tabasco (BC900-400).**

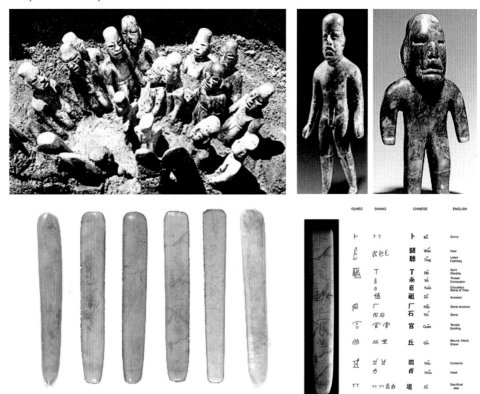

○ La Venta is famous for the largest ancestral rite historic site in Olmek civilization and Gǔdū 古都 (old capital) of Olmek. Since excavated from the central zone of the ancestral rite historic site, No. 4 cultural relic is very important. These relics consists of 16 pieces of small Yùrén玉人 and 6 pieces of Yùguī玉圭 and character signs are clearly engraved in No. 5, No. 6 Yùguī among them.

* Fànyùzhōu范毓周 studied them in detail and as a result, the form configuration of characters composed of slightly curved diagonals and seven straight lines engraved vertically in No. 5 Yùguī and Jiǎgǔwén excavated from Yīnxū殷 墟 were just consistent and compared to Jiǎgǔwén, they could be interpreted clearly as "十示二入三一报" in modern Chinese characters and the phrases could be divided into "十示二, 入三, 一报" according to Jiǎgǔwén grammar. Two letters are engraved in No. 6 Yùguī and were compared with Jiǎgǔwén and as a result, they clearly turned out to be "小示". Among Jiǎgǔwén, the character "示" is shown a lot and "世", the ancestor of the Shāng dynasty is referred to as

"示" and if ancestors of more than 10 generations among Jiǎgǔwén are combined, a method of writing "十" followed by "示" and then, the corresponding number was first used and this "十示二" on Jiǎgǔwén is consistent with the representation habit of Jiǎgǔwén and if translated into modern Chinese, it means the 12th ancestor. Interestingly, characters on Yùguī were compared and interpreted with Jiǎgǔwén and as a result, the described contents and position where relics are placed are surprisingly fit: 6 pieces of Yùguī form a line and a red Yùrén stands in front of Yùguī and 12 pieces of green Yùrén surround red Yùrén in the form of a concentric circle. 3 pieces of Yùrén form a line near No. 5, 6 Yùguī and their faces are toward red Yùrén and seem to come from the outside. If his interpretation is not wrong, Fànyùzhōu said that 12 pieces of green Yùrén are "十示二", 3 pieces of white Yùrén are "入三" and "一報" stands in front of Yùguī and refers to red Yùrén receiving greetings commonly from everyone.

Referring to the history of YīnShāng 殷商, Fàn presented a more advanced interpretation: He explains that there were 12 kings to Dìxīn帝辛 (Yīn zhòuwáng纣王) during the Yīn Dynasty that transferred its capital to Pángēng盤庚 and 12 green Yùrén among these relics are highly likely to represent them and the most highness red Yùrén standing in front of Yùguī may be their founder and 3 pieces of coming white Yùrén may be 3 kings handed down from Central America and No. 6 Yùguī engraved as "Xiǎoshì小示" (meaning collateral line in Jiǎgǔwén) is located next to them or they are seen as the descendants of the collateral line of Shāng royal family. <YīnréndōngdùfāxiànMěizhōu殷人東渡發現美洲>

■ «Shìjièxīnwénwǎng世界新聞網» 2010,11,28,

@ Mexico sign character materials: Related to the movement of the sun and the moon.

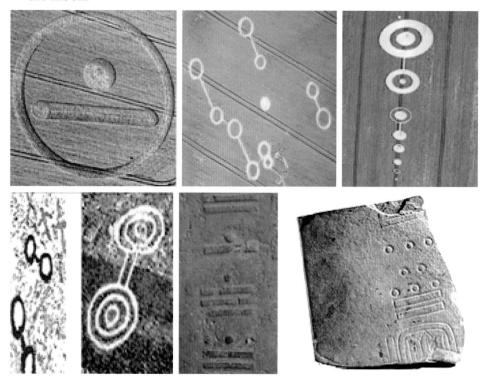

@ Sign character Petroglyphs: Atlatl Cliff in California, USA (5000-4000 years ago)

5 OTHERS

[1] Jade ritual vessel:

❀ Yùgū玉箍, Gōuyún勾雲 (cloud)-type jade jewelry etc.

Hēipíyù	Zhàobǎogōu	Hóngshān	Xiàjiādiàn xiàcéng	Liángzhǔ	Táosì	Gǔshǔ

❀ Yùbì玉璧: Jade disk with a hole in the center

Hēipíyù	Xīnglongwa	Hóngshān	Liángzhǔ	Táosì	Gǔshǔ

🌀 Yùcóng玉琮. Y-shaped jade jewelry.

Hēipíyù	Xīnglongwa	Hóngshān	Xiàjiādiàn xiàcéng	Liángzhǔ	Táosì	Gǔshǔ

🌀 Yùjiàn玉劍, Yùyuè玉鉞, Yùgōuxíngqì玉勾形器

Hēipíyù	Hóngshān	Lóngshān	Liángzhǔ	Táosì	Gǔshǔ

🌀 Yùjué玉玦 (Jade earrings), Qūyù, Mǔzǐqūyù 母子曲玉

Hēipíyù	Xīnglongwa	Hóngshān	Xiàjiādiàn xiàcéng	Korean Peninsula	Japanese Islands

(1) Hóngshān Culture

Three kinds of jadeware : Yùrén玉人+Yùgū玉箍+Yùfèng玉鳳.

🌀 Liúguóxiáng劉國祥: Tomb owner status Wūshī巫師,

Three kinds of jadeware (5000 years ago). Appeared as a price status.
Excavated from Jiànpíngxiàn Niúhéliáng 16th point No. 4 Tomb in 1984.

  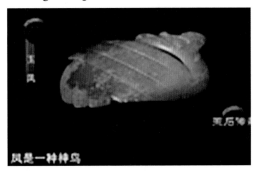

🌀 Three kinds of Shénqì 三種の神器 of Japan : Jìng鏡．Yù玉．Jiàn劍

Treasures inherited from generation to generation by the Japanese emperor
family. The entity is not visible.

- Bāchǐqiónggōuyù
  八尺瓊勾玉
  Yasakaninomagatama

- Tiāncóngyúnjiàn天叢雲劍
  Amenomurakumonotsurugi

- Bāzhǐjìng八咫鏡
  Yatanokagami

Three kinds of Shénqì are Jìng鏡 Yù玉 Jiàn劍 but many of them have been excavated as grave goods from Gǔfén古墳 (ancient tombs), the tombs of ancient king or royal family, heads. Finally, those valuably inherited by the Japanese emperor family are those cherished by the kings of ancient Japan.

✿ Gōuyù勾玉 (=Qūyù曲玉): "Role of rounded jade beyond ornaments"
"Larger trend than the period of ancient burial mounds"

- Excavated from Nàiliángxiàn Běigěchéngjùn Guǎnglíngtǐng Cháoshān 奈良縣 北葛城郡 廣陵町 巣山 ancient tomb. Talc 9.7cm long. The period of ancient burial mounds

- Excavated from Nàiliángxiàn Běigěchéngjùn Héhétǐng Bǎozhǒng 奈良縣 北葛城郡 河合町 宝塚 ancient tomb. Jadeite Qūyù (Gokok) Rounded jade 0.9-2.4cm long. The period of ancient burial mounds(3rd-6th century)

Materials of Gōuyù . bugle (guǎnyù管玉). Gōuyù used as headdress or arm ornaments is various such as agate . crystal . glass etc. but these remains are all made of jadeite. On the other hand, there are a lot of defective parts in 8 bugles. However, a significant high technology of drilling a hole of approximately 0.5cm in jade of less than 1cm in diameter can be seen.

■ «Tiānhuángjiāmíngbǎo 天皇家の名寶» 寶島社, Japan, 2014,8,10.

💮 **Yùgū:** Owned by Bālínyòuqí巴林右旗 Museum.

○ 12.5cm. Excavated from Bālínyòuqí Chágànmùlúnsūmù查干沐沦苏木,

○ 19cm. Excavated from Bālínyòuqí Bāyànchágànsūmù巴彦查干苏木.

○ 13cm. Excavated from Bālínzuǒqí in 1964, Owned by Bālínzuǒqí Museum. Excavated from Áohànqí Dàdiànzǐ No. 833 Tomb, Owned by Chinese Academy of Social Sciences Archeological Institute

(2) Gōuyúnxíngyùpèi勾云形玉佩:

💮 **Guōdàshùn:** Niúhéliáng first point already robbed tomb only one Wūrén巫人 (shaman, 7500-5500 years ago)

Function: Related to quánzhàng權杖 (Gōuyúnxíngyùpèi, Fǔyuè斧钺),

■ <Hóngshānwénhuàde"wéiyùwéizàng"yuLiáohéwénmíngqǐyuántèzhēngzàirènshi紅山文化的 "唯玉爲葬"與遼河文明起源特征再認識> 《Wénwù文物》 The 8th in 1997.

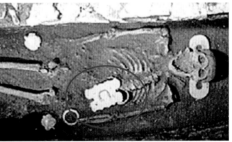

* Liúguóxiáng Researcher of Academy of Social Sciences Archeological Institute, Hóngshān Jadeware.

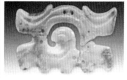

❧ Bok, Gi-dae :

Xiàjiādiàn Lower Culture Tāotièwén饕餮紋 (Hóngshān Culture relevance, Sānzuòdiàn三座店 Stone Fortress)

Gōuyún-type jade jewelry: Inherited Hóngshān Culture Jadeware as it is.

Hóngshān Culture and Xiàjiādiàn Lower Culture distribution map (Author's note: Red circle)

Hóngshān Culture	Xiàjiādiàn Lower Culture

○ Comparative diagram of Hóngshān Culture and Xiàjiādiàn Lower Culture jadeware (Author: Paper citation, life-size jadeware)

	Chìfēngshì wénwùdiàn suǒcáng		Áohànqí Dàdiànzǐ
	Bālínzuǒqí Yángjiāyíngzǐ		Áohànqí Dàdiànzǐ
	Niúhéliáng		Dàdiànzǐ

Hóngshān Culture is the culture with very developed jadeware. Some of this jadeware expressed beasts symbolically. If looking at the form engraved in the center of the object, there is an expression that can be regarded as the face of a beast. These are carved relatively simply. Rather than being solemn, various forms of expressions are shown in the face. If comparing this with the expression shown in colored earthenware of Xiàjiādiàn Lower Culture, it can be seen that the pattern of Xiàjiādiàn Lower Culture has become somewhat solemn. But, the basic framework is very similar in the two cultures. Therefore, given the similarities of two vessels, it can be seen that Tāotièwén of Xiàjiādiàn Lower Culture came from Hóngshān Culture.

<An Essay on the Relevance between Hóngshān Culture and Xiàjiādiàn Lower Culture>

■ «Cultural Historiography» No.27. Korea.

⚜ **Gōuyún-type jade jewelry:**

Xiàjiādiàn Lower Culture Chéngzǐshān城子山 Stone Fortress.

Hóngshān Culture Niúhéliáng historic site the 16th point is located in the southwest among Niúhéliáng Hóngshān Culture historic site group and is the straight-line distance of about 4000m from Niúhéliáng first point Goddess grave to the Northeast and Liáoníngshěng Língyuánshì凌源市 Língběizhèn凌北鎮 Sānguāndiànzǐcūn三官甸子村.

⚜ **Liúguóxiáng:** <Hóngshān Culture Gōuyún-type Jadeware Research> «Kǎogǔ考古» 5th in 1998

excavated from Niúhéliáng, Hútóugōu胡頭溝, Chéngzǐshān城子山 etc.

❀ **Yùxuánjī玉璇璣**: Excavated from Xiǎozhūshān小珠山 historic site. Xuán-huíxíngyùhuán旋回形玉環. Xuánjī璇璣 prince astronomical instrument.

○ Xiǎozhūshān Culture(5000 years BC).
○ Shāng Owned by Beijing Palace Museum.

❀ **Guōdàshùn:** Turning type jade disk with a hole in the center is likely to originate from Dàlián District

■ «Dàliánrìbào大連日報» 2014,4,21.

○ Hóngshān Culture Jadeware has received the attention of the world. The most typical turning type jade disk with a hole in the center found in Dalian District during the Hóngshān Culture period has been excavated in Dàwènkǒu of Shāndōng and Lóngshān Culture tombs and a turning type jade disk with a hole in the center has been also found in Shǎnxī陕西.

○ Excavated from Hútóugōu胡頭溝 No.1 tomb Niúhéliáng Second point No.1 ancient tomb No. 21 tomb jade disk with a hole in the center, 8-shaped jade disk (Shuāngliánbì 双聯璧).

○ Jade disk with a hole in the center 15.9x14.4cm. Hēilóngjiāng黑龍江 Museum jade disk Central Jilinshěng Báichéng白城 Area.

■ «Chángchūnrìbào長春日報» 2009,11,10

(3) Yùbì玉璧: Excavated from Hēilóngjiāng Province,

○ 4.32cm   ○ 4.57cm   ○ 7.15-8.93cm

○ Excavated from Tàiláixiàn Hóngshēngxiāng Dōngwēnggēnshān泰来县 宏升乡 东翁根山 ruins, 4.32cm. 4.57cm. 7.15-8.93cm.

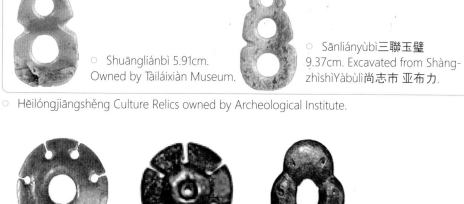

○ Shuāngliánbì 5.91cm.
Owned by Tàiláixiàn Museum.

○ Sānliányùbì三聯玉璧
9.37cm. Excavated from Shàng-
zhìshìYàbùlì尚志市 亚布力.

○ Hēilóngjiāngshěng Culture Relics owned by Archeological Institute.

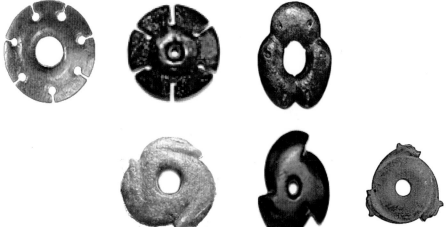

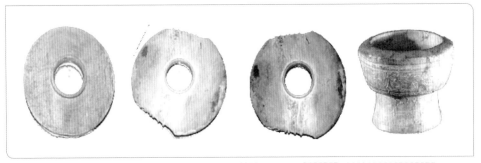

■ Táosì Culture. Qíjiā culture <yùshíchuánqí玉石传奇> Vol.2 巫神之玉 «CCTV-9» 2011,1,8.

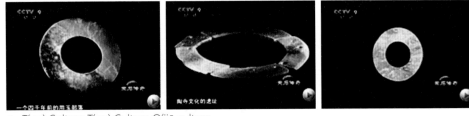

○ Táosì Culture Táosì Culture Qíjiā culture

❀ Sānxīngduī三星堆 Culture (5000~3000 years ago): Gǔshǔ古蜀 Culture, Sìchuān Guǎnghànshì广汉市 Sānxīngduī

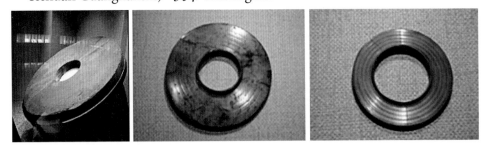

❀ Researcher Liúguóxiáng (Chinese Academy of Social Sciences): Bìyùduōtóuqì碧玉多頭器 (Jade ritual vessel).

Belonging to the late Hóngshān Culture and 5500-5000 years ago from now. Áohànqí Sàlìbāxiāng萨力巴鄉. A symbol of power.

The most important Lǐqì (ritual vessel) in Hóngshān Culture

 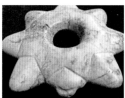 

○ Áohàn cultural relics purification, Bìyùduōtóuqì (Lǐqì), diameter：11cm. Áohànqí Museum.
○ Jílínshěng, Large octagonal type jadeware (vision of the universe)

(4) Yùbǎn玉版 (Augural jadeware): Língjiātān Culture.

Hánshānyùbǎnyǔrìguǐbǐjiào含山玉版与日晷比较.

Identifying winter solstice, summer solstice

 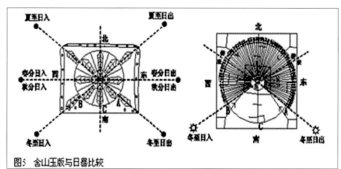

(5) Cóngxíngyù琮形玉: Navel position.

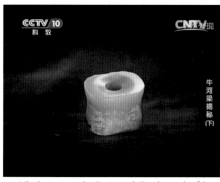 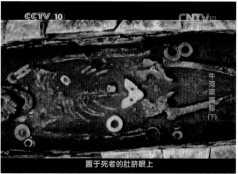

○ Likely to symbolize umbilical cord of human birth, Symbolizing the rebirth of the soul after death.

■ «Tànsuǒfāxiàn探索發現» Wǔqiānniánwénmíngjiànzhèng-Niúhéliángjiēmì 五千年文明見證-牛河梁揭秘 (下) «CCTV-10» 2014, 08, 17.

❁ Yùcóng玉琮: Black skin jade culture, Hóngshān Culture. Symbolizing Shén-quán神權 (divine power).

❁ Qīngdài清代 Yùcóng: Smithsonian Museum Freer Gallery.

○ Height: 5.2cm 5.7cm 20.3cm 6.3cm

❁ Yùcóng type Royal Kiln celadon: Southern Song 12th-13th century.

○ 19.7cm   ○ 22.7cm   ○ 21.8 cm
○ Japan Tokyo National Museum Important Cultural Property.
○ Smithsonian Museum Freer Gallery.
○ Míng明(Mid-16th century -17th century). Qīng清(18th Century) 景德鎮.

(6) Y-shaped jadeware: The original form of Jiǎgǔwén Dān單.

(7) Yùjiàn 玉劍 (Jade dagger)

<1> Mandolin-shaped jade dagger (Hóngshān Culture):

The original form of Mandolin-shaped bronze dagger.

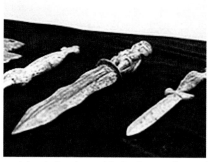

○ Mandolin-shaped jade dagger from already robbed tomb in the westernmost 16th point of Niúhéliáng historic site.
○ Mandolin-shaped bronze dagger was excavated from the right above the Hútóugōu ruins Hóngshān Culture occupation layer.
○ Hóngshān Cultivation associated with the Korean Peninsula.
■ <The Home of Koreans> 'Mysterious Kingdom' was found (12) «Jīngxiāngxīnwén京鄉新聞» 2007, 12, 19. Korea.

🌀 Found Mandolin-shaped bronze dagger made of jade.

'Xiàjiādiàn Lower Culture' excavated after that also attracts our attention. Because the place was the old territory of Gǔcháoxiǎn (Gojoseon). The year of remains was also about BC2200, similar to that of Gǔcháoxiǎn (Gojoseon) establishment and remains excavated were all the remains of Dōngyí東夷 Tribe. What is particularly noteworthy is the ruins of Bronze Age culture. Mandolin-shaped bronze dagger made of jade was also found. The common requirements for the ancient nation establishment that archaeologists say are fortress, city existence, palace, large tombs, bronze weapons etc. and most of them are prepared. Therefore, saying that 'history is science', Korean evidential historians have denied Gǔcháoxiǎn (Gojoseon) because there is no bronze culture. Now, this consumptive debate does not have a value any more.

■ «Qìngběirìbào慶北日報» 2009,11,2. Korea.

<2> Animal Totem inscription Yùjiàn (jade dagger):

Black skin jade culture. Hóngshān Culture inscription jade dagger. A certain making form.

<3> Yùgōuxíngqì玉勾形器:

Xiàjiādiàn Lower Culture (Excavated from Chìfēngshì Áohànqí Dàdiànzǐ).

○ Hóngshān Culture Yùgōuxíngqì: Completely the same as one excavated from Yīn Fùhǎomù 妇好墓.

* Owned by the aristocracy during the XiàShāngZhōu夏商周 period Hóngshān Culture Jadeware.

Jadeware excavated from Anyáng安陽 Yīn Fùhǎomù (755 pieces)

❀ Xíyǒngjié席永傑 (Head of Chìfēng Academy Hóngshān Culture International Research Center)

The most important cause is that jade artisans in the Shāng Dynasty were highly likely to see Hóngshān Culture Jadeware by themselves because it is more important in antient times when information transmission was not developed. 1 Yùgōuxíngqì excavated from Yīn Fùhǎomù and Yùgōuxíngqì Inner Mongolia Bālínyòuqí are completely identical and both are Hóngshān Culture Jadeware.

(8) Jade earrings : Yùjué玉玦 (=Qūyù曲玉)

<1> Yùjué:

Áohànqí Xīnglóngwā-KoreanPeninsula-Japanese Archipelago.

○ Áohànqí Xīnglóngwā Culture Diameter 2.9cm

○ Jiāngyuán gāochéng wényánlǐ 8000 years ago. 3.4-3.6cm

○ Quánnán Lìshuǐshì Nánmiàn Andǎolǐ Gwangju National Museum 6000 years ago 1.4cm.

○ Japan Fújǐngxiàn Jīnjīntǐng Sāngyě桑野 ruins Shéngwén shídài 6000 years ago

○ Fūyú (Buyeo) National Museum amazonstone.　　○ Quánnán全南 Wùānjùn務安郡　　○ National Museum of Korea Two rounded jade.

<2> Qūyù曲玉 (Rounded jade)

1. Bent jade (Rounded jade):

Professor Lee, Hyeong-gu: Bent jade (Rounded jade), Manchuria-Korean Peninsula-Japan, Transformation in fashion.

Symbol of power, civilization <The Root of Korean Culture>

■ «Jīngxiāngxīnwén京鄕新聞» 1989,2,3. Korea.

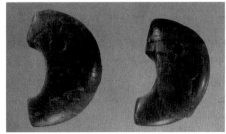

○ Dàlínghé Yùlóng. Zhōngběi忠北 Qūyù, Qìngběi慶北 Qūyù

2. Qūyù (Gokok): Smithsonian Museum Freer Gallery. Using Korean names.
http://www.asia.si.edu/collections/

○ H:4.0cm H:3.9cm H:3.1cm H:2.8cm H:2.4cm

3. Qūyù (Gokok): Relics excavated from Bǎijǐ百濟 area, Fūyú Sōngjúlǐ松菊里 stone-cists (8th-10th century BC).

○ Guāngzhōu光州 National Museum.
Bǎochéngjiāng Basin Lìshuǐ Peninsula

❀ **Mǎhán馬韓 Qūyù**: Ruins in Quánzhōu全州, Quánběi全北 (Quánběi National University Museum).

A total of 30 mounded tombs were investigated. About 150 main burial chambers.

Senior Researcher Professor Kim, Seung-ok (Quánběi National University) "A mounded tomb was known as a tomb of Proto-Three Kingdoms of Korea Mǎhán but Mounded Tomb return period could be readjusted because relics of early Iron Age were excavated from the bottom in this research."

❀ **Mǎhán Móulúbēilíguó牟盧卑離國. Gāochǎngjùn Yǎshānmiàn Fèngdélǐ高敞郡 雅山面 鳳德里.**

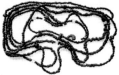

@ Jadeware excavated from Bǎijǐ百濟 area Língyán靈巖, Lìshuǐ (Research Center of Dolmens in Northeast Asia)

○ Quánnán Língyán Quánnán Lìshuǐ

@ Qūyù(Gokok) golden earrings of Bǎijǐ King Wǔníngwáng武寧王 (National Treasure No. 156) 8.3cm. Gōngzhōu公州 National Museum

@ Bǎijǐ Area Yìshān益山 Mílèsì彌勒寺 Pagoda circular box 'Shàngbùdálùmùjìn 上部達率目近' jewel box Qūyù:

Inscription on the lid of the bronze box and internal treasure 'Shàngbùdálùmùjìn 上部達率目近' were deciphered, It seems a jewel box.

○ Quánběi Yìshān <Mílèsì Pagoda bronze vessel opened> «Yonhap News» 2010,5,26. Korea.

4. Qūyù (Gokok): Gāyē伽倻(Gaya) Area. Yellow jade excavated from Jìnzhōu晋州 Yùfáng玉房.

○ Golden crown excavated from Gāolíng高靈. Around 5th-6th century. Golden crown of Gāyē Period. Height 11.5cm. National Treasure No. 138

○ Topaz Qūyù excavated from Jìnzhōu Yùfáng.

○ Jìnzhōu Yùfáng bronze Qūyù type decoration

■ Lee, Hyeong-gu «The Secrets of Korea Ancient Culture Found in Bohai Coast» pp. 174,176, 332. Gimmyoung Publishers, 2004,7. Korea.

※ Xīnluó新羅 Area Qūyù: Xīnluó's ruìzhì叡智 that overturned the Japan origin theory.

■ «Jīngxiāngxīnwén京鄉新聞» 1976,8,3. Korea.

Jīnmào金帽 Qūyù(Gokok). Excavated from Qìngzhōu慶州 Jīnlíngzhǒng金玲塚. National Museum of Korea

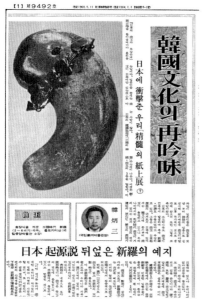

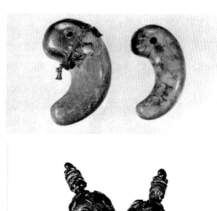

5. Qūyù (Gokok) golden crown:

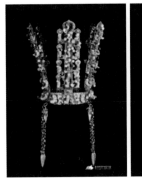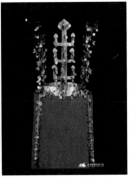

○ Tiānmǎzhǒng天馬冢 golden crown 6th century. National Treasure No. 188 golden crown Total 27.5cm National Treasure No. 87

☙ **Qūyù(Gokok): Xīnluó Area. Qìngzhōushì慶州市.**

6. Qūyù(Gokok): Unified Xīnluó Jewelry excavated from Jǐzhōushì濟州市.

○ Jǐzhōushì Digital Jǐzhōu Grand Culture

Qūyù identified in Jǐzhōu Island is divided into glass·earth·agalmatolite·stone depending on materials. Glass Qūyù was excavated from Guōzhī郭支 shell mound 5th district. The size of this Qūyù is 3cm long and head diameter is 1.5×1.7cm and the color is jade green. Of Qūyù types excavated from ancient tombs of the Three Kingdoms period, the type of this Qūyù is a relatively classic type and three carved lines are carved in the head. Earth Qūyù was made as a substitute for glass Qūyù. 4 pieces of agalmatolite Qūyù were excavated from Gāonèilǐ高內里 ruins of the 8th~9th century. Stone Qūyù was excavated from Sānyángdòng三陽洞 ruins and the length is less than 3cm. This stone Qūyù corresponds to the first century BC, the earliest period among Qūyù. Except earth, glass or agalmatolite Qūyù is not from Jǐzhōu Island. Like money excavated from Shāndìgǎng山地港, these Qūyù are determined to be elite grave goods as the products of foreign exchange.

(9) Japanese archipelago:

The oldest Three Sacred Treasures of Japan(三種の神器)

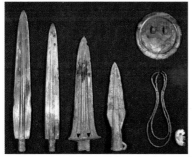 

○ Excavated from Fúgāngxiàn Jíwǔgāomù福岡県 吉武高木 Fukuokaken yoshitake ruins. Jiǔzhōu九州(Kyushu) National Museum http://www.kyuhaku.jp.
○ Lǎosī老司 ancient tomb No.3 stone chamber around Fúgāng福岡 Píngyě平野.
○ Fúgāngshì福岡市 Museum Yayoi period(2nd century BC)

@ **Japan's only golden Qūyù (Gokok). Assumed to be relics handed down from outside.**

○ 1.8cm. Middle period of ancient burial mounds. Cultural assets designated by Hégēshānxiàn和歌山県 (Wakayamaken).
○ Excavated from Chējiàzhīgǔzhǐ車駕之古址 Ancient Tomb. Whole length 86m Keyhole-shaped Burial Mounds.

(10) Mǔzǐqūyù母子曲玉:

1. Korean Peninsula Area: Quánnán全南, Qìngběi慶北.

○ Quánnán Shùntiānshì Sōngguǎngmiàn Yuèshānlǐ No.4 stone chamber. Owned by National Shùntiān University Museum.

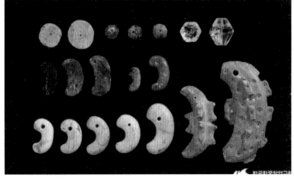

○ Length around 10㎝. Owned by Qìngzhōu(Gyeongju) National Museum

2. Japanese archipelago: Qúnmǎxiàn群馬縣. Bīngkùxiàn兵庫縣.

3. Japanese archipelago: The Gǔfénshídài古墳時代(around 250 to 538 AD)

Nàiliángxiàn奈良縣, Sānchóngxiàn三重県. Bìyùzhì碧玉製 Qiāoxíngshí鍬形石

○ Excavated from Nàiliángxiàn Běigěchéngjùn 奈良縣 北葛城郡 Guǎnglíngtǐng Cháoshān 廣陵町 巢山 ancient tomb. «Tiānhuángjiāmíngbǎo 天皇家の名寶» 寶島社, Japan, 2014,8,10. 21cm.

○ Excavated from Sānchóngxiàn Yīzhìjùn Xǐyětǐng shàngyědìqū 三重県 一志郡嬉野町 上野地区.19.7cm.

○ Agency for Cultural Affairs, Government of Japan Cultural Heritage Online http://bunka.nii.ac.jp/

○ Owned by Japanese e National Treasure National Museum National Treasure. Important Cultural Properties http://www.emuseum.jp/

○ Qiāoxíngshí important cultural property Nàiliángxiàn Shēngjūshì生駒市 (Objects excavated from Nàiliáng Fùxióngtǐng Wánshān 奈良 富雄町 丸山 ancient tomb) 17.4㎝ / 18.5㎝. Kyoto National Museum

✲ Wēixìncái威信財: Evidence of the alliance of the Great king.

Shellfish that started to be used for decorating a man's arm during the Míshēng彌生(Yayoi) period was moved to jasper as it is and it is called as Qiāoxíngshí. In particular, Qiāoxíngshí is a bracelet type stone product based on a bracelet made of shellfish in fashion from the Míshēng(Yayoi) period to the period of ancient burial mounds. Out of the original purpose, it was considered important as a sort of treasure during the former period of ancient burial mounds. Until now, it is excavated around large ancient tombs in the area and is assumed to be distributed from the great king of the area to the head of each place.

Chapter 3

Jade Culture of the Korean People

1 QūYÙ曲玉 (ROUNDED JADE)

Dolmens distribution in Chinese Continent: Pan Yellow sea coastal region

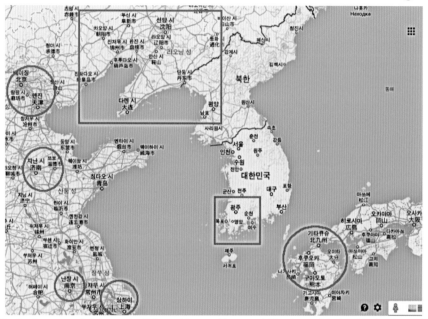

○ Distribution map of dolmens in Chinese Eastern Coast and Northeast District Báiyúnxiáng白云翔
■《Zhōngguózhīshímù中國支石墓》Korea Luózhōu羅州 National Research Institute of Cultural Heritage. 2011,10.

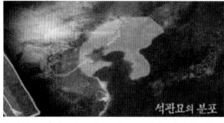

○ Hóngshānwénmíng stone cists distribution MBC-TV, Korea.

○ Mandolin-shaped bronze dagger distribution area and Gǔcháoxiǎn (Gojoseon) area

[1] Yùjué玉玦 (Qūyù曲玉):

Liáohé Area-Yellow River Basin-Yángzǐ River Basin-Taiwan
Liáohé Area-Korean Peninsula-Japanese archipelago.
Liáohé Area-Siberia-Japanese archipelago

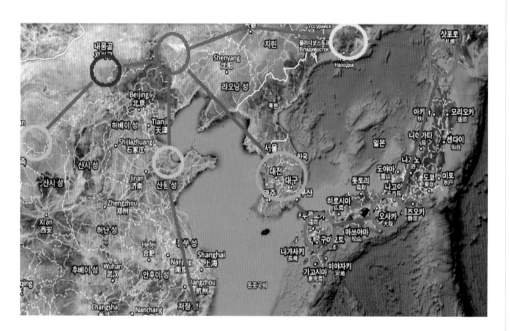

🌀 **Jade earrings:** Korea Peninshula

○ Quánnán Lìshuǐshì Nánmiàn Andǎolǐ, 1.4cm(6000 years ago), Gwangju National Museum

○ Jiāngyuán Gāochéng Wényánlǐ, 3.4cm (8000 years ago).

○ Qìngnán慶南 Yùshān蔚山 Chùrónglǐ處容里

Jade is a representative non-metallic ornament of the ancient society and has been identified from the Neolithic period in Korea. And then, in the Bronze Age when the northern cultural relics started to be introduced, various forms of

Jade represented as amazonite and jasper were used with bronze stone bone ornaments. After the spread of ironware culture, rapid increase and changing patterns appear in the quantity and quality of jade. Agriculture and iron production brought about the accumulation of wealth and development of economic life and such development resulted in the changes throughout the society. These changes are reflected in jade, the representative jewelry at that time. Therefore, by analyzing the distribution and characteristics of ancient jade, the characteristics and nature of decoration culture and burial rites can be identified and furthermore, even political and economic culture can be inferred

(1) Yùjué玉玦:

<1> Chinese Continent (Liáohé Area-Yellow River Area-Yángzǐ River Area

1. Liáohé Area : Black skin jade culture. Hóngshān Culture (Inner Mongolia, Liáoníngshěng, Jílínshěng, Hēilóngjiāngshěng)

These are the oldest juézhuàngěrshì玦狀耳飾 in Asia and items excavated from Liáoníng shěng Fùxīnshì Cháhǎi 遼寧省 阜新市 查海 historic site belonging to Xīnglóngwā興隆窪 Culture of Northeastern China and are the old type with thick cross section using kidney stone.--Therefore, Wényánlǐ juézhuàng ěrshì is more greatly related to China in terms of burial custom and materials, forms and is highly likely to be imported from Northeastern China and the Maritime province.

■ National Research Institute of Cultural Heritage «Jiāngyuán Gāochéng wényánlǐ yíjì 江原 高城 文岩里 遺蹟» pp.237-239, Korea. 2004,12,29.

❀ Xīnglóngwā Culture. Hóngshān Culture. Xiàjiādiàn Lower Culture.

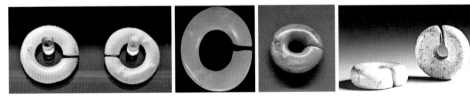

○ Aohànqí Xīnglóngwā excavated, Chinese Academy of Social Sciences,
○ Shànghǎi ZhèndànBówùguǎn上海 震旦博物館
○ Taiwan Natonal Palace Museum, Cháhǎi, Xiàjiādiàn Upper Culture
○ Inner Mongolia Chìfēngshì Kèshíkèténgqí克什克腾旗 excavated, Línxīxiàn Báiyīnchánghàn 林西县 白音长汗 excavated, Inner Mongolia Museum.

○ Jade earrings: Xīnglóngwā (8000 years ago) Jade earring inserted into the right eye. Girl Shamen (Nǚwū).

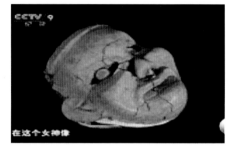

○ Bìyùl碧玉: Hóngshān Culture Niúhéliáng (5000 years ago) Bìyùl inserted into both eyes. Molded goddess statue.

■ <Rényǔshèhuìxúnyù人與社會尋玉> «CCTV-10» The 239th. 2010,10,20.
■ «Zhōngguówénwùbào中国文物报» 2008,4,9.

   * Based on the writing in «Zhōuyì周易» xìcí系辞, Chinese Yánxiángfù said in his book «Hóngshānwénhuàyùqìyánjiū红山文化玉器研究», " yīn陰 and yáng陽 culture is the basis of the Eight Trigrams 八卦 for divination. " Fúxī made the Eight Trigrams for divination" is inseparable from yīn and yáng culture and explains the fact that yīn and yáng culture already existed before Fúxī (4000 BC or much earlier). When is the specific origin of yīn and yáng culture. There is no clear answer yet. Many jade earrings excavated from Xīnglóngwā Culture (6200 years BC) historic site were analyzed and as a result, the big and small, yīn and yáng phenomenon evenly existed in each jade earring. This explains that these Xīnglóngwā Culture former inhabitants already used yin and yang culture.

❀ Black skin jade culture

○ human face pattern jade earring.

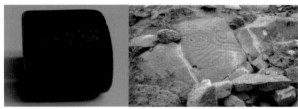

○ Inner Mongolia Wēngniútèqí Sānzuòdiàn Human face petroglyphs

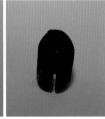

○ Shòumiànwénguǎnyùxíngyùjué獸面紋管玉形玉玦

2. Yellow River area: Zhōngyuán region (Hénánshěng Wǔyáng Gǔhú贾湖 historic site).

Lǜsōngshíqiú綠松石球 found in head left and right eyes of a middle-aged woman. 3 pieces from the right eye, 2 pieces from the left eye. 1 piece outside the left lower jawbone (Guessed it fell from the left eye).

○ KǎogǔxìhéHénánshěngwénwùkǎogǔYánjiūsuǒhézuò考古系和河南省文物考古研究所合作 <HénánWǔyángGǔhúYízhǐ2001niánfājuéjiǎnbào 河南舞阳贾湖遗址2001年发掘简报>

❀ Lóngshān Culture Shòumiànwén兽面纹 Guǎnxíngshíjué 管形石玦 (Beast face pattern)

3. Yīn殷

❀ **Professor Lee, Jong-ho (KAIST)** : Dōngyí Tribe moved to Zhōngyuán.

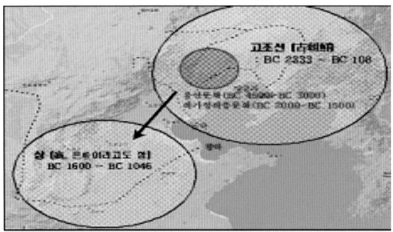

■ <Gǔcháoxiǎn (Gojoseon) found by Science> p.334.

It is explained that Dōngyí Tribe started from 6000 years BC (Cháhǎi, Xīnglóngwā Culture) formed Xiàjiādiàn Lower Culture (2000-1500 BC, that is, Gǔcháoxiǎn (Gojoseon) Period) through Hóngshān Culture (4500-3000 years BC) and moved to Zhōngyuán, China while going through the founder of the Shāng Dynasty Xiè契, his grandson Xiàngtǔ相土, 7th Wánghài王亥 and 8th Shàngjiǎwēi上甲微 and finally, defeated the Xià夏 Dynasty completely in around 1600 BC and unified the whole world.

❀ **Archaeologist Fùsīnián傅斯年:**

It was concluded, "Yīn (Shāng Dynasty) flourished in the northeast and went back to Northeast after ruined." In the case of HuánběiShāngchéng洹北商城 excavated this time, the central axis is tilted to the northeast by 13°. This is the typical direction of a capital city of the Shāng Dynasty and is interpreted to "show deep nostalgia for the home (Bóhǎi渤海 coast)

@ **Yīn Dynasty Jadeware** : Inheritance of Hóngshān Culture Jadeware

What Peking University professor Fùsīnián said during the speech in the conference opened to celebrate the 80th anniversary of the Yīnxū excavation in 2008 is even more meaningful. He concluded "The Yīn Dynasty flourished in the northeast and went to the northeast after the fall."

Bronzeware excavated from Yīnxū is more than 5000 pieces and Bronze Fāngdǐng方鼎 with the text written as Sīmǔqu司母戌 weighed a whopping 832.75kg. 2600 pieces of Jadeware were identified and inherit Jadeware culture originated in China Northeastern Cháhǎi-Xīnglóngwā as it is.

2008, Yīnxūfājué 80 zhōuniánjìniànxuéshùdàhuì 殷墟發掘 80周年記念學術大會 Fùsīnián (Peking University).

@ **Yùshízhilù玉石之路 (Approximately 2000 km):** Wǔdīng (3250-3192 years ago).

○ Yīn Jiǎgǔwén Yù玉: zhēngyù征玉, qǔyù取玉, guǐfāng鬼方 (Westsouthern nomadic tribes).
○ «Zhōuyì周易» Gāozōng fáguǐfāng sānniánkèzhī 高宗 伐鬼方 三年克之, Gāozōng: Wǔdīng武丁 (BC1250-1192 years ago)
○ Excavated from Yīn Fùhǎomù, Hóngshān Culture Yùgōuxíngqì玉勾形器.
○ Why was distant Hétiányù和田玉 taken without taking Xiuyanyù岫岩玉 of Yīn
○ Liáoníngshěng?

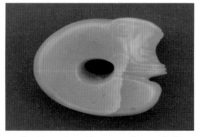

○ Yīn Fùhǎomù jade earrings. Yīnxū殷墟 Museum.

○ Smithsonian Museum Freer Gallery 3.1cm

❀ Spring and Autumn jade earrings Lóngshǒuwén龍首紋 jade earrings Lù'ānshì 六安市 Wǎnxī皖西 Museum

❀ Yānguó燕國, Běijīng Liúlíhé琉璃河, Hóngshān Culture Jadeware excavated, Yānguó燕國 Shòuxíngyùpèi兽形玉佩 (1 piece).

■ Chényìmín «Hóngshānyùqìtújiàn紅山玉器圖鑑» p.15, ShànghǎiDàxuéchūbǎnshè 上海大學出版社, 2004

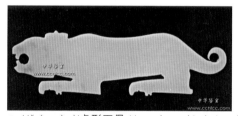

○ Hǔxíngyùpèi虎形玉佩 (tiger-shaped jade jewelry) 7.4cm.
○ Běijīng Liúlíhé 北京 琉璃河 Yānguómùdìchūtǔ 燕国墓地出土, XīzhōuYānjīngYízhǐBówùguǎn西周燕京遗址博物馆

❀ Hánguó韓國 Jadeware: Yùzhūlóng玉猪龍 (14cm)

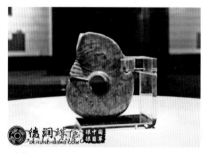

○ Shǎnxī Liángdàicūn Xīzhōugǔmùcángchūtǔ 陝西 梁带村 西周古墓藏 出土.
○ <5000 niánqiándeYùzhūlóng 5000年前的玉猪龙 Guóbǎo zhèngguǎnzhībǎo 国宝"镇馆之宝"> Guóbǎodàng'àn国宝档案«CCTV-1,4,10»

■ Rénmínwǎng人民網 http://culture.people.com.cn/ 2006,1,10.

❦ Guóguó虢国 Jadeware excavation site

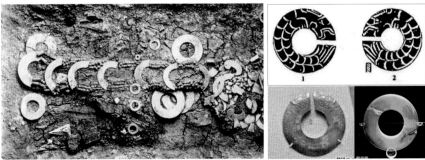

○ Jade earrings, jade disk with a hole in the center. Guóguó Sānménxiáshì三门峡市, Guóguó Museum, Hénán.

4. Yángzǐ River Basin: Hémǔdù Culture, Língjiātān Culture, Liángzhǔ Culture.

❦ Hémǔdù河姆渡 Culture (7000-5000 years ago)

○ Zhèjiāngshěng Museum 5.8cm in diameter.

❦ Língjiātān凌家滩 Culture (6000 years ago)

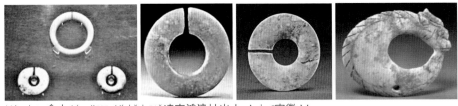

○ Hánshān含山 LíngjiātānYízhǐchūtǔ凌家滩遗址出土, Anhuī安徽 Museum

❦ Mǎjiābāng马家浜 Culture (5000-4000 years ago).

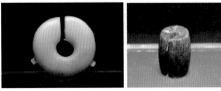

○ Shànghǎi Museum Chinese Ancient Jadeware Hall

❀ **Liángzhǔ良渚 Culture.**

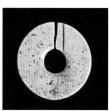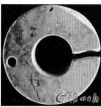

○ Yúháng Píngyáo cǎijí 余杭瓶窑采集, Yúháng Xīngqiáo Hòutoushān chūtǔ 余杭星桥后头山出土, Jiāngsū Xúzhōu 江苏徐州 Museum

[2] Yùshòuxíngjué玉獸形玦: various animals as totems

❀ **Yùlóng玉龍, Yùxiónglóng玉熊龍, Yùzhūlóng玉猪龍, Yùniǎolóng玉鳥龍 etc.**

As shown above, jade earrings of Hóngshān Culture seem to have been developed from the simple form of decorative earrings to complex carving as the representative symbols of a tribe or clan with various animals as totems such as pigs, bears, birds, etc. in the head with the round body of a snake as the base. As can be seen from the name of Yùshòuxíngjué (China Běijīng Natonal Palace Museum), it is called as Yùzhūlóng (dragon and pig) in the case of a pig (Zhū猪) and Yùxiónglóng (dragon and bear) in the case of a bear. On the other hand, while varying forms slightly, jade earrings (Yùjué玉玦 =Yùshòuxíngjué) influenced even the Korean Peninsula and Japanese Archipelago internationally and directly affected the later dynasties such as Yīn殷, Guó虢 etc. in China. In particular, China Běijīng National Palace Museum revealed that jade earrings are artifacts not by the recent archaeological excavation but those which have been owned by the Qīng清 imperial family. At the same time, jade earrings were also developed into C-shaped dragon (Yùlóng: The shape of a dragon made of jade), the representative Jadeware of Hóngshān Culture and animals of tribal totem seem to have been carved symbolically. A Hóngshān Culture expert of Chinese Chìfēng Academy, Xíyǒngjié席永傑 said, "Yùzhūlóng of this modeling was given to the chief of each village in the country area by the leader of the country after going through Hóngshān homeland-centered unified design and machining and the chief could represent the symbol of his identity and power and honor by wearing this Yùzhūlóng. In a Hóngshān country, a loose coalition relation with a certain type of the shape of a country existed between villages."

Yùshòuxíngjué (Usually referred to as Yùlóng. Classified by beasts: Yùzhūlóng. Yùxiónglóng etc.)

○ Běijīng Natonal Palace Museum British Museum. France Louvre Museum.

 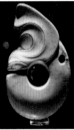 

○ Liáoníng Province Museum Excavated from Cháhǎi
○ Black skin jade culture

○ China's best Shíilóng石龍 (Stone dragon): Zuǒjiāshān左家山 Culture, Jílínshěng Nóng'ānxiàn 農安縣 (5000-4000 years ago)

■ Owned by National Museum of China. «Chángchūnrìbào長春日報» 2012,2,16.

❀ Yùniǎoxíngjué玉鳥形玦

○ 5.5x 5cm Owned by Bālínyòuqí Museum. Black skin jade culture

○ Yīn (Shāng) Guóguó虢國 Museum, http://www.guostate.com/

Rounded jade excavated from Yīnxū Fùhǎomù has the most dragon-shaped pieces among hundreds kinds of Jadeware excavated from the tomb of Fùhǎo, Queen Wǔdīng武丁 in the Yīn Dynasty.

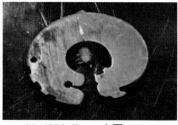

○ Beast shaped jade earrings, excavated in 1986. Shānxī山西 Museum.
○ Spring and Autumn period, excavated from Yíshuǐ沂水 Jìwánggù纪王崮, Shāndōng Museum.

2 ROUNDED JADE : THE KOREAN PENINSULA, THE JAPANESE ISLANDS

[1] Jīngjī京畿 and Zhōngqīng忠淸

Jīngjīdào京畿道 Pōzhōu坡州 area: Many kinds of Yùzhūlóng of Pōzhōu Zhōuyuèlǐ, Hóngshān Culture excavated.

Jīngjī (Gyeonggi) Province Museum Curator Lee, Hun-jae. Ornaments of the Neolithic people, Jadeware.

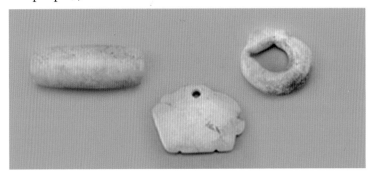

Jīngjīdào Museum Curator Lee, Hun-jae:

Yùzhūlóng is Jadeware symbolizing an animal head. Originally, Yùzhūlóng was named after 'Yùzhūlóng (Dragon and Pig) known in China Liáoníng Neolithic Age Hóngshān Culture and means 'Pig and dragon made of jade.' Jadeware in Zhōuyuèlǐ, Pōzhōu may be also included in the classification of Yùzhūlóng of Hóngshān Culture. There is a groove for a string in two places of the middle hole and the groove shape has something in common with the technique of jade products excavated from Xiǎozhūshān小株山 2nd group Ojiācūn 吳家村 in China. The shape of jadeware in Zhōuyuèlǐ, Pōzhōu is similar to that of Jadeware of Neolithic Hóngshān Culture in Liáohé Basin in Northeastern China. Hóngshān Culture belongs to the late Neolithic Age of China and is mainly distributed in Chìfēngshì in Western Liáoníngshěng.

(1) Relics excavated from stone-cists in Bǎijǐ百濟 area

<1> Zhōngqīng忠淸 Province

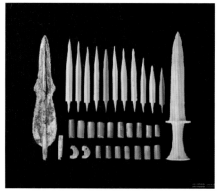

○ Fúyú Sōngjúlǐ扶餘 松菊里 (8th-10th century B.C.).

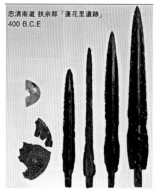

○ Fúyú Liánhuālǐ蓮花里 relics(400 BC)

⚜ Fúyú National Museum : Rounded jade, amazon stone.

⚜ Golden hood rounded jade: Golden hood rounded jade gold earrings of Bǎijǐ 百濟 Wǔníngwáng武寧王.

○ National Treasure No. 150. National Museum of Korea
○ National Treasure No. 156. Gōngzhōu National Museum
○ Jīnmào金帽 rounded jade excavated from Royal Tomb of Wǔníngwáng:

○ Quánběi Yìshān盆山 <Mílèsì彌勒寺 Pagoda bronze vessel opened> «Hánliánshè韩联社» 2010,5,26. Korea.

<2> Quánnán全南 Province

❀ Bǎochéngjiāng寶城江 basin Lìshuǐshì Peninsula:

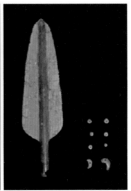

○ Liáoníng bronze-dagger, Ground stone, Jade (bronzeware 33.0cm long). Guāngzhōu National Museum. Naewoo dolmen ruins Mandolin-shaped bronze dagger in Quánnán Shùntiānshì Shēngzhōu NiúShānlǐ 全南 順天市 昇州 牛山里.

❀ Bronze rounded jade decorated with gold: Same as rounded jade decorated with gold of Tomb of Wǔníngwáng

■ «Hánliánshè韩联社» 2009,2,22.

○ Quánnán Hǎinán海南 Wànyìzhǒng萬義塚 tomb No.1.
○ Bronze rounded jade decorated with gold recently excavated from 'Hǎinán Wànyìzhǒng tomb No.1' in Hǎinánjùn海南郡, Quánnán. This rounded jade is decorated with the same gold decoration as Qūyù曲玉 (Tomb of Wǔníngwáng) decorated with gold of Bǎijǐ百濟. Rounded jade refers to crescent-shaped decorative beads. Dōngxīn東新 University Culture Museum

※ **Western Quánnán region:** Relics excavated from dolmen burying objects.

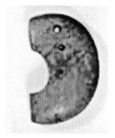

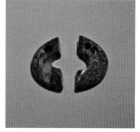

○ Língyánjùn靈巖郡 Wàngshānlǐ望山里 jade earrings(Research Center of Dolmens in Northeast Asia) Bronze Age

○ Dolmen in Yìlǎoyì一老邑, Wùānjùn務安郡

○ Rounded jade excavated from Cǎopǔlǐ草浦里, Xiánpíngjùn咸平郡. National Museum of Korea

※ **Lìshuǐshì Pyeongyeodong:**

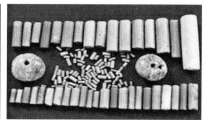

○ Group C No.2 Dolmen in Pyeongyeodong, Lìshuǐshì, rounded jade 2 pieces, xiǎoyù小玉 235 pieces, guǎnyù管玉(jades attached to the front part of a crown) 35 pieces, Assumed to be used for decorating clothes.

<3> Quánběi 全北 Province

※ **Bǎijǐ Area Yìshān益山 Mílèsì彌勒寺 Pagoda circular box 'Shàngbùdálǜmùjìn 上部達率目近' jewel box Qūyù:**

Inscription on the lid of the bronze box and internal treasure 'Shàngbùdálǜmùjìn 上部達率目近' were deciphered, It seems a jewel box.

❀ **Mǎhán馬韓 Qūyù:** Ruins in Quánzhōu全州, Quánběi全北 (Quánběi National University Museum).

Senior Researcher Professor Kim, Seung-ok (Quánběi National University) "A mounded tomb was known as a tomb of Proto-Three Kingdoms of Korea Mǎhán but Mounded Tomb return period could be readjusted because relics of early Iron Age were excavated from the bottom in this research."

○ Relics in Sangwoon-ri, Quánzhōushì全州市, Quánběi University Museum

❀ **Quánběi Gāochǎngjùn Yǎshānmiàn Fèngdélǐ 高敞郡 雅山面 鳳德里**

○ Rounded jade buried in Wàndòng 萬洞 No. 8 tomb main chamber.

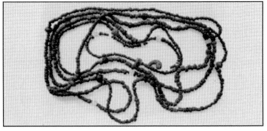

○ Rounded jade excavated from Wàndòng No. 8 tomb No. 1 pit tomb

○ Wàndòng No. 9 tomb No. 6 earthenware coffin

○ Wàndòng Zone 2 No. 5 pit tomb

☸ **Chinese Literature records**: Beads were considered more precious than gold, silver, silk.

«Sānguózhì三國志» 券30, 魏書 韓專條

"以瓔珠爲財寶 或以綴衣爲飾 或以懸頸垂耳 不以金銀繡爲珍".

«Hòuhànshū後漢書» 東夷列傳 韓條.
«Jìnshū晉書» 列傳 四夷傳 馬韓條.

It is said "The people of the Three Hans regarded beads as treasures and hung on clothes for decoration or hung them on the neck or ear but did not regard gold and silver, silk embroidery as treasure." These records are proven to be true as a large amount of jade was identified in the ruins of tombs understood as a memorial service held before the grave of Mǎhán馬韓.

☸ **Professor Im, Young-jin**: "Jade excavated in this region belongs to the Proto-Three Kingdoms of Korea so it not only tells that jade products have been made to the late period but archaeologically supports' «Hòuhànshū後漢書» Dōngyíchuán東夷傳' saying that beads were considered more precious than gold, silver, silk so they were sewn on clothes for decoration or hung on the neck or ear in Mahan Area."

■ «Hánliánshè韩联社» Bǎijǐ百濟 gilt bronze shoes were excavated from the 5th century mounded tombs. 2009,9,28

(2) Relics excavated from stone-cists in Gāyē伽倻, Xīnluó新羅 Area

<1> Qìngcháng慶尙 Province:

☸ **Lee, Hyeong-gu**:
Gāyē伽倻 Area. Yellow jade excavated from Jìnzhōu晋州 Yùfáng玉房.

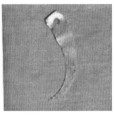

○ Golden crown excavated from Gāolíng 高靈. Around 5th-6th century. Golden crown of Gāyē Period. Height 11.5cm. National Treasure No. 138

○ Yellow jade rounded jade excavated from Jìnzhōu Yùfáng.

○ Jìnzhōu Yùfáng bronze rounded jade type decoration.

■ «The Secrets of Korea Ancient Culture Found in Bóhǎi渤海 Coast» pp.174,176, 332. Gimmyoung Publishers, 2004,7. Korea.

🕸 **Gāyē Area:** Jadeware excavated from Royal tomb-grade large wood coffin tomb
■ «Hánliánshè韩联社» 2012.8.8

○ JīnguānGāyē 金冠伽倻 Ancient Tombs around 4th century. Jadeware excavated from Qìngnán Jīnhǎishì Dàchéngdòng 慶南 金海市 大成洞 (left).

○ Smithsonian Museum Freer Gallery. 10.4cm (right)

🕸 **Xīnluó新羅 Area Qūyù:** Xīnluó's ruìzhì叡智 that overturned the Japan origin theory. «Jīngxiāngxīnwén京鄕新聞» 1976,8,3. Korea.

Jīnmào金帽 Qūyù(Gokok). Excavated from Qìngzhōu慶州 Jīnlíngzhǒng金玲塚. National Museum of Korea

○ A unique shape of combining Bóhǎi Coast Qūyù culture and gold culture of Xīnluó. Lee, Hyeong-gu «The Secrets of Korea Ancient Culture» 2012.12.27. Saenyok Publisher. Korea.

○ Gold hood rounded jade excavated from Qìngzhōu Jīnlíngzhǒng金玲塚 (Life size in the article content). National Museum of Korea.

❧ Qūyù (Gokok) golden crown:

 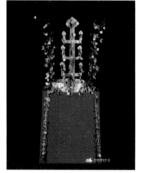

○ Tiānmǎzhǒng天馬冢 golden crown 6th century. National Treasure No. 188

○ Jīnguānzhǒng金冠塚 golden crown, 27.5cm National Treasure No. 87

❧ Qūyù(Gokok): Xīnluó Area. Qìngzhōushì慶州市.

  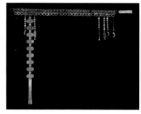

○ Qìngzhōu Lùxīdòng 路西洞 gold necklace, Length 16.8㎝, Weight 35.6g.

○ Qìngzhōu Huáng-chéngdòng 隍城洞

○ Southern mound of Huángnándàzhǒng皇南大塚. Gold belt. 33.2cm National Treasure No. 194. Gold necklace.

○ 41.6㎝. Huángnándàzhǒng Qìngzhōu.
○ Tiānmǎzhǒng Total length 64.0 ㎝ (Right)

(3) Relics excavated from stone-cists in Jǐzhōu濟州 Island:

❀ **Qūyù(Gokok):** Unified Xīnluó Jewelry excavated from Jǐzhōushì濟州市.

○ Jǐzhōushì Digital Jǐzhōu Grand Culture

Qūyù identified in Jǐzhōu Island is divided into glass·earth·agalmatolite·stone depending on materials. Glass Qūyù was excavated from Guōzhī郭支 shell mound 5th district. The size of this Qūyù is 3㎝ long and head diameter is 1.5×1.7㎝ and the color is jade green. Of Qūyù types excavated from ancient tombs of the Three Kingdoms period, the type of this Qūyù is a relatively classic type and three carved lines are carved in the head. Earth Qūyù was made as a substitute for glass Qūyù. 4 pieces of agalmatolite Qūyù were excavated from Gāonèilǐ高內里 ruins of the 8th~9th century. Stone Qūyù was excavated from Sānyángdòng三陽洞 ruins and the length is less than 3cm. This stone Qūyù corresponds to the first century BC, the earliest period among Qūyù. Except earth, glass or agalmatolite Qūyù is not from Jǐzhōu Island. Like money excavated from Shāndìgǎng山地港, these Qūyù are determined to be elite grave goods as the products of foreign exchange.

❀ **Qūyù (Gokok):** Smithsonian Museum Freer Gallery. Using Korean names.

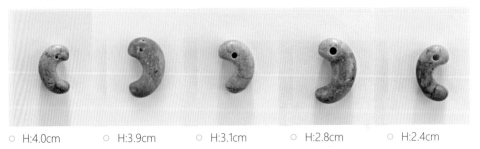

| ○ H:4.0cm | ○ H:3.9cm | ○ H:3.1cm | ○ H:2.8cm | ○ H:2.4cm |

■ http://www.asia.si.edu/collections/

[2] Mǔzǐqūyù母子曲玉: Attached Qūyù (Gokok).

Related to the birth of new life.

○ Excavated from No. 4 dolmen in Quánnán Shùntiānshì Sōngguǎngmiàn Yuèshānlǐ. Owned by National Shùntiān University Museum.

○ Lee, Geum-hwa«Black Skin Jade» p.37, Pan Hóngshān Culture Lee Geum-hwa Gallery, 2014. Korea.

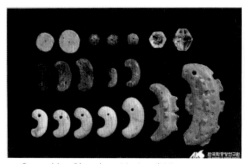

○ Owned by Qìngzhōu National Museum
○ Owned by National Shùntiān University Museum: Bǎijǐ百濟. Length 8.5cm.
○ Pagodite. Excavated from No.3 settlement in Lóngjiānglǐ龍江里 Guāngyáng光陽

❀ Bǎijǐ Mǔzǐqǔyù母子曲玉: Connected with prehistoric Qūyù (Gokok).

In particular, attached Qūyù (Mǔzǐqǔyù) draws attention in Qūyù of Bǎijǐ. This is made by attaching a couple of smaller rounded jade to the surface of rounded jade. Such rounded jade has been considered to be Japan's specialty because a lot of talc was found in the ruins of the period of ancient burial mounds of Japan but it was proved that attached Qūyù was made also in Korea because

1 talc rounded jade was recently found in Fúyú 扶餘 and there is also reporting about excavation in Qìngnán慶南. On the other hand, 2 small rounded jades of 2.2cm made of Tiānhéshí (天河石: amazon stone were excavated from the Sōngpíngdòng松坪洞 ruins of Xiánběi Xióngjī 咸北 雄基 and it is implied that they are the original shape of rounded jade in the Three Kingdoms era because both of them have one hole in the head.

And Yìngyùzhì硬玉製 rounded jade carving was found in Kuīyánmiàn窺岩面, Fúyú, Zhōngnán and Juéxíng玦形 rounded jade was also excavated from stone-cists near Fúyú. This was also found in a stone grave of the Bronze Age in Eastern Mǎnzhōu滿洲 Jílínshěng, China so rounded jade of the ancient tomb period mentioned in the above is assumed to be connected with rounded jade of prehistoric times. Only 5, 6 pieces were found in Korea and the findspot of the cases found in Jūnshǒulǐ軍守里, Fúyú, Zhōngnán, near Jìnzhōu, Shùntiān is only confirmed. Things found in Shùntiān were found in the lower dolmen and this shows that dolmen, the tomb of the Bronze Age became the target of a kind of ceremonial conduct during the period of the Three States.

3 THE JAPANESE ISLANDS

Southwest of Japanese archipelago - Southwest of Korean Peninsula - China Shāndōng Peninsula Línzī臨淄

Shānkǒuxiàn山口県 (Yamaguchiken) Tǔjǐngbāng土井が浜 Doigahama ruins (2300-2000 years ago Míshēngshídài 弥生時代).

○ Human bones buried in the direction of Xiǎngtān響灘 (Hibikinada) (Museum of Anthropology)

[1] Japanese archipelago:

🌀 **Three kinds of Shénqì三種の神器**: The oldest Three Sacred Treasures of Japan. Rounded jade+bronze sword+bronze mirror.

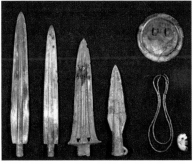

○ Excavated from Fúgāngxiàn Jíwǔgāomù 福岡県 吉武高木 Fukuokaken yoshitake ruins. Jiǔzhōu九州 (Kyushu) National Museum http://www.kyuhaku.jp.

○ Lǎosī老司 ancient tomb No.3 stone chamber around Fúgāng福岡 Píngyě平野.

○ Fúgāngshì福岡市 Museum Yayoi弥生 period (2nd century BC)

'Jade' among 'Three kinds of Shénqì' of Japanese imperial family is Bāchǐqióng八尺瓊 Gōuyù勾玉(まがたまMagatama). This is, it is Gōuyù (=Qūyù 曲玉). C-shaped rounded jade appeared from the mid-Shéngwén繩文 (Jomon) Period. It is guessed that hunting people carried a stone in their body, being afraid of the soul of animals or fish and thinking they wanted to protect themselves by the power of the Holy Spirit. It was changed to Gōuyù (=Qūyù) and materials are jewelry such as jade . agate . crystal etc. and the shape was also complicated. Entering the period of ancient burial mounds, it became the symbol of an authority. That is why it may have been one of 'Three kinds of Shénqì'. Three kinds of Shénqì are Jìng鏡 . Yù玉 . Jiàn劍 but many of them have been excavated as grave goods from Gǔfén古墳 (ancient tombs), the tombs of ancient king or royal family, heads. Finally, those valuably inherited by the Japanese emperor family are those cherished by the kings of ancient Japan.

(1) Jiǔzhōu 九州 (Kyushu) Area

<1> Fúgāngxiàn 福岡縣(Hukuokaken) Chūnrìshì Xūjiǔgāngběn 春日市 須玖岡本 Kasugashi Sukuokamoto ruins (The largest producing area in the same period)

🌀 Núguówángmù奴國王墓 Dolmen: Three kinds of Shénqì 三種の神器 Jìng鏡 . Yù玉 . Jiàn劍, original shape excavated.

○ Dolmen called as the top seat of 'Wángmù王墓'

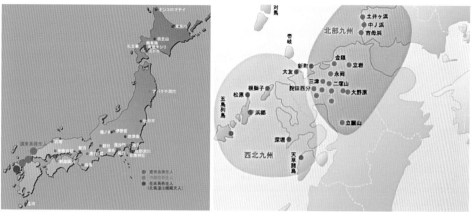

●渡來係 弥生人 ●中間形 弥生人 ●在來係 弥生人(北海道 續繩文人)

■ Japan's National Museum of Nature and Science http://www.kahaku.go.jp/

🌀 Jíwǔgāomù 吉武高木 (yoshitake) ruins: Yayoi弥生 2nd century BC
Excavated from Fúgāngxiàn Jíwǔgāomù (Fukuokaken yoshitake) ruins.
The oldest Three Sacred Treasures of Japan.

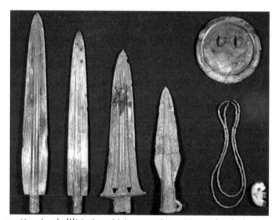

○ Kyushu九州National Museum http://www.kyuhaku.jp.

○ Mǔzǐqūyù母子曲玉: Attached Qūyù (Gokok) excavated from Fúgāngxiàn Jíwǔgāomù (Fukuokaken yoshitake) ruins.

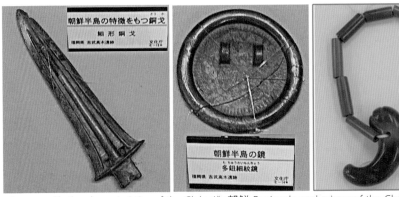

○ Copper with the characteristics of the Cháoxiǎn朝鮮 Peninsula and mirror of the Cháoxiǎn Peninsula.

○ Owned by Jiāoshì 萩市 (hagishi) Museum. Yuánguāngsì 円光寺 (Enkouji) ancient tomb, about 30m in diameter, assumed to be a round shape tomb built in the mid and late 6th century.

○ 4 pieces of rounded jade, 1 bugle, 2 earrings and 3 handles of a sword with round pommel are present.

○ Lǎosī 老司 Rouji ancient tomb No.3 stone chamber around Fúgāngxiàn plain area. Fúgāng 福岡市 (Fúgāngshi) Museum

<2> Xióngběnxiàn 熊本縣 (Kumamotoken). Zuǒhèxiàn 佐賀県 (Sagaken)

○ Excavated from Xióngběnxiàn (Kumamotoken) Jiāngtián 江田 (Eda) Chuánshān 船山 (Hunayama) ancient tomb, glass rounded jade (Japanese period of ancient burial mounds 5~6th century)

○ Important cultural property designated by Zuǒhèxiàn (Sagaken), Yīwànlǐshi伊万里市 (Imarishi). Excavated from Qiánguī錢亀 (Zenigame) ancient tomb. History and Folk Reference Center.

✿ Lùérdǎoxiàn 鹿兒島縣 (Kagoshimaken). Chōngshéng 沖繩 (Okinawa).

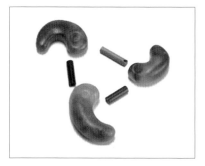

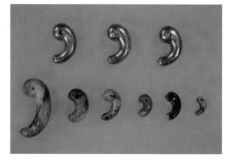

○ Left: Lùérdǎoxiàn (Kagoshimaken) Lùwūshì鹿屋市 (kanoyashi) Gāngqí岡崎 Okazaki Ancient Tombs. Period of ancient burial mounds Gōuyù and bugle excavated.

○ Okinawa Shàngshì尚氏 (Shousi) 1st, 2nd Royal line. Gold, jade, glass rounded jade. Japanese National Treasure, important cultural property

(2) Běnzhōu本州 (Honshu) Xīnánbù西南部

<1> Shānkǒuxiàn山口県 (Yamaguchiken)

1. Tǔjǐngbāng土井が浜 (Doigahama) ruins: Shānkǒuxiàn (Yamaguchiken) 2300-2000 years ago, Míshēng弥生 (Yayoi) period.

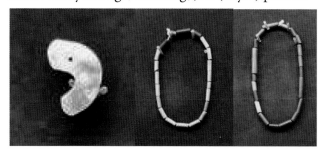

2. Shānkǒuxiàn (Yamaguchiken) Língluómùxiāng綾羅木郷 (Ayaragigo) ruins: XiàguānshìlìKǎogǔbówùguǎn下關市立考古博物館

Resources of Tokyo National Museum: Exchange between Southern Korean Peninsula and Japanese archipelago (bronzeware. patternless earthenware. yùlèi 玉類) proved. Míshēng (Yayoi) Culture of the west end of Běnzhōu (Honshu)

特集陳列
本州最西端の弥生文化 —響灘と山口・綾羅木郷遺跡—
Thematic Exhibition
Yayoi Culture at the Westernmost Point of Honshu:
The Hibikinada Area and the Ayaragigo Site in Yamaguchi Prefecture
10月29日[火]—2014年3月9日[日]
平成館1F 考古展示室
HEISEIKAN 1F Japanese Archaeology Gallery

❀ Guǎngdǎoxiàn広島県 (Hiroshimaken). Shānkǒuxiàn 山口県 (Yamaguchiken).

○ Guǎngdǎoshì広島市 (Hiroshimashi) Important Tangible Cultural Property. Excavated from Anyúnqū Chuányuèxīngōng 安芸区 船越 新宮 ancient tomb.

○ Tangible cultural property designated by Shānkǒuxiàn (Yamaguchiken). Excavated from Yuánguāngsì (Enkouji) ancient tomb.

(2) Běnzhōu 本州 (Honshu) Běibù北部

<1> Excavated from Běihǎidào 北海道 (Hokkaido) Area: Mid Shéngwén繩文 Period (7000-6000 years ago)

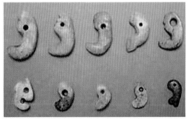

○ Shéngwén (Jomon) Period Lónglǐ 滝里 (Takisato) ruins group (About 2300 years ago) excavated.

○ Tangible cultural property designated by Lúbiéshì 芦別市 (Ashibetsushi) No.67.

○ Excavated from Gōngchéngxiàn Shàngchuānmíngbèizhǒng 宮城縣 上川名貝塚 Miyagiken kamikawana kaizuka. Manager of Dōngběidàxué 東北大學 (Tohokuuniversity)

(3) Běnzhōu 本州 (Honshu) zhōngbù中部

<1> Guāndōng 關東 (Kanto) Area:

1. Dōngjīng 東京 (Tokyo). Héngbāng 横浜 (Yokohama)

○ Excavated from Tokyo 北區 田端 不動坂 Ki-daku Tabata Hudouzaka ruins.

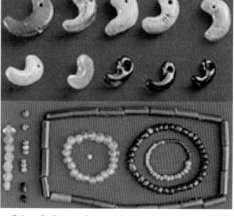

○ Excavated from Héngbāng (Yokohama)

○ Qúnmǎxiàn Ānzhōngshì Liānglàièrzǐzhǒng 群馬県 安中市 簗瀬二子塚 Gunmaken Annakashi Yanasehutagotsuka Ancient Tomb (Early 6th century)

2. Shānlíxiàn Díchuīshì 山梨県 笛吹市 Yamanasiken Fuefukishi
Jìnggāngxiàn 静岡県 (Shizuokaken). Shānxíngxiàn 山形県 (Yamagataken)

○ Díchuīshì笛吹市 (Fuefukishi) Period of ancient burial mounds (Late 6th century)

○ Jìnggāngxiàn (Shizuokaken) 浜松市 Hamamatsushi Museum. Late period of ancient burial mounds.

○ Shānxíngxiàn (Yamagataken) 羽山 Hayama ancient tomb.

○ Higashiokitamagun Takahatamachi 東置賜郡高畠町, 6-7th century, 安久津Akutsu ancient tombs

■ Shānlíxiàn Díchuīshì (Yamanasiken Fuefukishi) Burial Cultural Center Report Vol.175, 2000.

3. Cultural assets designated by Qíyùxiàn Xiónggǔshì 埼玉県 熊谷 市 (Saitamaken Kumagayashi).

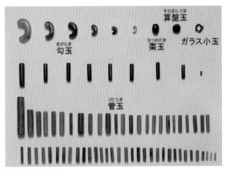

○ Xióngyě 熊野 (Kumano) Shrine ancient tomb built Late 4th century, Qíyùxiàn (Saitamaken) History and Folk Museum

○ Ancient decorative beads Zhùxíng鑄型, original shape excavated. Qíyùxiàn (Saitamaken) Běnzhuāngshì本庄市 (Honjoshi).

■ Glass small jade mold excavated. 7th century, Fēiniǎo飛鳥 (Asuka) period «Asahishinbun 朝日新聞» 2013,5,29. Japan.

<2> Guānxī 關西 (Kansai) Area:

1. Nàiliáng 奈良 (Nara) Basin: Qūyù曲玉, Míshēng (Yayoi) period.

○ Qūyù and pottery carving taken from the limonite container

○ Míshēng (Yayoi) period largest rounded jade. Length 4.64cm. Length 3.63cm.

Japan Karago唐古．Kagi鍵 ruins, Míshēng (Yayoi) period largest Qūyù: Possessions of priest class. Rounded jade contained in the Hètiěkuàng褐鐵鑛 (Limonite) container found in 2001 from Karago唐古．Kagi鍵 ruins located almost in the center of Nari Basin in Japan was found to be the largest jade product of Míshēng (Yayoi) Period. One rounded jade is 4.64cm. The 10th largest in the country as a Míshēng (Yayoi) period jade product. Another piece is small, 3.63cm long but has clear green sheen and turned out to be good quality jade.

TaharaHoncho田原本町 Education Committee thinks <We do not know why they put it in the limonite but it may be a possession of the priest class>. The limonite container was excavated from the ditch in the vicinity of the building group shown as the center of a community. Turned out to be a thing of the first century BC.

2. Hégēshānxiàn Hégēshānshì 和歌山県 和歌山市 (Wakayamaken Wakaya-mashi) : Gold Qūyù (Jīnzhìgōuyù金製勾玉).

- 1.8cm. Middle period of ancient burial mounds.
- Cultural Heritage designated by Hégēshānxiàn (Wakaya-maken). Japan's only gold Qūyù. Assumed to be relics handed down from outside. Excavated from Chējiàzhīgǔzhǐ 車駕之古址 (Shakanokoshi) Ancient Tomb
- Whole length 86m Keyhole-shaped Burial Mounds.

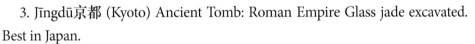

- Excavated from Jīngdūfǔ Zhīyuán 京都府 芝ケ原 (Kyotofu Hagahara) ancient tomb (Late Yayoi period-Early period of ancient burial mounds 3rd century) Owned by Chéngyáng-shì城陽市 (Joyoshi) Education Committee

3. Jīngdū京都 (Kyoto) Ancient Tomb: Roman Empire Glass jade excavated. Best in Japan.

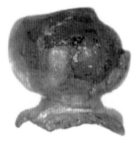

1mm

- Zhòngcéng重層 glass jade excavated from Yǔjīnjiǔzhì宇津久志 (Utukushi) No.1 ancient tomb, found to be the same ingredients as that manufactured in the Roman Empire territory.

Chánggāngjīngshì長岡京市 (Nagaokakyoshi) Burial Cultural Center and Nara Cultural Heritage Institute announced on 21st that 3 pieces excavated from Yǔjīnjiǔzhì (Utukushi) No.1 ancient tomb (the former of 5th century) located in Jīngdū (Kyoto) Chánggāngjīngshì (Nagaokakyoshi), layered glass jade turned out to have the same ingredients as the one manufactured in the Roman Empire territory in the 1-4th century. It is the best in Korea as layered glass. A researcher Tamura田村朋美 at Nàiliáng (Nara) Cultural Heritage Institute said, "layered glass jade of the same period was found also in southern China and tere is also a possibility that it was passed down to Japan by sea." Yǔjīnjiǔzhì (Utukushi) No.1 ancient tomb is a square tomb with one side of 7m and 3 pieces of layered glass jade of 5mm in the maximum diameter were excavated with grave goods such as bugle in 1988 but elemental analysis was not performed. «Asahishinbun朝日新聞» 2012,11,17, Japan.

4. Dàbǎnfǔ Téngjǐngsìshì 大阪府 藤井寺市 (Osakafu Hujiiterashi)

○ Téngsēn藤の森 (Hujinomori) ancient tomb corridor-style stone chamber (late 5th century)

5. Dǎogēnxiàn島根県 (Shimaneken). Gāngshānxiàn岡山県 (Okayamaken)

 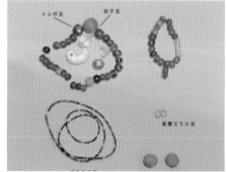

○ Dǎogēnxiànlì gǔdài Chūyún 島根県立古代出雲 History Museum.

○ Okryu excavated from Zhǒngduàn塚段 (Tsukanodan) ancient tomb Owned by Gāngshānshì岡山市 (Okayamashi) Burial Cultural Center

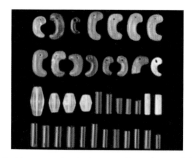

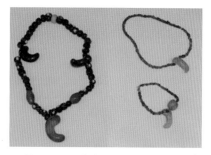

○ Excavated from Jīnshānshì Wěishíshēnggǔkǒu 津山市 尾石生谷口 Tsuyama Muroyishudanikuchi ancient tomb.

○ Excavated from Wánzishān丸子山 Marukoyama ancient tomb. Aochūyúnduōgēn 奧出雲多根 (Okuizumotane) Nature Museum

6. Fújǐngxiàn Jīnjīntǐng Sāngyě 福井県 金津町 桑野 (Fukuiken Kanazucho kuwano)

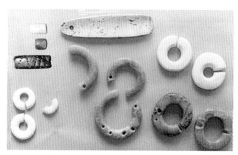

○ Early-end Shéngwén 繩文 (Jomon) Period - former period (6000 years ago)
○ Téngtiánshìfū藤田士夫 (Hujita): Argued that Japan Shéngwén (Jomon) Period and Liángzhǔ 良渚 Culture jade culture Yùjué玉玦 of China Yángzǐ River downstream are connected.

■ Edited by Nàiliáng 奈良 Nara Cultural Heritage Institute 《Rìběnkǎogǔxué日本の考古學》學生社, 2005,12.

7. Qífùxiàn Hángjīsì 岐阜県 行基寺 (Gifuken Gyokiji): Jìng鏡, Qūyù曲玉, Guǎnyù 管玉 etc. excavated. Hǎijīnshì 海津市 (Kaizushi) Tangible Cultural Property Qífùxiàn Hǎijīnshì Hángjīsì (Gifuken Kaizushi Gyokiji) ancient tomb(End of 4th century).

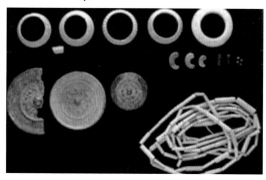

8. Chángyěxiàn長野県 (Nagano Prefecture).

Niǎoqǔxiàn鳥取縣 (Tottori Prefecture)

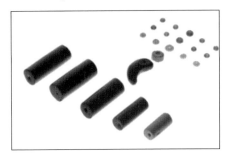

Excavated from Guǐfǔ鬼釜 (Onigama) ancient tomb, Fàntiánshì Shàngjiǔjiān 飯田市 上久堅 (Iidashi Kamihisakata)

⚜ Zōufǎngshì yìshíbǎn 諏訪市 一時坂 (Suwashi Ittokizaka) ancient tomb (Period of ancient burial mounds) Zōufǎngshì (Suwashi) Museum.

Niǎoqǔxiàn (Tottoriken) Burial Cultural Center

[2] Mǔzǐqūyù母子曲玉: Attached Qūyù (Gokok). Related to the birth of new life.

(1) Shénnàichuānxiàn神奈川県 (Kanagawaken)

○ Shénnàichuānxiàn Xiāngmóyuánshì Shèngbǎnyǒulùgǔ 神奈川県 相模原市 勝坂 有鹿谷 (Kanagawaken Sagamihar-asi Katsusaka Arukatani) Memorial relics.

○ Mǔzǐqūyù excavated from Qúnmǎxiàn Sānsì群馬縣 三ツ寺 (Gunmaken Mitsu-dera) ruins: The late fifth century

○ Length 10.2cm. Owned by Qúnmǎxiàn (Gunmaken) Burial Cultural Center. About 80m Square ancient tomb. Large talc.

○ Known to be relics excavated from Méilín 梅林 (Bailin)

(2) Excavated from Bīngkùxiàn 兵庫県 (Hyogoken), Nàiliángxiàn 奈良県 (Naraken):

○ Bīngkùxiànlì兵庫県立 Archeological Museum. Im-portant cultural property designated by prefecture.
○ Artifacts of Nándànlùshì Zhìzhīchuān Yǔliú 南淡路市 志知川 雨流 (Minamiawajisi Shichikawa uryu) ruins

○ Yīngjǐngshì Sōngzhīběn 桜井市 松之本 (Sakuraisi Matsunomoto) ruins (late 6th century-early 7th century).

(3) Jīngdū 京都 (Kyoto). Aizhīxiàn愛知県 (Aichiken)

○ Jīngdū (Kyoto) Burial Culture Research Center. www.kyotofu-maibun.or.jp
○ Chíkāo 池尻 Jigo ruins (Late 6th century), Mǔzǐqūyù (late 5th century) excavated.

○ Excavated from Báishí白石 (Shiroishi) ruins. Excavated from Bǎoměibèizhǒng保美貝塚 (Hobigaitsuka). Fēngqiáoshì豊橋市美術博物館(Toyohashisi) Artmuseum, Middle period of ancient burial mounds (About 5th century)

[3] Yùzhàng 玉權杖: Recommended.

○ Excavated from Nàiliángxiàn (Naraken) Ancient Tomb.

○ Important cultural property long jasper product Zhàngxíng Bìyùzhìpǐn 杖形 碧玉製品 28.7cm. Period of ancient burial mounds 4th century.
○ Known to be Sānchóngxiàn 三重縣 Mieken artifacts. Tokyo National Museum

○ Yīngjǐng Chájiùshān 桜井 茶臼山 (Sakurai Chausuyama) Ancient Tomb. Nàiliángxiàn Chájiùshān (Naraken Sakurai) Burial Mounds.

[4] Jadeware excavated historic sites:

Ruins, ancient tombs in Jiǔzhōu 九州 Kyushu Area http://www.netpia.jp

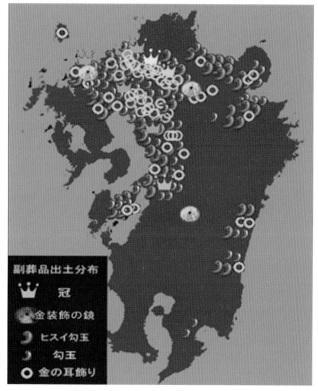

○ Green: Fěicuìgōuyù翡翠勾玉 (HisuiMagatama)
○ Red: Gōuyù勾玉 (Magatama). Rounded jade.
○ Yellow: Gold earrings decoration.

3 GUĪ圭 (=HÙ笏)

[1] Guī圭 (=Hù笏)

❀ **Hù笏**: Cultural Heritage Administration www.cha.go.kr

Hù is a thing held in their hands when servants meet the king and 1st rank to 4th rank held Hù made of ivory and 5th rank to 9th rank held Hù made of wood. It was originally used to record king's teachings or writings offered to the king and not to forget them but was institutionalized for simple courtesy later. Hù was kept by 1st rank to 4th rank and one point is 24㎝ in length, 5㎝ in width and blue Yúnwénsī雲紋絲 was put around the handle. The other point is 30.5㎝ in length, 4㎝ in width and the upper part is slightly round and the handle is wrapped with blue satin.

❀ **Guī圭**: Long bar type, top triangle, bottom angle type.

lǐqì礼器 (ritual vessels) during Cháopìn, ancestral rites, funeral rites of Chinese ancient aristocrats. Aristocrat and plebeian hierarchy depending on the size.

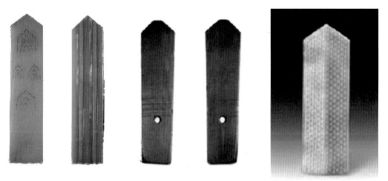

○ Mountain shape shuānggǔwén双谷紋 Guī. Míng明 Dìnglíng定陵

❀ Yángbǎidá (Chinese Cultural Relics Society Jadeware Research Committee) <巫·玉·神简论> 2006,11,8.

In the archeology, the Lóngshān龍山 Period was a turning point of shamanism, jade, god. Wū巫 just helped the king to destroy one old system and things and furthermore, the king took away priesthood, regime, zōngquán 宗權, military right and reduced people in the divine position at the same time. Accordingly, the king replaced Cóng琮, Bì璧 as Guī, Zhāng璋 and Shénshì神事 of Wū, YùShénqì玉神器 also disappeared. Since the end of prehistoric times, "Dì帝 (Wǔdì五帝)" has ruled the priesthood era reigned by Wū巫 but it entered into the kinghood era when not called as king all the time. This period were just a step away from the civiliaztion age.

■ Yángbǎidá <tǒngyīgédiàodeXià,Shāng,XīzhōuYùwénhuà统一格调的夏,商,西周玉文化> 2007,1,19.

«Zhōulǐ周礼 Chūnguān春官·Dàzōngbó大宗伯» : "We made six jade with jade and used them as Bāngguó邦國. The king had Zhènguī鎮圭, Huánguī桓圭 as Gōng公, Xìnguī信圭 as Hóu侯, Gōngguī躬圭 as Bó伯, Gǔbì谷璧 as Zǐ子, Púbì蒲璧 as Nán男". "By making six vessels with jade, we showed courtesy to the world everywhere. We showed courtesy with Cāngbì蒼璧, Huángcóng黃琮, Qīngguī青圭, Chìzhāng赤璋, Báihǔ白琥, Xuánhuáng玄璜 for sky, land, east, south, west, north, respectively.

(1) Gǔcháoxiǎn 古朝鮮 (Gojoseon) Guī圭

<1> Mandolin-shaped jade dagger:

Hóngshān Culture stone cists (Consistent with Gǔcháoxiǎn (Gojoseon) Mandolin-shaped bronze dagger distribution area).

■ <The fifth Civiliazation, Go to Liáohé遼河> «KBS-TV» History Special, 2009,8,29. Korea.

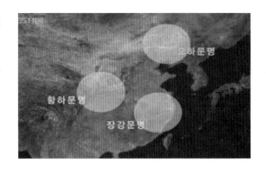

○ Stone graves (Shímù石墓) distribution map of Bóhǎi渤海 Coast «The Secrets of Korea Ancient Culture» p.95. Gimm-Young Publishers,2004,7.Korea.

○ Donga.com http://news.donga.com 2008,3,10. Korea.

❧ **Mandolin-shaped jade dagger excavated**: Hóngshān Civilization associated with the Korean Peninsula.

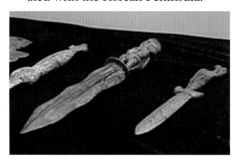

❧ **Original form of Mandolin-shaped bronze dagger**:

The central dàmù大墓 of the westernmost 16th point in the Niúhéliáng ruins, this place is especially characterized by shaman dolls and Phoenix made of jade. The amazing thing is Mandolin-shaped dagger made of jade was also found. In the meantime, scholars have wondered how the mandolin shape of Mandolin-shaped bronze dagger totally different from China's bronze dagger appears in the bronze dagger of Dōngyí東夷 and as the mandolin shape is discovered in jadeware of Hóngshān Culture, it can be seen that the mandolin shape did not occur suddenly and was significantly stamped on Hóngshān people also in the Hóngshān Culture period.

■ <The Home of Korean, 'Mysterious Kingdom' was found> (12). December 19, 2007 «Science Times» http://www.sciencetimes.co.kr. Korea.

❀ Mandolin-shaped bronze dagger made of jade found.

Especially noteworthy things are the ruins of Bronze Age Culture. Mandolin-shaped bronze dagger made of jade was also found. The common requirements for the ancient nation establishment that archaeologists say are fortress, city existence, palace, large tombs, bronze weapons etc. and most of them are prepared. Therefore, saying that 'history is science', Korean evidential historians have denied Gǔcháoxiǎn (Gojoseon) because there is no bronze culture. Now, this consumptive debate does not have a value any more.

■ «Qìngběiríbào慶北日報» 2009,11,2. Korea.

❀ <The fifth Civiliazation, Go to Liáohé遼河>

■ «KBS-TV» History Special, 2009,8,29.

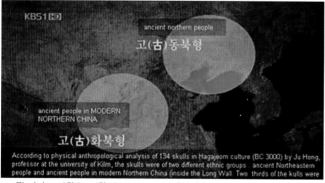

○ Zhūhóng (China Jílín University): Xiàjiādiàn Lower Culture remains (134 pieces: 5000 years ago)

Human bone constitutional anthropological analysis: Old Northeast type 2/3 or more. We tried the constitutional anthropological analysis of 134 human bones from Xiàjiādiàn Lower Culture. According to the research findings, they were largely divided into two tribes and the old Northeast type around Liáohé civilization was found to account for more than 2/3.

The professor Bok, Gi-dae (University of Brain Education Department of

Korean Studies): More than 60% of ancients in the Liáoxī遼西 area are the old Northeast type affinitive with Koreans. "It seems right to think that the ancient culture of the Liáoxī area was established by Korean ancestors and Korean ethic groups."

    * The professor Bok, Gi-dae argues that Inner Mongolia Xīnglónggōu興隆溝 figure statue shows a high cultural level of the northern race who entered the national phase earlier than the Chinese Hàn漢 Dynasty. He explains, "A figure statue newly found in Xīnglónggōu in recent years received the major attention of Chinese academics but this was made in the late Hóngshān Culture which was in fashion in the driest period and is clearly the unique culture of the northern people." He also argues "This figure statue showing a practicing powerful man strongly suggests that he must have been a being like Tánjūn Wángjiǎn 檀君王儉 (Dangun Wanggeom) of Gǔcháoxiǎn (Gojoseon) in the future combining the roles of a chief priest and secular powerful man."

■ «jiàoshòuxīnwén教授新聞» 2012,9,24. Korea.

<2> Fax ax (Shànxíngtóngfǔ扇形銅斧)

Mandolin-shaped bronze dagger and Qūyù曲玉 are excavated together. Distributed around Liáoníngshěng.

  ○ Excavated from Jiāngyuándào Shùcǎoshì Cháoyángdòng 江原道 束草市 朝陽洞.

■ «National Museum of Korea»

  ♲ Fax ax <Shànxíngtóngfǔ>

■ «Doosan Encyclopedia»

Bronze axes are divided into fax axes with the fanwise head part and rectangular bronze axes showing overall rectangle but fax axes are typical and are excavated with Mandolin-shaped bronze dagger. These special types of axes are distributed around Liáoníngshěng and most of them are found in the ruins of Mandolin-shaped bronze dagger Culture. They are excavated in large quantities in Cháoyáng Shí'èrtáiyíngzǐ 十二臺營子, Jǐnxī 錦西 Wūjīntáng 烏金塘, Shěnyáng Zhèngjiāwāzǐ 鄭家窪子, Liáoyáng 遼陽 èrdàohézǐ 二道河子, Dàlián 大連 Lóushàng 樓上 and casts (Róngfàn 鎔范) were found in èrdàohézǐ·Gǎngshàng 崗上. Korean fax axes seem to have been produced under the influence of Liáoníngshěng Bronze Age Culture because Měisōnglǐ 美松里 (Misongri)· Yǒngxīngyì 永興邑 (Yeongheungeup) ruins etc. in Korea show the similar nature to Bronze Age culture of Liáoníngshěng. Fax ax middle and old bronze axes are exported with Mandolin-shaped bronze dagger so the period can be generally compared to the former Bronze Age.

<3> Gǔcháoxiǎn (Gojoseon) King Zhǔn 準 (Jun): Granted 圭 to Wèimǎn 衛 滿 (Wiman).

■ «Sānguózhì 三國志» Wèishū 魏書 Dōngyíchuán 東夷傳 Hán 韓

Wèilüè 魏略 said: As the Hàn 漢 Dynastiy appointed Lúwǎn 盧綰 as Yānwáng 燕王, Cháoxiǎn 朝鮮 determined Xiùshuǐ 溴水 as the border with Yān 燕. As Lúwǎn betrayed Hàn 漢 and went to the Xiōngnú 匈奴, a Yān person Wèimǎn 衛滿 sought asylum and wore Húfú 胡服 and crossed Xiùshuǐ eastward and went to Zhǔnwáng 準王 to surrender and said, "If you let me live in the Western border, I will use those who came from the country of Zhōngyuán 中原 to seek asylum as the fence of Cháoxiǎn" and Zhǔnwáng believed and cherished Wèimǎn and appointed him as Bóshì 博士 and gave the land of 100 lǐ 里 as fief while giving Guī 圭 and ordered him to protect the western border well.

魏略曰：及漢以盧綰臺陌王, 朝鮮與燕界於 浿水. 及綰反, 入匈奴, 燕人衛滿亡命, 爲胡服, 東度浿水, 詣準降, 說準求居西界, 中國亡命爲朝鮮藩屏.準信寵之, 拜爲博士, 賜以圭, 封之百里, 令守西邊.

■ «Source: National History Compilation Committee Korean History Database http://db.history.go.kr»

☸ **Gǔcháoxiǎn (Gojoseon) Guī 圭 Gyu:** Zhèngyínpǔ鄭寅普 衛滿亂 Wèimǎnluàn <Sprit> of Cháoxiǎn for five thousand years.

"He did not permit only what he requested. He favored him so much and appointed him as Bóshì博士 and gave the land of 100 lǐ里 as fief while giving Guī and ordered him to protect the western border well."

<Sprit> of Wǔqiānniánjiān Cháoxiǎn

This is the historical record through which you can see the process of Zhǔnwáng準王 of Gǔcháoxiǎn (Gojoseon) accepting the asylum of Wèimǎn and the late Cháoxiǎn situation. In fact, however, we have missed a crucial description because of interest with a focus on the history about the dynasty replacement around political history. It is the part "giving Guī as a faith object" and is the historical fact that although facing the end of the dynasty, Zhǔnwáng of Gǔcháoxiǎn (Gojoseon) gives Guī made of 'jade'. The author's stance is that it is necessary to examine 'jade' Guī圭 appearing in the process of overcoming a national crisis situation of Gǔcháoxiǎn (Gojoseon) at that time in the historical continuum of 'jade culture' rather than limiting it to mere political act or policy means.

■ «Dōngyàrìbào東亞日報» 1935,3,3. Korea.

328 |

<4> Gāojùlì 高句麗 (Goguryeo) Guī圭 (=Hù笏)

❀ **Hébó-Zhūméng shénhuà** 河伯-朱蒙 神話: Later Hàn漢 Shāndōngshěng Wǔliángcí武梁祠 Huàxiàngshí畫像石. Hù笏(=Guī圭)

■ Jeong, Jae-seo «Angtti-Oedipus's Mythology» pp.178-179, Changbi. 2010,9. Korea.

○ Procession of Hébó or Hǎishén海神. Hòuhàn後漢 Huándì桓帝 Built in about 148.

Looking at Huàxiàngshí, a god assumed to be Hébó or Hǎishén rides a wagon led by three fish with holding a whip. A person in front of the wagon greets the wagon with holding Hù and kneeling down and one person behind the wagon sees off the wagon politely with holding Hù. In the front and left and right of the wagon, warriors riding fish escort him with holding arms of a spear type and many fish are following around the wagon. In addition, beasts of gǒukē狗科 system are chasing behind wagon and people of a mermaid type with fish fin are swimming behind it. Unlike previous emperor or Tàirìshén太日神, escorting by fish, mermaid and warriors riding fish is distinctive like the procession of Hébó or Hǎishén, the ruler of the underwater world. Through this picture, we can imagine one scene of Zhūméng Myth. A story that when being chased by the troop of Dōngfūyú東夫餘 and coming to the river, Zhūméng prayed to his grandfather Hébó and fish and terrapin came in flocks to make a bridge can be said to feel more realistic with the prestige of Hébó in mind leading fish.

@ **Gāojùlì 高句麗 (Goguryeo) ānyuè 安岳 Anak Tomb Mural:** Hù(=Guī圭)
ānyuè (Anak) No.3 Tomb Mùzhǔfūfùxiàng墓主夫婦像: Northeast Asian History Foundation http://contents.nahf.or.kr/ Korea.

○ Zhǔshì主室 Xiǎoshǐ小史 Shěngshì省事 Ménxiàbài門下拜
○ Hù笏　　　　　 Bǐ筆　　Zhǐ紙　　　　　Hù笏

@ **Professor Lee, Hyeong-gu «The Secrets of Korea Ancient Culture Found in Bóhǎi Coast» p.257, Gimm-Young Publishers. 2004,7. Korea.**

According to «Jiùtángshū舊唐書», in the Gāolì高麗 (Goryeo), Gāojùlì高句麗 (Goguryeo) Dynasty, "A king wear clothes in the five colors and báiluó白羅 Crown (唯王五綵, 以白羅爲冠)" and actually, the main character in the ānyuè (Anak) No.3 Tomb mural is wearing Báiluóguàn白羅冠 made of white silk. In the left and right of the main character drawn on the west side room wall, great servants such as Zhǔshì Xiǎoshǐ Shěngshì Ménxiàbài etc. are holding paper, pens and ink or hù.

❀ Yùěrbēi玉耳杯: Excavated from Jílín (JílínshěngBówùyuàn吉林省博物院).

○ Excavated from Jílín Province Jí'ānxiàn集安縣, provision store in the province. Height 3.2cm. Width 13cm.1958.

○ Yùbì玉璧 Táng唐, excavated. Jílín Dàhǎiměng大海猛 historic site.

■ «Chéngshìwǎnbào城市晚报» 2012,6,6.

<5> Xīnluó新羅 (Silla) Hù笏: Yáhù牙笏 is a hol made of ivory.

❀ Zhēndéwáng眞德王 gives Yáhù to zhēngǔ眞骨.
«Sānguóshǐjì三國史記» juǎn dìwǔ Xīnluóběnjì 卷 第五 新羅本紀 第五
Zhēndéwáng gives Yáhù to 四年夏四月 zhēngǔ. (April 650 unknown lunar).
In the summer April, <King> ordered people in government office as zhēngǔ to have Yáhù. «National History Compilation Committee», Korea.

❀ Fǎxīngwáng 法興王 Yáhù.
«Sānguóshǐjì三國史記» juǎn dìsānshísān zázhì dì'èr 卷 第三十三 雜志 第二
Sèfú色服 clothing system of Fǎxīngwáng reign
法興王制自太大角干至大阿湌紫衣阿湌至級湌緋衣並牙笏
During the reign of Fáxīngwáng, Dàjiǎogàn大角干 to Dàācān大阿湌 wear a purple robe. Acān阿湌 to Jcān級湌 wear a red cloth and Yáhù牙笏.

<6> Gāolì 高麗 (Goryeo) Guī圭 (=Hù笏)

«Gāolìshǐ高麗史» Yùguī玉圭, Yùcè玉冊:
juǎn bā shìjiā juǎn dìbā Wénzōng 卷八 世家 卷 第八 文宗 19年 (1065)
juǎn shíqī shìjiā juǎn dìshíqī Rénzōng 卷十七 世家 卷 第十七 仁宗 20年 (1142)

\<7\> Cháoxiǎn 朝鮮 (Joseon) Guī圭 (=Hù笏):

○ Cháoxiǎn Gāozōng高宗 Yīngqīnwáng
英親王 Yùguī玉圭 17.3cm

○ Related rituals: Ancestral rites祭祀,
Cháopìn招聘

However, as Gāozōng rose to the throne during Korean Empire, Báiyùguī白玉圭, 1 chǐ尺 2cùn寸, 12 liúmiǎn旒冕, 12 zhāngfú章服 were used for Miǎnfú冕服and Guī圭 like the emperor of Míng. At this time, Guī is Zhènguī鎮圭 and the above end is pointed and 4 mountain shapes were carved on the outside and the bottom was tied with Huángqǐ黃綺.

■ 《National Palace Museum》 Korea.

✿ Hù笏: Important folk cultural assets No. 13-5 Cultural Heritage Administration: www.cha.go.kr

○ National Folk Museum of Korea

Hù is a thing held by servants when meeting a king and 1st rank to 4th rank held Hù made of ivory and 5th rank and 9th rank held Hù made of wood. Originally, it was used to record King's teachings or writings offered to the king and not to forget them but institutionalized as for simple rites later.

(2) Japan Guī圭 (=Hù笏)

○ Hù笏«Tokyo National Museum» Japan.

○ Zhèngcāngyuàn正倉院 tōngtiānyáhù通天牙笏 34.9cm.

○ Dàomíngsì Tiānmǎngōng Jiāngōng yáhù 道明寺 天滿宮 菅公 牙笏 (平安 Heian Period 794-1185/1192) National Treasure. Japan.

(3) Mexico Guī圭 (=Hù笏):

Mexican Jiǎgǔwén characters inscription Yùguī玉圭
Yùguī and 16 Yùrén 玉人 statue: La Venta, Tabasco(BC900-400).

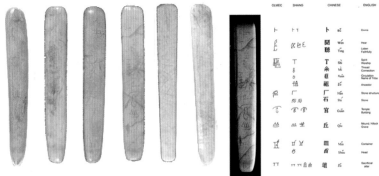

○ La Venta is famous for the largest ancestral rite historic site in Olmek civilization and Gǔdū古都 (old capital) of Olmek. Since excavated from the central zone of the ancestral rite historic site, No. 4 cultural relic is very important. These relics consists of 16 pieces of small Yùrén玉人 and 6 pieces of Yùguī玉圭 and character signs are clearly engraved in No. 5, No. 6 Yùguī

○ among them.

[2] Yùyī玉衣 (=Yùxiá玉匣)

✆ Lǐjìnyún李縉云, Yúbǐngwén于炳文:

The life size materials of Yùyī have been found since the 1950s. In archaeological materials, Yùyī begins to appear in early Xīhàn西漢 Wéndì文帝, jǐngdì景帝 years and early Yùyī has no top and bottoms because it consisted of three parts of the mask, gloves, shoes and was excavated from Shāndōng Línyí臨沂 Liúcī劉疵 Tomb, for example. The regulations on Yùyī were strict in the Later Hàn of a little late Xīhàn Wǔdì武帝 beginning. The currently found complete ones are relatively less. As Cáowèi曹魏 Huángchū黃初 3rd year (222) 文帝 Cáopī曹丕 "prohibited the use of Yùxiá玉匣" in the period of the Three States, the production and use of Yùyī玉衣 came to an end.

■ «Wénwùshōucángtújiěcídiǎn文物收藏圖解辭典» p.85, Zhèjiāng浙江 People's Publishing House, 2002,9.

(1) Fūyú 夫餘 (Buyeo) Yùyī玉衣: Traditional jade culture of Dōngyí Tribe.

«Sānguózhì三國志»

juàn30 Wèishū Wūwán Xiānbēi Dōngyíchuán 卷三十 魏書 烏丸 鮮卑 東夷 傳

«Hòuhànshū後漢書»

juàn 85 Dōngyílièzhuàn東夷列傳 (2) Fūyúguó Guāngwǔběnjì 夫餘國 光武 本紀

«Wèilüè魏略» juǎn 185 Dōngyí東夷 Top "Fūyú夫餘"

«Wèizhì魏志» Dōngyízhuàn東夷傳

«Yùhǎi玉海» Vol.97. 154.

«Tōngdiǎn通典» Biānfángdiǎn邊防典, Tōngdiǎn Vol.185 Biānfáng邊防一 Biānfángxù邊防序 Dōngyíshàng東夷上

«Tàipínghuányǔjì太平寰宇記» Vol.174, 東夷三 Fūyúguó夫餘國

«Cèfǔyuánguī册府元龜» Vol.959 wàichénbù外臣部 sì四 tǔfēng土風

«Tàipíngyùlǎn太平御覽» Vol.804 sì四 zhēnbǎobù珍寶部, Vol.805 sì四.

«Jìnshū晉書» Vol.97 lièzhuàn列傳 The 67th Dōngyí東夷

«Zīzhìtōngjiàn資治通鑑» Vol. 18 Hànjìshí 漢紀十 Shìzōngxiàowǔhuángdì世宗孝武皇帝 (Yuánshuò元朔 yuánnián元年 B.C.128)

«Hòuhànshū後漢書»

juàn 85 Dōngyílièzhuàn東夷列傳 (2) Fūyúguó夫餘國 Guāngwǔběnjì光武本紀

«Hòuhànshū後漢書»

juàn 85 Dōngyílièzhuàn東夷列傳 (2) Fūyúguó夫餘國

其王葬用玉匣, 漢朝常豫以玉匣付玄菟郡, 王死則迎取以葬焉⊠

If a king dies, a funeral was held by using a box made of jade and this Yùxiá 玉匣 was ordinarily given to Xuántùjùn during the Hàn Dynasty.

«Hòuhànshū後漢書» Guāngwǔběnjì光武本紀

漢時, 夫餘王葬用玉匣, 常豫以付玄菟郡,, 王死則迎取以葬. 公孫淵伏誅, 玄菟庫猶有玉匣一具. 今夫餘庫有玉璧·珪·瓚數代之物, 傳世以爲寶, 耆老言先代之所賜也.

During the Hàn Dynasty, Fūyú (Buyeo) used Yùxiá玉匣 during the king funeral and always left it to Xuántùjùn and immediately brought it to the funeral if a king died. When Gōngsūnyuān was dead, there was a pair of Yùxiá in the Xuántùjùn warehouse. Now in the Fūyú warehouse, there are things such as Yùbì, Guī, Zàn which have been handed down over the generations and have been regarded as treasure for generations and an old man said they were handed down from ancestors.

«Hòuhànshū後漢書» zhì志 6th Yùxiáyínlǚ玉柙銀縷

(2) The last king of YinZhòu殷周:

<1> Yīn Yùyī 殷玉衣

❀ Shāngxiāngtāo商湘濤:

> «Shǐjì史記» "甲子日, 紂兵敗. 紂走入, 登鹿台, 衣其宝玉衣, 赴火而死"
> "On jiǎzirì, when lost in the war, Zhòu紂 ran in and went up to Lùtái and wore the treasure Yùyī and jumped into the fire and died." So called"Yùxiá玉匣" is Yùyī and is Liànfú worn after the death of emperor or high nobleman and is written a lot in the records of the Hàn Dynasty.

> «Yìzhōushū逸周書» 世俘 "甲子夕, 紂取天智玉琰五,環身以自焚"
> In the evening of jiǎzixī, Zhòu took five Tiānzhìyùyǎn and wrapped it around the body and killed himself in the fire."

■ «Zhōngguógǔyùjiàncáng中國古玉鑒藏» Shanghai Culture Publisher, 2006,8.

<2> Xīhàn西漢(=Qiánhàn前漢) Yùyī玉衣 (=Yùxiá玉匣)

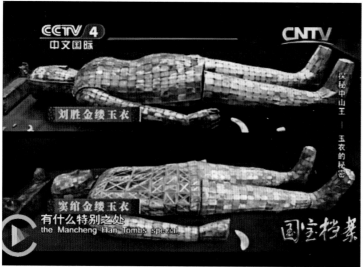

○ Hànmù漢墓 Liúshèng劉勝 Zhōngshānjìngwáng中山靖王 Jīnlǚyùyī金縷玉衣1.88m

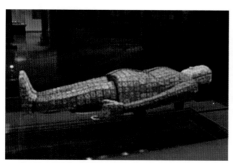

○ Earlier Xīhàn西漢 Nányuèwáng南越王 Sīlǚyùyī絲縷玉衣 1.73m.
○ 1980 Excavated from Guǎngdōngshěng Guǎngzhōushì Xiànggāng 廣東省 廣州市 象岡 Nányuèwáng tomb
○ Earlier Xīhàn西漢 (206-25 BC) Zhōngshānhuáiwáng中山懷王 Liúxiū劉修 tomb.
○ 1.82m 1973 Héběi河北 Dìngxiàn定縣

■ <TànmìZhōngshānwáng-yùyīdemìmì探秘中山王-玉衣的秘密>国宝档案 《CCTV-4》 2014.12.10.

❀ **Fàndéwěi范德偉 (Vice researcher of Héběi河北 Museum):** China State Seismological Bureau and Geological Institute concluded that the material of Yùyī of MǎnchéngHànmù滿城漢墓 belongs to Liáoníng XiùyánXiuyan岫岩 District.

[3] Yùguān玉棺: Xúzhōu Shīzishān Hànmù
徐州 獅子山 漢墓.

Xúzhōu Shīzishān Hànmù Xiāngyùqīguān鑲玉漆棺

■ <Tànsuǒfāxiàn探索發現>Lóngtángxiàdewánglíng龍塘下的王陵(二) «CCTV-10» 2015,4,3.
■ Xīhàn Jiāngdūwáng Liúfēi 西漢江都王劉非

[4] Yùyìn玉印. Yùxǐ玉璽

(1) Fūyú: Huòwángzhīyìn濊王之印 use related literature records.

　«Tōngdiǎn通典» Biānfángdiǎn邊防典, Tōngdiǎn Vol.185 Biānfáng邊防一 Biānfángxù邊防序 Dōngyíshàng東夷上 (Compiled by Táng Dùyòu 唐 杜佑).

🌀 **Professor Sin, Yong-ha**

■ <The Formation of Gǔcháoxiǎn (Gojoseon) Country> «Society and History» Vol.80 (2008) Korean Sociological Association

　"Ye濊" was a tribe originated from 嫩江 basin. "Yegang" is the old name of current Nènjiāng嫩江 (Nungang, tributary of Songhua river). Ye Tribe was originated from the land where Fūyú扶餘 (Buyeo) Country was built. In «Hòuhànshū後漢書», there is a statement 'Fūyúguó is originally the land of Ye' and according to «Jìnshū晋書», 'There is an old castle in Fūyú (Buyeo) Country and its name is Huòchéng濊城. Mostly, it is originally the land of Yemò濊貊' and the name can be seen based on these records.

(2) Cháoxiǎn朝鮮 yùbǎo玉寶 : «National Palace Museum»

○ Zhézōng哲宗 yùbǎo 9.6cm

○ Zhézōngfēi哲宗妃 yùbǎo 9.9cm

○ Gāozōng yùbǎo Korean Empire Jade 9.8cm

(3) Yùcè玉冊 :

CháoxiǎnTàizǔjiāshàngshìhào 朝鮮太祖加上諡號 «National Palace Museum»

○ Yùcè made and offered by granting a posthumous epithet of Zhèngyìguāngdé正義光德 and creating Yùbǎo御寶 with addition to the meaning of Wēihuàdǎo 威化島 Retreat to exiting Tàizǔshìhào太祖諡號 in the 9th year of Cháoxiǎn Sùzōng肅宗 (1683).

○ Yùyìn玉印 (jade seal) of installing Zhèngzǔ正祖 as the eldest son of the Crown Prince / Shìsūn(Zhèngzǔ) cèfēngyùyìn世孫(正祖)冊封玉印. Yīngzǔ 英祖 in 1759 (Yīngzǔ 35) Yùyìn玉印 (9.8×9.8×10.1cm). Zhúcè竹冊.

[5] Ornament:

(1) Yùdài玉帶: «National Palace Museum»

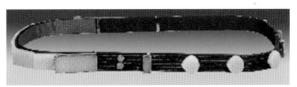

○ Yīngqīnwáng Yùdài 英親王 玉帶. Length 118cm, width 4.3cm

○ The only existing Dài for royal offspring. Length 80.0cm width 2.0cm

(2) Yùguànzǐ玉貫子

○ It is Fùzàngpǐn副葬品 (Grave goods) excavated from the tomb of Chāngchéngwèi昌城尉 Huángréndiǎn黃仁點 couple and Héróuwēngzhǔ和柔翁主(?-1777), the 10th daughter of Yīngzǔ and is made of jade.

(3) Jade ornaments: Cháoxiǎn «National Palace Museum»

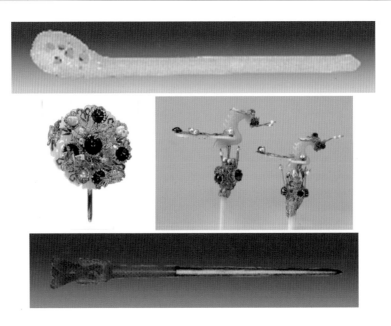

[6] jìjù祭具: Yùzhìxiānglú玉製香爐. Cháoxiǎn «National Palace Museum»

This artifact is an incense burner made of jade and Yíshìyòngjù儀式用具 (ritual utensils) during rituals. Since used in the Confucian ritual, the shape of its body is Dǐng鼎 different from an incense burner used in Buddhism. It has sān zú三足 (three feet) with the animal leg-shaped nodes.

○ Height: 21.0cm. Diameter: 13.7

[7] Crystal Sarira bottle: Sarira Reliquary (offerings).

(1) Shèlìzhuāngyánjù 舍利莊嚴具: Sarira Reliquary.

1. Huáyánsì Xīwǔcéngshítǎ 華嚴寺 西五層石塔

■ «Hánliánshè韩联社» Huáyánsì Sarira Reliquary designated as treasure 2002,10,21.

Remains for Sarira solemnity of North South States Period found inside the Huáyánsì Xīwǔcéngshítǎ (West Five-story Stone Pagoda) in Quánnán Qiúlǐjùn Mǎshānmiàn HuángTiánlǐ 全南 求禮郡 馬山面 黃田里. During dismantling and maintenance of Huáyánsì Xīwǔcéngshítǎ in August 1995, Báizhǐmòshūtuóluóníjīng白紙墨書陀羅尼經, tǎyìn塔印, Sarira bottle contained in celadon bottle and 22 Sarira etc. were found in the pagoda body of the 1st floor and various artifacts including bronze Buddha framework, bronze bells and decoration, iron sword, matallic strips, crystal were found in the basement of the stylobate.

Designated as Treasure No. 1348 on October 19, 2002, it is preserved in Huáyán-sì. Others are artifacts through which we can collectively review the society of the period of united Xīnluó新羅 (Silla) such as Shèlìzhuāngyánfǎ舍利莊嚴法 or sculptural form, technique of metal craft, use and perception of celadon, ornaments of women, negotiations with China etc. and are materials greatly helpful for research of Korean Buddhism development history, art history etc.

2. Yìshān益山 Wánggōnglǐ王宮里 Wǔcéngshítǎ Shèlìzhuāngyán舍利莊嚴

○ Bǎijǐ (Baekjae) Kingdom is a 'cultural hub' of East Asia
○ Sarira solemnity relics·enshrinement system is a unique style affected by the
○ Suí隋 Dynasty. And then, it was handed down to Japan and significantly affected Fǎlóngsì Wǔchóngtǎ 法隆寺 五重塔 (Horyuji gojunoto). Precious relics to reveal cultural exchange aspect of Xīnluó, China, Japan, etc. Revealed diversity and openness, internationality of Late Bǎijǐ百濟 Buddhism and Royal Culture. The existence of pearl beads showed the possibility that may have directly exchanged with Southeast Asia.

■ «Yìshān Newspaper» http://www.iksannews.com/

3. Yìshān益山 Mílèsì彌勒寺 Stone Pagoda Sarira Reliquary: Beads

○ Sarira   ○ Beads

4. Stupa Sarira Reliquary of Shuǐzhōngsì水鐘寺 in Nányángzhōu, Jīngjīdào Nányángzhōu Shuǐzhōngsì 南陽州 水鐘寺

Yínzhìdùjīnshěliqì銀製鍍金舍利器 (Silver gold coated Sarira vessel) contained with Jīnzhìjiǔcéngtǎ金製九層塔 (Gold nine-story pagoda) in Jīngcíyǒugàihú青磁有蓋壺 is 17.3㎝ high and a hexagonal roof was put on the hexagonal body carved by drilling lotus pattern and cloisonne pattern on the stylobate with double lotus flower patterns alternately each side. At the roof top, the orb is decorated on the lotus shape. A ball-shaped Sarira bottle made of crystal is contained in this Yínzhìdùjīnshěliqì銀製鍍金舍利器 and Sarira was kept by punching here.

Owned by Central Buddhist Museum. Cultural Heritage Administration

5. Shùntiān Xiānyánsì Sāncéngshítǎ 順天 仙巖寺 三層石塔 Sarira Reliquary: Octagonal cylindrical crystal bowl.

There are three pieces of remains found when dismantling and repairing Xiānyánsì Three-story Stone Pagoda. It is the first time that a sari hole was found in the lower part of 1st floor of the pagoda. Remains from the sari hole were one celadon jar and one white porcelain jar as Sarira Reliquary and Sari device came from the white porcelain jar. There is a gilt bronze sarira pagoda wrapped with silk in this white porcelain jar and 1 light gray oval sari in the sarira pagoda and sari is in the octagonal cylindrical shaped crystal bowl.

6. Yuèjīngsì月精寺 Octagonal Nine-story Stone Pagoda Sarira Reliquary

(Treasure No. 1375): Buddhist Art Exhibition of Korea

Yuèjīngsì bājiǎojiǔcéngshítǎ shèlìzhuāngyánjù 月精寺 八角九層石塔 舍利莊嚴具 is batch artifacts found in Octagonal Nine-story Stone Pagoda in Yuèjīngsì in Píngchāngjùn平昌郡, Jiāngyuán江原 and is in Yuèjīngsì Shèngbǎo 聖寶 Museum. It was designated as Treasure No. 1375 of Korea on June 26, 2003. Shuǐjīngshèlìpíng水晶舍利瓶 (crystal sarira bottle) is a Piáoxíng瓢形、Húlúxíng葫蘆形 bottle and sarira was kept by drilling the center vertically and then, the hole was blocked with Xiāngmù香木 and the shape is the same as Piáoxíngliúlíshèlìpíng瓢形琉璃舍利瓶 including a silk pouch among reliquaries excavated from Anchéng安城 Chángmìngsì長命寺 five-story stone pagoda (997). Such Piáoxíngliúlíshèlìpíng is not common and was in fashion in the 11th century after Wǔdài五代 period in China and it was especially excavated in some pagodas related to Quánshēnshèlìjīng全身舍利經 and is a material requiring the meaning analysis in the future.

7. Gǎn'ēnsì感恩寺 Temple Site Stone Pagoda Sarira Reliquary :

Crystal orb: Gǎn'ēnsìzhǐ xīsāncéngshítǎ shèlìzhuāngyánjù感恩寺址 西三層 石塔 舍利莊嚴具. Cultural Heritage Administration
■ http://www.cha.go.kr/

○ Crystal Sarira bottle and Sarira

Crystal orb: Sarira Reliquary made of bronze consists of three parts of square stylobate, body including a sarira bottle and orb made of crystal and reminds us of a wooden structure. The stylobate and body part of the reliquary are in a relatively good state of preservation but the top baldachin was corroded enough not to know the original form.

8. Jade prayer beads:

Chuán傳 Xiūdésì修德寺 Stone Pagoda Sarira Reliquary (Red, green, white)
These sari supplies known to be found in Xiūdésì Pagoda in Lǐshān禮山, Zhōngnán are a bulk product with Tuóluónídíng陀羅尼經, copper mirror, boul-

ders, shellfish, herbs including the copper box lid. Of them, the lid of a box is severely damaged and there are two tóngjìng銅鏡 and the bigger one has no decoration while the smaller one is decorated with Liánzhūwén連珠紋 etc. And three kinds of prayer beads were made with Yù of red, green, white and there are 10 shells. Owned by Korea University Museum

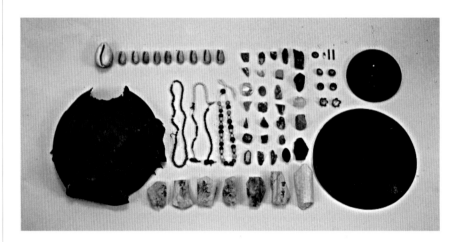

9. Jade candlestick:

Pǔjuéguóshītǎ普覺國師塔 at jīnglóngsì靑龍寺, Zhōngzhōu忠州, Zhōngběi忠北. National Treasure No. 197.

This stupa is the stupa of Pǔjuéguóshī普覺國師, a high priest in the late Gāolì高麗 (Goryeo). A stupa is a sturcture where a monk's sarira is enshrined and has a structure of octagonal circular type, the typical form of stupa from the period of united Xīnluó (Silla) to early Cháoxiǎn (Joseon) and bell-shapes have been made a lot since then.

■ <Source: Zhōngzhōu Cityl>

[8] Yùrén玉人:

(1) Animal-shaped decorative jade: Excavated from Wángxīngsìzhǐ 王興寺址 Temple Site.

Saying, "Various artifacts such as beads and jade, gold products, bronze products, silver products used as ornaments such as necklaces and bracelets, traditional ornamental hairpins, gold earrings around wooden pagoda central foundation stone south side were found", an official of National Fúyú Cultural Heritage Research Institute also said, "These relics not only show the excellence and internationality of Bǎijǐ百濟 (Baekjae) Buddhist culture well but are evaluated as important materials for research on Bǎijǐ (Baekjae) era ornaments and jewelry making, research on foreign relations." Gold, sliver, copper Sarira Reliquary showing the essence of the heyday of Bǎijǐ (Baekjae) culture was excavated from the Zhōngnán Fúyú Wángxīngsì historic site, attracting extraordinary attention of academia. On 24th, National Fúyú (Buyeo) Cultural Heritage Research Institute opened the excavated artifacts including sarira cases to the public.

Jade products excavated with Sarira Reliquary.

○ Owned by National Fúyú Cultural Heritage Research Institute. Tiger Shape, zhènmùshòu鎭墓獸 shape

○ Tāotièwén饕餮紋 Jade Products

■ «Cháoxiǎnrìbào朝鮮日報» 2007,10,25.

The original body was cut into the fan shape and halved again and delicate patterns are engraved on both sides and bronze chopsticks are 21㎝ and the length and shape are the same as those excavated from Royal Tomb of Wǔníngwáng武寧王.

■ «Electronic Times» October 26, 2007. Korea.

(2) Jade figure statue: Offerings.

Băijĭ (Baekjae) Tomb of Wŭníngwáng. Găn'ēnsì stone pagoda sari supplies.

<1> 'Glass Young Boy Statue' excavated from Băijĭ (Baekjae) Tomb of Wŭníngwáng. Excavated in pairs.

Glass Young Boy Statue excavated from Băijĭ (Baekjae) Tomb of Wŭníngwáng (2.8㎝, Băijĭ, Owned by Gōngzhōu公州 National Museum).

@ **Young Boy Statue of the period of the Three States**

Young boy faith has been followed since the period of the Three States. There are several stories about young boys in «Sānguóyíshì三國遺事» and Young Boy Statue also has a long history. Looking at the history of Korean Young Boy Statue, the oldest Young Boy Statue in Korea is Liúlítóngzĭxiàng琉璃童子像 (Glass Young Boy Statue) excavated with glass beads from Băijĭ Wŭníngwánglíng, Reign (501~523). Tomb of Wŭníngwáng was found in 1971 after 1448 years and excavation has been carried out four times in total. Including Mùzhishí墓地石, gold Diadem Ornament of the king and queen, many glass ornaments were excavated from Tomb of Wŭníngwáng. <Glass Young Boy Statue>excavated from Tomb of Wŭníngwáng is a small Young Boy Statue of 2.8㎝. Although a young boy statue for protection·decoration wearing over the body, the appearance of a young boy surprisingly resembles existing Jĭzhōu Island young boy stone. The young boy statue has a round face and shaven head, stands neatly and bows down by gathering two hands on the belly. This <Glass Young Boy Statue> was excavated in a pair and a small hole in the waist makes us assume that a queen carried it on the clothes like a patron saint while alive (Kim, Chun-sil, 2003). Hands, pants, socks, etc. as well as ěrmùkǒubí耳目口鼻 (ears, eyes, mouth, and nose) of the face were expressed with simple carved lines on Shítòuxìng實透性 glass. The impression of the figure and expression technique of this work are evaluated to demonstrate the Korean aspect (Gwon, Young-pil, 1997). Based on this case, it can be said that Korea people have already regarded a young boy as the object of faith for a long time. The custom of carving a very small young boy statue and burying it in a tomb was established as a tradition of standing a young boy made of stone in the Cháoxiǎn Dynasty. «Kim, Yu – Jeong's Aesthetics Journey Style and Beauty» 23. Brief history of Korean Tóngzǐxiàng童子像 (young boy statue)

<2> Yùzòuyuètóngzǐxiàng玉奏樂童子像 (Pipe), Lǜyùwǔyuètóngzǐxiàng綠玉舞樂童子像 (Xīnluó, owned by National Museum of Korea)

Gǎnēnsì Stone Pagoda Sarira Case: Treasure No. 366

○ Yùzòulètóngzǐxiàng   ○ Lǜyùwǔtóngzǐxiàng

There is also a young boy statue in Shèlìjù舍利具(Sarira Case) found in United Xīnluó (682) Gǎn'ēnsìshítǎ. This is the representative young boy statue among early examples of Korean Buddhist young boy statues shown as carving. The whole Sarira Case where two young boy statues are carved is designated as Treasure No. 366. These two young boy statues are a young boy playing music (奏樂童), a dancing young boy (舞童) (Im, Jin-gwang, 2003). This Sarira Case is a pavilion form and a crystal sarira bottle with convex belly in the center and the bamboo-shaped handrail was installed delicately around it and Tiānrénxiàng天人像 playing Gokdu Korean mandolin, fiddle, hourglass-shaped drum, Dàcén 大笒 was seated on the edge. Again, Zòuyuètóngzǐxiàng made of jade and Lǜyùwǔtóngzǐxiàng dancing naked and made of green jade were established in between. It can be seen that these young boy statues were directly accepted to United Xīnluó through Táng because they are deeply ingrained in Central Asia style (Jiāngshùnxīn姜舜馨,1994).

<3> Yùrén玉人: Gāolì 高麗 (Goryeo) Dynasty

* Gāolì (Goryeo) Dynasty. Kim, Yong-man «Korea Life History» Jade, jewelry that has been loved since ancient times.

■ Owned by Our History Culture Institute. 2011.11.09

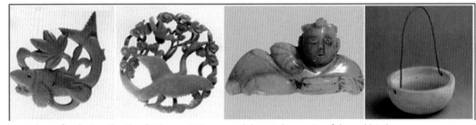

○ Jade crafts during the Gāolì (Goryeo) Dynasty elaborately carving fish and birds.

Conclusion

Recently, the direction of research on Jade culture in China is moving from individual Jadeware of jade culture to the whole jade culture. Under such circumstances, in order to newly identify the historical affinitive relationship mainly around Dōngyí東夷 Tribe and the culture subject of Black skin jade culture and Hóngshān Culture that built its own cultural area and existed as the historical subject in a certain area called Liáohé Basin of the current Chinese Continent for at least over 5000 years, this study tried a new experimental study for the first time out of the typical framework of the existing historical research leading to Neolithic Age-Bronze Age-Iron Age by analyzing the jade culture of the East Asian international community that appeared on the historical stage in the late 20th century as a major study target under the premise of the 'jade culture and jade totem' society.

Therefore, in order to identify the historical basis on jade carving of Black skin jade culture and Hóngshān Culture, this study used literature records such as «Shījīng詩經» «zuǒzhuàn左傳» «Mèngzǐ孟子» «zhuāngzǐ莊子» «Shǐjì 史記» «Shānhǎijīng山海經» etc. and Petroglyphs around Inner Mongolia, Gāojùlì (Goguryeo) tomb murals, Hàndàihuàxiàngshí漢代畵像石 etc. as the study target. In order to accomplish this research purpose, we set the society at that time that created Black skin jade culture which is difficult even for modern people in the 21st century to understand under the premise of 'jade totem' and comprehensively compared and analyzed by dividing it into the following areas to prove this:

1. Nature worship:

Sun-shaped jade disk with a hole in the center, gōuyún (cloud)-shaped jade jewelry, rainbow-shaped jade and Yùhuáng etc. based on nature worship are included.

2. Animal Totem: Snakes, cows, birds, bears, pigs, deer, fish, etc.

Yùlóng (C-shaped dragon) of snake totem, Yùxiónglóng (bear-shaped dragon made of jade) and bear crown Yùdiāo Shénrén of bear totem, Niúshǒurénshēn of cattle totem, Yùniǎo of bird totem, Rénmiànniǎoshēn (人面鳥; human face, bird body) and Rénmiànyúshēn (human face, fish body) of fish totem etc. are included. Original animals shaped and Bànrénbànshòu半人半獸 (half man and half beast) shaped Jadeware based on the worship of animals is supposed to be a collective symbol of a certain specific tribal society. In particular, this type of Jadeware is not only standard Jadeware representing two cultures in Black skin jade culture and Hóngshān Culture Jadeware but accounts for the most majority.

3. Ancestor worship: Sex worship.

The figure formation made of jade is closely related to each other of reproduction worship, genital organ worship, sex worship, ancestor worship given by God to human beings so the prosperity of reproduction, that is, survival issue of a tribe was the most important key task determining the continuous existence of a clan or tribe. The appearance of such an intercourse figure shape is the result reflecting the transition process of sex worship rituals the most directly in order to express the reproductive ability and other divine power given by God to human beings to the gods of heaven.

According to the above division method, «Shānhǎijīng山海經», Gāojùlì (Goguryeo) tomb murals and Jadeware representing Black skin jade culture were first compared and analyzed as follows:

1) Yùlóng (C-shaped dragon); Snake(dragon) totem.

«Shānhǎijīng» Dàhuāngběijīng; The morphological relevance can be seen in Shòushǒushéshēn獸首蛇身 (Animal head, snake body). And the shape of the sun god, moon god (Chinese Fúxī, Nǚwā) appearing in Gāojùlì (Goguryeo) tomb murals is also identical with Rénmiànshéshēn (human face and snake body) recorded in «Shānhǎijīng». But most of all, the mythical topics of Gāojùlì

(Goguryeo) tomb murals can be obtained from «Shānhǎijīng» and those of «Shānhǎijīng» can be morphologically seen in Black skin jade culture and Hóngshān Culture.

2) Niúshǒurénshēn: Cattle totem.

As for Niúshǒurénshēn (Cow head and human body) Statue of cattle totem attracting attention enough to account for about 30% of Black skin jade culture, the relevance can be seen in Rénmiànniúshēn人面牛身 (human face, cow body of «Shānhǎijīng» Xīcìèrjīng. And the basis of this Niúshǒurénshēn shape can be also found in Yándì of Niúshǒurénshēn appearing even three times in Gāojùlì (Goguryeo) tomb murals. Finally, like Yùlóng explained in the above, for the shape of Yándì of cattle totem, the mythical topics of Gāojùlì (Goguryeo) tomb murals can be obtained from «Shānhǎijīng» and those of «Shānhǎijīng» can be morphologically seen in Black skin jade culture and Hóngshān Culture.

3) Rénmiànniǎo: Bird totem.

For the shape of Rénmiànniǎo (human face, bird body) reflecting the bird totem of Hóngshān Culture and Black skin jade culture, the morphological relevance can be seen in Rénmiànniǎoshēn人面鳥身 of «Shānhǎijīng» Dàhuāngběijīng. If including unidentified Rénmiànniǎo such as Hèniǎo, Qiānqiū), Wànsuì etc. of Gāojùlì (Goguryeo) tomb murals, the grounds of the shape of these Rénmiànniǎos can be found as many as we like. In addition, records on Rénmiànniǎo are also written in «Shānhǎijīng». Finally, like Yùlóng, Niúshǒurénshēn Statue explained in the above, for the shape of Yándì of the Cattle totem, the mythical topics of Gāojùlì (Goguryeo) tomb murals can be obtained from «Shānhǎijīng» and those of «Shānhǎijīng» can be morphologically found in Black skin jade culture and Hóngshān Culture.

4) Zhūshǒurénshēn: Pig totem

For the shape of Zhūshǒurénshēn (Pig head, human body) reflecting the pig totem of Black skin jade culture, the morphological relevance can be found in Shǐshēnrénmiàn豕身而人面 (pig body, human face) of «Shānhǎijīng». Finally, for the shape of the pig totem, the mythical topics of «Shānhǎijīng» can be morphologically seen in Black skin jade culture.

In addition, the bear totem highly associated with the foundation myth of Gǔcháoxiǎn (Gojoseon) can be fully seen through the records of «Shānhǎijīng» Zhōngshānjīng: 熊山. 有穴焉, 熊之穴, 恒出神人, relief sculpture of the Later HàndàiWǔshìCítánghuàxiàngshí, Xióngshǒurénshēn of Black skin jade culture. In particular, if contrasting the records of «Shānhǎijīng» Dàhuāngdōngjīng: Dōnghǎizhīwàidàhè東海之外大壑, Shǎohàozhīguó少昊之國 and those of «Shíyíjì拾遺記» 卷一 <Shǎohào少昊> "Fèngniǎoshì鳳鳥氏", «Zuǒzhuàn左傳» 昭公17th year "Fèngniǎo凤鸟" etc., the vice researcher of Xúchūnlíng (Tiānjīnshì Museum in China) argued in recent years, "The whole area of Shāndōng, Jiāngsū, Zhèjiāng through Southern Yānshān from the ancient Northeast is a place where the new totem clan of Dōngyí Tribe used to live." («CCTV-4» 2012,5,7) and what does his argument imply?

And the mythical topics appearing in «Shānhǎijīng» can be found relatively easily because a series of shapes of half man and half beast Gods combined with human body such as dog totem of Quǎnérrénmiàn (Dog, human face) of Běishānjīng, horse totem of Mǎshēnrénmiàn (horse body, human face) of Běishānjīng Běicìsānjīng, fish totem of Rénmiànyúshēn(human face, fish body) of Hǎinèinánjīng and Rényú人魚 of Běishānjīng, tiger totem of Hǔshǒurénshēn (tiger head, human body) of Xīshānjīng and Dàhuāngběijīng are recorded in «Shānhǎijīng».

However, the correlation between «Shānhǎijīng» and Jade culture is not limited only to Black skin jade culture and Hóngshān Culture. It is based on the fact that in the case of Shímǎoyùrén excavated from the Shímǎo historic site of the Late Neolithic Age in Shǎnxī, China, the morphological relevance can be also found in Yīmùguó and Dàhuāngběijīng, Hǎinèiběijīng appearing in «Shānhǎijīng».

As described above, the morphological basis of the mythical topics of Gāojùlì (Goguryeo) tomb murals and that of the mythical topics of «Shānhǎijīng» can be easily found in «Shānhǎijīng» and Black skin jade culture and Hóngshān Culture jade carving, respectively and is the fact mere coincidence? Or is it historic naturalness. It is no wonder that the most important thing here is the geographic location of «Shānhǎijīng». For this, a Chinese professor Léiguǎngzhēn said that the secret of Hóngshān Culture and other prehistoric cultures could be solved by confirming the exact geographical position of '海 (sea)' of «Shānhǎijīng» as Bóhǎi.

In particular, the dual sculpture or complex sculpture shape appearing in Black skin jade culture and Hóngshān Culture is not only the historical relics for meeting and parting according to natural disasters, alliance, war, marriage, peace among different animal totem tribal groups but reflects the "Jade Totem" Society showing the cultural level mature enough to leave the consciousness world of the religious dimension such as heavenly gods worship, nature worship, ancestor worship, reproduction worship etc. as jade carving. Therefore, these jade carving relics are not only contemporary self-portraits showing the ultimate of a three-dimensional space art of the highest level of the Neolithic Age in the East Asian region but highly likely to be parties such as Tàihào Fúxī and Nǚwā (human face and snake body), Shénnóng Yándì (God of agriculture and God of fire: Cow head and human body), Chīyóu, Huángdì etc. among main characters of legends and myths of each country and nation in East Asia.

As historical artifacts from the prehistoric age between about 8000 years ago and 4000 years ago that has been only considered the uncivilized society which is uncertain and distant and where civilization is not open yet to the great transition period getting into historic times on the premise of the emergence of an ancient country in the initial form, such a series of Black skin jade culture and Hóngshān Culture and jadeware remind us that they should be reviewed historically.

This study is the first experimental result of the comprehensive analysis of Black skin jade culture and Hóngshān Culture jade carving artifacts in the Neolithic Age, literature records such as «Shījīng詩經» «zuǒzhuàn左傳» «Mèngzǐ 孟子» «zhuāngzǐ莊子» «shàngshū尙書» «Shǐjì史記» «Shānhǎijīng山海經» etc., Gāojùlì (Goguryeo) tomb murals, Hàndàihuàxiàngshí etc. and as a culture with strong international nature directly related to communal cultural wish of three countries of Korea, China and Japan in East Asia, jade culture based on these series of 'jade totem' societies not only can transcend the scope and boundaries current ethnic groups or countries but are the origin of the communal civilization to recover the identity of the international community in East Asia.

Index